An Introduction to Isaiah 1–39

An Introduction to Isaiah 1–39

A Foundational Prophetic Work

Marvin A. Sweeney

CASCADE *Books* • Eugene, Oregon

AN INTRODUCTION TO ISAIAH 1–39
A Foundational Prophetic Work

Copyright © 2025 Marvin A. Sweeney. All rights reserved. Except for brief quotations in critical publications or reviews, no part of this book may be reproduced in any manner without prior written permission from the publisher. Write: Permissions, Wipf and Stock Publishers, 199 W. 8th Ave., Suite 3, Eugene, OR 97401.

Cascade Books
An Imprint of Wipf and Stock Publishers
199 W. 8th Ave., Suite 3
Eugene, OR 97401

www.wipfandstock.com

PAPERBACK ISBN: 978-1-6667-7036-0
HARDCOVER ISBN: 978-1-6667-7037-7
EBOOK ISBN: 978-1-6667-7038-4

Cataloguing-in-Publication data:

Names: Sweeney, Marvin A. (Marvin Alan), 1953– [author].

Title: An introduction to Isaiah 1–39 : a foundational prophetic work / Marvin A. Sweeney.

Description: Eugene, OR: Cascade Books, 2025 | Includes bibliographical references and index.

Identifiers: ISBN 978-1-6667-7036-0 (paperback) | ISBN 978-1-6667-7037-7 (hardcover) | ISBN 978-1-6667-7038-4 (ebook)

Subjects: LCSH: Bible.—Isaiah, I–XXXIX—Criticism, interpretation, etc. | Bible.—Isaiah—Criticism, interpretation, etc. | Bible.—Isaiah—Textbooks.

Classification: BS1515.55 S94 2025 (paperback) | BS1515.55 (ebook)

VERSION NUMBER 10/07/25

For Gamward Quan

Ish Ḥayil

Contents

Preface | ix
Abbreviations | xi

1   Introduction | 1
    I. Isaiah 1–39 Within the Book of Isaiah | 1
    II. The Book of Isaiah as a Whole | 3
    III. The Synchronic Internal Structure of Isaiah 1–33 | 9
    IV. The Synchronic Internal Structure of Isaiah 34–66 | 18
    V. Conclusion | 23
    VI. Appendix: Structure Diagram of the Book of Isaiah | 24

2   Isaiah 1–12 | 26
    I. Overview | 26
    II. Isaiah 1 | 27
    III. Isaiah 2–4 | 36
    IV. Isaiah 5–12 | 43

3   Isaiah 13–27 | 57
    I. Overview | 57
    II. Isaiah 13:1—14:32 | 59
    III. Isaiah 15:1—16:14 | 62
    IV. Isaiah 17:1—18:7 | 64
    V. Isaiah 19:1—20:6 | 67
    VI. Isaiah 21:1–10 | 69

VII. Isaiah 21:11-12 | 71
VIII. Isaiah 21:13-17 | 72
IX. Isaiah 22:1-25 | 72
X. Isaiah 23:1-18 | 76
XI. Isaiah 24-27: Overview | 78

4   Isaiah 28-33 | 88
    I. Overview | 88
    II. Isaiah 28:1-29 | 90
    III. Isaiah 29:1-24 | 93
    IV. Isaiah 30:1-33 | 94
    V. Isaiah 31:1-9 | 96
    VI. Isaiah 32:1—33:24 | 98

5   Isaiah 34-39 | 104
    I. Isaiah 34-35: Overview | 104
    II. Isaiah 36-39: Overview | 108

6   Isaiah 1-39: Concluding Remarks | 122

Appendix: Form Criticism and the Structure of Isaiah | 127
Bibliography | 133
Index | 143

Preface

I HAVE BEEN PREOCCUPIED with the book of Isaiah throughout my entire life. As a boy, born in Springfield, Illinois, and growing up in Decatur, Illinois, where my family were members of Temple B'nai Abraham, I encountered the book of Isaiah in many contexts. The Shabbat Torah service quotes Isaiah 2:3, "for from Zion, Torah will go forth!" I remember the song I learned in Hebrew school, "*lo' yissa goy el goy ḥerev' velo' yilmedu 'od milḥamah*," "Nation shall not lift up a sword against (another) nation, and they shall no longer learn war." For my Bar Mitzvah Torah and Haftarah portion, under the guidance of Rabbi Dr. J. Jerome Pine, z"l, I read from Parashat Eqev in which my Torah portion began with Deuteronomy 10:1, "In that time, YHWH said to me, 'Carve for yourself two tablets of stone like the first, and come up to me to the mountain where you will make for yourself a wooden ark,'" and the Haftarah portion began with Isaiah 49:14, "And Zion said, 'YHWH has abandoned me, and my L-rd has forgotten me,'" but I didn't forget. As an undergraduate student at the University of Illinois Urbana-Champaign, I wrote a paper on Isaiah 36–39 for my introductory Hebrew Bible class, team-taught by David Petersen and Neil Irons, and I continued with a focus on Isaiah in Petersen's Prophecy in Ancient Israel class and Irons's Isaiah seminar. During my graduate studies in Claremont, Rolf Knierim asked me to lecture on Isaiah 1–5 in his Old Testament Theology of the Eighth Century B.C.E. class—in which I was a student! And that led to insights in Isaiah 1–4, which became the topic of my 1983 PhD dissertation, later published as *Isaiah 1–4 and the Post-Exilic Understanding of the Isaianic Tradition*, BZAW 171 (Berlin: de Gruyter, 1988). I was later honored to be invited to write the Isaiah 1–39 commentary for the Forms of the Old Testament Literature Series. And

Preface

when my friend and colleague Roy F. Melugin informed me of his terminal illness, it became my task to write the FOTL commentary on Isaiah 40–66 at his request. Although I have turned to other subjects, Latter Prophets, Former Prophets, Pentateuch, Jewish Biblical Theology, and Jewish Mysticism, throughout my career, I continue to write many articles and reviews on the book of Isaiah.

When I was asked to write this students' guide to Isaiah 1–39 by my Cascade Wipf and Stock editor, Robin Parry, and seconded by the editor-in-chief, K. C. Hanson, my old friend and classmate from graduate school, I was delighted to accept! Although I was working on an Exodus commentary at the time, which will appear about the same time as this volume, Isaiah has always remained central to my thinking. I began writing shortly after having the honor of giving a plenary lecture on Isaiah at the Leuven Biblical Colloquium in August 2024, at the gracious invitation of Ulrich Berges, and I have written this volume in the aftermath of that lecture. Although I am near to retirement, *be'ezrat ha-Shem*, "with the help of G-d," I will teach my Isaiah seminar once more.

In keeping with some circles in Judaism, I employ the terms YHWH, G-d, and L-rd in reference to the Deity.

All translations from Hebrew, Greek, Aramaic, Akkadian, Ugaritic, and German are mine.

I would like to thank my Cascade editor, Dr. Robin Parry, for the thorough job he did in securing and editing the volume throughout the process of its composition. I would also like to thank my Claremont Research Associate, Mr. Hyunghee Kim, for his work in preparing the Index. In both cases, any remaining problems are my own responsibility.

I thank all those who are mentioned here—and many who are not mentioned—for their roles in developing my preoccupation with Isaiah! I also thank my lovely wife, Dr. Soo Jung Kim Sweeney, also a Hebrew Bible scholar, for her support and her own engagement in Hebrew Bible studies.

I would like to dedicate this volume to my good friend Gamward Quan, formerly chief financial officer at the Claremont School of Theology. He is truly an *Ish Ḥayil*, "a capable man" and an astute administrator like the *Eshet Ḥayil* honored in Proverbs 31:10–31!

Kislev 5785
Marvin A. Sweeney
December 2024
Salem, Oregon

Abbreviations

AASOR	Annual of the American Schools of Oriental Research
AB	Anchor Bible
ABD	*Anchor Bible Dictionary.* Edited by D. N. Freedman et al. 6 vols. Garden City, NY: Doubleday, 1992.
ANAO	Avhandlinger uitgitt av Der Norske Videnskaps-Akademi Oslo
AnBib	Analecta biblica
ANET	*The Ancient Near Eastern Texts.* Edited by J. B. Pritchard. Princeton: Princeton University Press, 1969.
ANEP	*The Ancient Near East in Pictures Relating to the Old Testament.* Edited by J. B. Pritchard. Princeton: Princeton University Press, 1969.
AOAT	Alter Orient und Altes Testament
ASORDS	American Schools of Oriental Research Dissertation Series
AThANT	Abhandlungen zur Theologie des Alten und Neuen Testaments
BASOR	*Bulletin of the American Schools of Oriental Research*
BBB	Bonner Biblische Beiträge
BDB	Brown, Francis, S. R. Driver, and Charles A. Briggs. *A Hebrew and English Lexicon of the Old Testament*
BEATAJ	Beiträge zur Erforschung des Alten Testaments und des antiken Judentum
BETL	Bibliotheca Ephemeridum Theologicarum Lovaniensium
BibSem	The Biblical Seminar

Abbreviations

BibInt	Biblical Interpretation Series
Bib	*Biblica*
BIS	Biblical Interpretation Series
BJS	Brown and Judaic Studies
BKAT	Biblischer Kommentar Altes Testament
BN	*Biblisiches Notizen*
BO	Berit Olam
BZAW	Beihefte zur Zeitschrift für die Alttestamentliche Wissenschaft
CBQ	*The Catholic Biblical Quarterly*
CBQMS	Catholic Biblical Quarterly Monograph Series
CBS	Core Biblical Studies
CCC	Contextual Critical Commentary
ChrH	The Chronicler's History
ConBibOT	Coniectanea biblica: Old Testament Series
ContCom	Continental Commentaries
CR:BS	*Currents in Research: Biblical Studies*
CRIANT	Compendia rerum Iudaicarum ad Novum Testamentum
DCLS	Deutero-Canonical and Cognate Literature Studies
DDD2	*Dictionary of Deities and Demons in the Bible.* Edited by K. van der Toorn et al. 2nd ed. Leiden: Brill, 1999.
DJD	Discoveries in the Judean Desert
DtrH	Deuteronomistic History
EB	Études Bibliques
EBR	*Encyclopedia of the Bible and Its Reception.* Edited by H. Spickermann et al. 22 vols. Berlin: de Gruyter, 2001–present.
ECC	Eerdmans Critical Commentary
EncJud	*Encyclopaedia Judaica.* Edited by C. Roth et al. 16 vols. Jerusalem: Keter, n.d.
ET	English translation
ETL	*Ephemerides Theologicae Lovanienses*
FAT	Forschungen zum Alten Testament
Fest.	Festschrift
FOTL	Forms of the Old Testament Literature

ABBREVIATIONS

FRLANT	Forschungen zur Religionen und Literatur des Alten und Neuen Testaments
HALOT	*Hebrew and Aramaic Lexicon of the Old Testament*. Edited by L. Koehler and W. Baumgartner. 5 vols. Leiden: Brill, 1994–99.
HAT	Handbuch zum Alten Testament
HBS	Herders Biblisches Studien
HBT	*Horizons in Biblical Theology*
HKAT	Handkommentar zum Alten Testament
HR	*History of Religions*
HS	*Hebrew Studies*
HSM	Harvard Semitic Monographs
HThKAT	Herders Theologischer Kommentar zum Alten Testament
HUCA	*Hebrew Union College Annual*
IBT	Interpreting Biblical Texts
ICC	International Critical Commentary
IDB[S]	*The Interpreter's Dictionary of the Bible Supplementary Volume*
JAOS	*Journal of the American Oriental Society*
JBL	*Journal of Biblical Literature*
JNES	*Journal of Near Eastern Studies*
JPS	Jewish Publication Society
JR	*Journal of Religion*
JSJSup	Journal for the Study of Judaism Supplement Series
JSOT	*Journal for the Study of the Old Testament*
JSOTSup	Journal for the Study of the Old Testament Supplement Series
KAT	Kommentar zum Alten Testament
KHAT	Kurzer Handbuch zum Alten Testament
LBT	Library of Biblical Theology
LHBOTS	Library of Hebrew Bible and Old Testament Studies
LXX	Septuagint
NCBC	New Cambridge Bible Commentary
NCeB	New Century Bible Commentary
NEAEHL	*New Encyclopaedia of Archaeological Excavations in the Holy Land*. Edited by E. Stern et al. 4 vols. Jerusalem: Israel Exploration Society; Carta, 1993.

Abbreviations

NICOT	New International Commentary on the Old Testament
OBO	Orbis Biblicus et Orientalis
OBT	Overtures to Biblical Theology
OT Guides	Old Testament Guides
OTL	Old Testament Library
POS	Pretoria Oriental Studies
SAC	Studies in Antiquity and Christianity
SBL	Society of Biblical Literature
SBLDS	Society of Biblical Literature Dissertation Series
SBLMS	Society of Biblical Literature Monograph Series
SBLResBS	Society of Biblical Literature Resources for Biblical Study
SBLSym	Society of Biblical Literature Symposium Series
SBS	Stuttgarter Bibelstudien
SBT	Studies in Biblical Theology
SBTS	Sources for Biblical and Theological Study
SHBC	Smyth and Helwys Biblical Commentary
SJSJ	Supplements to Journal for the Study of Judaism
SSN	Studia Semitica Neerlandica
SOTSMS	Society for Old Testament Study Monograph Series
TDNT	*Theological Dictionary of the New Testament*. Edited by G. Kittel et al. 10 vols. Grand Rapids: Eerdmans, 1964–76.
TDOT	*Theological Dictionary of the Old Testament*. Edited by G. J. Botterweck et al. 17 vols. Grand Rapids: Eerdmans, 1974–2021.
ThLZ	*Theologische Literaturzeitung*
TSAJ	Texte und Studien zum antiken Judentum
VT	*Vetus Testamentum*
VTSup	Vetus Testamentum Supplements
WBC	Word Biblical Commentary
WMANT	Wissenschaftliche Monographien zum Alten und Neuen Testament
ZAW	*Zeitschrift für die alttestamentliche Wissenschaft*

I

Introduction

I. Isaiah 1–39 Within the Book of Isaiah

A. Overview

ISAIAH 1–39 IS PART of the book of Isaiah. The book of Isaiah is the best-known book of all the prophetic books of the Hebrew Bible, including both the Tanak, the Jewish form of the Bible, and the Old Testament, the first portion of the Christian form of the Bible. Portions of the book of Isaiah are read more frequently as Haftarot readings of the Prophets, which complement the Torah readings in the Jewish worship service. And Isaiah is quoted more times than any other prophetic book in the Christian New Testament. Isaiah is especially well-known in Judaism for its inclusion of the oracle in 2:2–4, which envisions all the nations streaming to Zion to learn G-d's "Instruction" (i.e., Torah), which is quoted as part of the Jewish service for reading the Torah.[1] This procession, of which Israel/Jacob will be a part, will result ultimately in the nations beating their swords into plowshares and their spears into pruning hooks so that no nation shall lift up the sword against another nation and all of them shall never again learn war.

---

1. Although the Hebrew word *tôrâ* is often translated as "law," particularly in the Christian New Testament, where it is rendered in Greek as *nomos*, the word actually means "instruction." The Hebrew word for "law" is *mišpāṭ*, which is often translated as "justice."

An Introduction to Isaiah 1–39

Christians read texts from Isaiah as predictions concerning the coming of Christ, such as Isaiah 7:4, which is quoted in Matthew 1:23 to demonstrate that Jesus was born to a virgin (Greek, *parthenos*), although the Hebrew term, ʿalmâ, actually refers simply to a woman of child-bearing age. Likewise, passages concerning an ideal Davidic king, such as Isaiah 9:1–6, are read as announcements of Jesus's future coming.

The book of Isaiah is a work of sacred scripture in both Judaism and Christianity, but it is also a work of literature, and it must be read as such. Isaiah includes sixty-six chapters, and it is identified in Isaiah 1:1 as "the vision of Isaiah ben Amoz which he saw concerning Judah and Jerusalem in the days of Uzziah, Jotham, Ahaz, and Hezekiah, Kings of Judah" (cf. Isa 2:1; 13:1). The reigns of these kings would extend from 783–686 BCE, according to the dating system of reckoning employed by the American Albright school. But whereas Isaiah appears repeatedly in the book through Isaiah 39, beginning in Isaiah 40, Isaiah never appears again. However, King Cyrus of Persia, who ruled from ca. 550–530 BCE, appears by name as YHWH's messiah and temple builder in Isaiah 44:28 and 45:1. Consequently, modern scholars, beginning with the Swiss scholar Bernhard Duhm,[2] are accustomed to dividing the book into: First or Proto-Isaiah in Isaiah 1–39, emerging from the work and life of the late eighth-century prophet Isaiah ben Amoz; Second Isaiah in Isaiah 40–55, emerging from the work of a late sixth-century exilic prophet known by scholars as Deutero-Isaiah; and Third Isaiah in Isaiah 56–66, emerging from the works of a number of prophets from the Persian period (late sixth through late fourth century BCE), known collectively as Trito-Isaiah. Some scholars, however, view Isaiah 56–66 as part of the work of Second Isaiah.[3]

Isaiah 1–39 is part of the whole book of Isaiah, and no ancient manuscript of Isaiah 1–39 circulating independently of 40–66 has ever appeared. The book of Isaiah appears among the Dead Sea Scrolls in a number of manuscripts, but most are fragmentary, except for 1QIsaiah^a, the "Great Isaiah Scroll" from Cave 1, which dates to 125–100 BCE, and 1QIsaiah^b, another Isaiah scroll also from Cave 1, albeit heavily damaged and incomplete, which dates to 50–25 BCE.[4] The Great Isaiah Scroll, apparently the

---

2. Duhm, *Jesaia*. Unfortunately, this commentary has never been translated into English, despite its importance as the foundation for modern scholarship on the book of Isaiah.

3. E.g., Paul, *Isaiah 40–66*.

4. For the publication of 1QIsaiah^a and 1QIsaiah^b, see now Ulrich and Flint, *Isaiah Scrolls*. For the dating of 1QIsaiah^a, see Ulrich and Flint, *Isaiah Scrolls*, 61–64, and for 1QIsaiah^b, see Ulrich and Flint, *Isaiah Scrolls*, 199–200.

Introduction

oldest and most complete surviving manuscript of the book of Isaiah, is particularly important to us because it divides the book into two portions, Isaiah 1–33 and Isaiah 34–66.

II. The Book of Isaiah as a Whole

In order to understand fully the place and function of Isaiah 1–39 within the entire book of Isaiah, we must first understand the final, received form of the entire book of Isaiah.[5] Interpreters have known since antiquity that Isaiah is an edited book. The Babylonian Talmud, completed in the sixth century CE, states in b. Baba Batra 15a that the book of Isaiah was written by "Hezekiah and his colleagues" and not by Isaiah himself. The twelfth-century CE medieval Rabbinic biblical commentator R. Abraham ibn Ezra (1089–1164 CE) notes in his commentary on Isaiah 40:1 the references to the Babylonian exile and to King Cyrus of Persia together with the message of comfort evident in this verse, and states that the message "refers to a period yet to come." He adds that the orthodox maintain that the book of Samuel was written by Samuel until the mention of the death of Samuel in 1 Samuel 25:1, that Chronicles contains the names of David's descendants until Zerubbabel, and that kings and princes will arise on hearing the name of the prophet (Isaiah) even after his death. He concludes with the recommendation, "the reader will adopt the opinion which recommends itself most to his judgment," apparently to avoid stating that Isaiah did not write the entire book.[6]

With the beginning of modern scholarship in the Age of Enlightenment, interpreters continued to view Isaiah as an edited book, based especially on its references to the Babylonian exile and Cyrus in Isaiah 40–66 and in Isaiah 1–39.[7] Johann Gottfried Eichhorn, beginning in the first edition of his *Introduction to the Old Testament*, originally published in three volumes in 1780–83, maintains that later writers supplemented Isaiah's original oracles with material written during the Babylonian exile and beyond.[8]

---

5. For surveys of research on the formation of the entire book of Isaiah, see Sweeney, "Book of Isaiah in Recent Research"; especially useful studies on the formation of Isaiah include Ackroyd, *Studies*; Sweeney, *Isaiah 1–4*; Rendtorff, *Canon and Theology*; Williamson, *Book Called Isaiah*; Clements, *Old Testament Prophecy*; Berges, *Buch Jesaja*; Stromberg, *Isaiah After Exile*; Wieringen and Jang, *Function of the Reader*.

6. Friedländer, *Commentary of Ibn Ezra*, 169–71.

7. For discussion, see Sweeney, "On the Road to Duhm."

8. See Eichhorn, *Einleitung*, 76–146.

Eichhorn was followed by Wilhelm Gesenius, who argued in his 1820–21 commentary on Isaiah that the work of an exilic writer, whom he named "Pseudo-Jesaia," appeared in Isaiah 40–66 and in some texts from Isaiah 1–39, such as Isaiah 13–14; 21; 24–27; 34; and 35.[9] Other interpreters who argued that an exilic writer authored portions of Isaiah included Ferdinand Hitzig, Heinrich Georg August Ewald, and August Dillmann.[10] When Duhm published his commentary in 1892, he revolutionized the field by arguing that a third prophet, whom he designated as Trito-Jesaiah, wrote Isaiah 56–66.[11] It is noteworthy that all of these scholars focused especially on the prophets and writers who wrote the book of Isaiah, so that in his interpretation, the book became collections of quotations of their prophetic oracles and the narratives that portrayed their activities. Consequentially, Isaiah 1–39 presented collections of the oracles of Isaiah ben Amoz and narratives about him; Isaiah 40–55 presented collections of oracle by Deutero-Isaiah; and Isaiah 56–66 presented oracles by Trito-Isaiah. The result was commentaries that were written on each of these sections as if they were independent and self-standing prophetic books.

But contemporary interpreters have learned that the book of Isaiah—and indeed, all biblical books—are first and foremost works of literature that also stand as sacred scripture.[12] Consequently, the book of Isaiah must be read first as a work of literature before any conclusions are drawn about the history of its composition. This calls for reading the book of Isaiah first from a synchronic literary perspective, that is, as a work of literature without any historical presuppositions.[13] Only after a synchronic literary reading has been completed, so that the reader may understand the book's overall literary structure and viewpoint, can a diachronic or historical reading of the book take place in an effort to reconstruct its compositional history, if the book presents evidence that such a history is possible to construct. In the case of the book of Isaiah, both a synchronic literary reading of the book and a diachronic historical reading are justified.

9. Gesenius, *Jesaia*.

10. Hitzig, *Jesaja*; Ewald, *Propheten*; Dillmann, *Jesaia*.

11. Duhm, *Jesaia*, 1892, V-XXI, 390–458; Duhm, *Jesaia*, 1968, 7–22, 418–90.

12. For commentaries that treat Isaiah as a unified literary work, see Sweeney, *Isaiah 1–39*; Sweeney, *Isaiah 40–66*; Childs, *Isaiah*; Blenkinsopp, *Isaiah 1–39*; Blenkinsopp, *Isaiah 40–55*; Blenkinsopp, *Isaiah 56–66*; Kim, *Reading Isaiah*.

13. For methodological reflection on reading biblical books, see Knierim, "Form Criticism Reconsidered"; Knierim, "Criticism of Literary Features." See also Sweeney, "Form Criticism"; Sweeney, "Synchronic, Diachronic, and Intertextual Dimensions."

Introduction

The book of Isaiah presents difficulties to readers who attempt to understand its literary form and structure. Other prophetic books offer ready clues to their individual forms and structures. Both Jeremiah and Ezekiel include superscriptions throughout that introduce each structural element of the book. And the book of the Twelve Prophets presents a sequence of twelve constitutive prophetic writings that form the structure of the book in both its Masoretic Hebrew and Septuagint Greek forms.

Isaiah is different. Although Isaiah has superscriptions in Isaiah 1:1; 2:1; and 13:1 that play important roles in the book, they do not explain the structure of the book of Isaiah as a whole. Isaiah 1:1 identifies the book as "the vision of Isaiah ben Amoz, which he saw concerning Jerusalem and Judah in the days of Uzziah, Jotham, Ahaz, and Hezekiah, Kings of Judah," which introduces the entire book. But Isaiah 2:1 and 13:1 have more limited functions. Isaiah 2:1, "The word that Isaiah ben Amoz saw concerning Judah and Jerusalem," introduces only Isaiah 2–4, insofar as Isaiah 5–12 addresses both Judah and Israel. Isaiah 13:1, "The Pronouncement of Babylon, which Isaiah ben Amoz saw," introduces the oracle concerning Babylon in Isaiah 13:1—14:27 as well as a sequence of "pronouncements" concerning various nations that appear throughout Isaiah 14:28—23:18, insofar as Isaiah 24–27 focuses once again on the land of Israel.

The key to understanding the formal structure of the book of Isaiah lies elsewhere. Indeed, there are several keys that work together to disclose the formal literary structure of the book. They include the parallel but contrasting narratives concerning King Ahaz of Judah in Isaiah 7:1–25 and King Hezekiah of Judah in Isaiah 36:1—39:8; intertextual references that connect statements in Isaiah 40–66 to statements in Isaiah 1–39; the parallel addresses to Israel in Isaiah 1:1–31 and to the nations, exemplified by Edom, in Isaiah 34:1—35:10 concerning the punishment and restoration of Israel and Judah to Jerusalem; the contrasting scenarios of an Assyrian threat against Jerusalem and Judah in Isaiah 1–33 and the conclusion of the Babylonian threat against Jerusalem and Judah in Isaiah 40–66; and the indication of a gap between Isaiah 1–33 and Isaiah 34–66 in the Great Isaiah Scroll from Qumran, 1QIsaiah^a. Altogether, these keys will indicate that the final form of the book of Isaiah is to be read as "A Prophetic Exhortation to Adhere to YHWH," and they point to a two-part structure for the book, viz., the Prophetic Announcement of YHWH's Plans for Worldwide Sovereignty at Zion in Isaiah 1–33 and the Prophetic Announcement of the

An Introduction to Isaiah 1–39

Realization of YHWH's Plans for Worldwide Sovereignty at Zion in Isaiah 34–66.[14]

From the late 1960s to the early 1980s, Peter R. Ackroyd published six studies, often in obscure, hard to find publications, that grew out of his work on a brief commentary on Isaiah published in *The Interpreter's One-Volume Commentary on the Bible*.[15] These studies focused especially on the narrative accounts of King Hezekiah of Judah in Isaiah 36–39, which also appeared in somewhat different forms in 2 Kings 18–20 and 2 Chronicles 29–32, and King Ahaz of Judah in Isaiah 7 (cf. 2 Kgs 16; 2 Chr 28). Ackroyd's studies made several important points that enabled interpreters to think of the book of Isaiah as a unified literary work. They demonstrated that Hezekiah was a very special figure who functioned in relation to Isaiah ben Amoz, and that he was idealized as a righteous king in Isaiah, Kings, and Chronicles. They also demonstrated that the allegedly righteous Hezekiah was contrasted with the allegedly wicked King Ahaz in all of these works. Ackroyd's studies further demonstrated that the Hezekiah narratives in Isaiah 36–39 and 2 Kings 18–20 each concluded with Isaiah's condemnation of Hezekiah for making an alliance with Prince Merodach-Baladan of Babylon to support their joint revolt against King Sennacherib of Assyria. As part of Isaiah's condemnation of Hezekiah, the prophet announced that Hezekiah's sons would someday be exiled to Babylon, which anticipated the Babylonian exile. Kings concludes with the Babylonian exile in 2 Kings 25, and so the story of Hezekiah's alliance with Merodach-Baladan in 2 Kings 18–20 points toward this conclusion of the book. Insofar as Isaiah 40 begins the section of the book of Isaiah concerned with the Babylonian exile, Isaiah 36–39 provides a literary bridge that links Isaiah 1–39 to Isaiah 40–66. The concerns with the Babylonian exile evident in Isaiah 36–39 (e.g., Isa 39:1–8) prompted scholars to consider if other portions of Isaiah, such as Isaiah 1–12, had been edited in later times to relate Isaiah's message to the Babylonian exile (see chapter 6 at the end of this volume).

Ronald E. Clements built upon Ackroyd's work during the 1980s and the early 1990s by demonstrating further links between Isaiah 1–39 and

---

14. See Sweeney, *Isaiah 1–39*, 31–62; Sweeney, *Isaiah 40–66*, 1–40; Sweeney, *Prophetic Literature*; Sweeney, "Isaiah (Book and Person)."

15. Ackroyd, "Book of Isaiah." For the studies, see Ackroyd, "Isaiah 1–12"; Ackroyd, "Isaiah 36–39"; Ackroyd, "Historians and Prophets"; Ackroyd, "Interpretation of the Babylonian Exile," 152–71; Ackroyd, "Death of Hezekiah"; and Ackroyd, "Biblical Interpretation."

INTRODUCTION

Isaiah 40–66 in relation to his own commentary on Isaiah 1–39.[16] Clements pointed to Deutero-Isaiah's development of First Isaiah's themes, such as Israel's blindness and deafness (Isa 42:16–19; 43:8, from Isa 6:9–10; 29:18; 35:5); the divine election of Israel (Isa 40:1; 41:8–9; 43:6–7; 44:1–2, from Isa 2:6); G-d's future actions toward Israel (Isa 44:26 from Isa 6:11); G-d's signal to nations (Isa 49:22–23 from Isa 5:26). Other indications of unity in Isaiah include the role of Isaiah's "disciples" in developing the prophet's earlier words and applying them to later times (see Isa 8:6); the downfall of Babylon (Isa 47 from Isa 13:1—14:23); and the emphasis on Hezekiah's psalm of thanksgiving for deliverance from illness in Isaiah 38:9–20 and Israel's deliverance in Isaiah 40–55. Finally, Clements pointed to the differentiation of narratives in Isaiah 36–39 so that the account of YHWH's deliverance of Jerusalem in chapters 36–37 would have been written in the late monarchic period, due to its knowledge of Sennacherib's assassination by his own sons in 681 BCE, whereas Isaiah 38–39 had later, exilic associations.

Other scholars continued to develop the links between Isaiah 1–39 and Isaiah 40–66. Rolf Rendtorff published several key essays during the 1980s and 1990s that pointed to the roles of Isaiah 6 and Trito-Isaiah in contributing to the unity of Isaiah.[17] H. G. M. Williamson argued that Deutero-Isaiah must have been a disciple of Isaiah who both wrote Isaiah 40–55 and edited Isaiah 1–39 so that it would join with Isaiah 40–55.[18] Patricia Tull Willey employs an intertextual perspective to point to Second Isaiah's references to the former things (e.g., Isa 43:18–19; 46:9–10) as references to earlier texts in Isaiah as well as to other texts, such as Lamentations; Jeremiah; Nahum; and Psalms.[19] And Jacob Stromberg most recently developed the work of both Rendtorff and Williamson to argue that the author of Trito-Isaiah was both the reader and redactor who produced the final form of the book of Isaiah.[20]

Building on the work of Ackroyd, Clements, Rendtorff, and others, Sweeney published a study that focused on Isaiah 1 as a post-exilic,

---

16. Clements, *Isaiah 1–39*. See also Clements, *Old Testament Prophecy*, which includes his studies "Prophecies of Isaiah"; "Immanuel Prophecy"; "Beyond Tradition History"; "Unity of the Book of Isaiah"; and Clements, *Isaiah and the Deliverance of Jerusalem*.

17. Rendtorff, *Canon*. See his essays, Rendtorff, "Composition of the Book of Isaiah"; Rendtorff, "Isaiah 6"; and Rendtorff, "Isaiah 56:1."

18. Williamson, *Book Called Isaiah*.

19. Tull Willey, *Remember the Former Things*. See now Tull, *Isaiah 1–39*. She is currently writing a second volume on Isaiah 40–66.

20. Stromberg, *Isaiah After Exile*.

An Introduction to Isaiah 1–39

Persian-period redactional composition and Isaiah 2–4 as an exilic period redactional composition that read earlier oracles by Isaiah in relation to their later application to their later redactional settings. In addition, the study focused on both the changing nature of the Davidic promise and the role of exodus and wilderness motifs in the final form of the book of Isaiah. This study led ultimately to Sweeney's two FOTL commentaries on Isaiah 1–39 and Isaiah 40–66.[21] Isaiah 1 functioned as an introduction to the final fifth/fourth-century edition of the book of Isaiah as a whole,[22] and Isaiah 2–4 functioned as an introduction to the earlier sixth-century edition of the book.[23] Whereas the first part of the book in Isaiah 1–39 focuses especially on the eternal promise to the House of David (e.g., Isa 9:1–6; 11:1–16; 32:1–20), the second part of the book in Isaiah 40–66 dispenses with the notion of eternal Davidic kingship and assigns the Davidic promise to Israel in Isaiah 55, allowing for the recognition of YHWH as King in Isaiah 66. By contrast, the exodus and wilderness motifs—which call for return to the land of Israel following exile in Assyria, Babylonia, and elsewhere—permeate the entire book of Isaiah.[24]

Finally, the last key to reading the book of Isaiah as a synchronic, formal, literary unity is the recognition that the synchronic form of the book comprises two major sections, Isaiah 1–33 and Isaiah 34–66, and not Isaiah 1–39, 40–55, and 56–66, which represent diachronic divisions of the book. This conclusion is based on the division of the Great Isaiah Scroll from Qumran, 1QIsaiah[a], and a number of key arguments.[25] One is the deliberate contrast between the portrayal of King Ahaz of Judah in Isaiah 7:1—9:6 and that of Hezekiah in Isaiah 36–39. Both narratives focus on the upper pool by the Fuller's Field as the location of the primary encounters depicted in each narrative. Whereas Ahaz allegedly shows great faithlessness in YHWH so that the nation suffers Assyrian invasion, Hezekiah shows great faithfulness in YHWH and thereby saves Jerusalem. Second are the major parallels between Isaiah 1 and Isaiah 34–35. Isaiah 1 points to coming punishment and restoration for Israel due to its neglect of YHWH and

---

21. Sweeney, *Isaiah 1–4* (1988); Sweeney *Isaiah 1–39* (1996); Sweeney, *Isaiah 40–66* (2016).

22. Cf. Fohrer, "Jesaja 1."

23. Cf. Clements, "Prophecies of Isaiah"; Wiklander, *Prophecy as Literature*.

24. In addition to the works noted above in note 21, see Sweeney, "Synchronic, Diachronic, and Intertextual Dimensions."

25. Sweeney, *Isaiah 1–39*, 39–51; Sweeney *Isaiah 40–66*, 10–25; Evans, "Unity."

need for purging or cleansing whereas Isaiah 34–35 point to coming judgment against the nations, exemplified by Edom, and subsequent restoration for Israel. Both texts begin with a call to attention (Isa 1:1 and 34:1) and they continue with other parallels, such as focus on YHWH's vengeance (Isa 1:24 and 34:8), the unquenchable burning of YHWH's enemies (Isa 1:31 and 34:10), "the mouth of YHWH that speaks" (Isa 1:20 and 34:16), YHWH's sword of punishment (Isa 1:20 and 34:5, 6), the sacrificial blood and fat of cattle (Isa 1:11–15 and 34:6–7), references to Sodom and Gomorrah (Isa 1:7–9, 10 and 34:9–11), and references to wilting leaves (Isa 1:30 and 34:4). Whereas Isaiah 1 announces to Israel the judgment of Jerusalem and its subsequent restoration, Isaiah 34–35 announces the judgment of the nations followed by subsequent restoration for both the nations and Israel/Jerusalem. Consequently, Isaiah 1 and 34–35 each function as introductions to their respective portions of the book of Isaiah 1–33, which announces the *coming* worldwide sovereignty of YHWH at Zion, and Isaiah 34–66, which announces the *realized* worldwide sovereignty of YHWH at Zion.

III. The Synchronic Internal Structure of Isaiah 1–33

Isaiah 1–33, which contains the book of Isaiah's presentation of YHWH's plans for worldwide sovereignty at Zion, displays a two-part structure. Isaiah 1 presents a sequence of Isaian oracles that constitute the prologue for the book of Isaiah, and Isaiah 2–33 presents a sequence of four textual blocks concerned with prophetic instruction concerning YHWH's projected plans to establish worldwide sovereignty at Zion. The four blocks include the prophetic announcement concerning the preparation of Zion for its role as the center for YHWH's worldwide rule in Isaiah 2–4; prophetic instruction concerning the significance of Assyrian judgment against Jacob/Israel to prepare for the restoration of Davidic rule in Isaiah 5–12; a prophetic announcement concerning the preparation of the nations for YHWH's world rule in Isaiah 13–27; and prophetic instruction concerning YHWH's plans for Jerusalem where a royal savior will emerge in Isaiah 28–33.

A. Isaiah 1

Isaiah 1 constitutes the prologue of the book of Isaiah, which focuses on introductory parenesis, a form of announcement that calls for both punishment for alleged wrongdoing and restoration after the punishment has been completed. The reason for this understanding is that the chapter includes oracles that accuse Jerusalem and Judah of wrongdoing in Isaiah 1:2–26 and 29–31, but it also portrays the restoration of Jerusalem and Judah following repentance in Isaiah 1:27–28. The pattern of announcement of punishment and announcement of restoration was noted by Georg Fohrer, who argued that Isaiah 1 served as a summation of the prophetic proclamation of Isaiah ben Amoz and that Isaiah 1 therefore served as the prologue for Isaiah 1–39, based on the assumption that Isaiah 1–39 constituted a distinct prophetic book.[26] This argument was followed by Christopher R. Seitz, who argued that the entirety of the book of Isaiah was ultimately concerned with the history, experience, and well-being of the city of Jerusalem.[27]

With the recognition that Isaiah constituted a single, unified prophetic book, Sweeney argued that Isaiah 1 constituted the prologue for the entire book of Isaiah.[28] This conclusion includes two essential components.

The first is the role of the superscription in Isaiah 1:1. Superscriptions by their very nature stand apart from and introduce the material that they identify.[29] Consequently, the superscription in Isaiah 1:1 both introduces the following material and stands apart from it. In the case of Isaiah 1:1, the superscription identified the following material as "the vision of Isaiah, which he saw concerning Judah and Jerusalem in the days of Uzziah, Jotham, Ahaz, and Hezekiah, Kings of Judah." Several issues appear in this text. First, it identifies the genre of Isaiah as "the *vision* of Isaiah ben Amoz." Although "vision" in English describes a strictly visual event, the Hebrew word, *ḥāzôn*, means more than merely "vision," insofar as it includes both visual and auditory perception. The book of Isaiah contains some visionary elements, such as Isaiah's inaugural vision in Isaiah 6, but it also contains many oracular speeches, generally made by YHWH to the prophet or by the prophet to the people of his time, or speeches that are addressed to later generations. Consequently, the initial element of Isaiah 1:1 is best translated "the perception of Isaiah, which he perceived . . . ." Secondly, the entire book is attributed to Isaiah ben Amoz, but not all of the book could have been written by the prophet, particularly the narrative accounts in Isaiah 7 and 36–39, which would have been written by someone other than Isaiah ben Amoz, and the references to the Babylonian exile in Isaiah 40–66 as well

---

26. Fohrer, "Jesaja 1" (see note 22).
27. Seitz, *Zion's Final Destiny*.
28. Sweeney, *Isaiah 1–39*, 71–87; cf. Sweeney, *Isaiah 1–4*, 27–34.
29. Tucker, "Prophetic Superscriptions."

INTRODUCTION

as the references to King Cyrus of Persia in Isaiah 44:28 and 45:1, which would not have been known to the prophet in his own lifetime. Those who argue that Isaiah must have predicted these events miss some important points about prophecy. Prophecy was not understood to be predictive until the Hellenistic period, and even then, specific names and events could not have been known to those making predictions.[30] Prior to the Hellenistic period, prophecy in the ancient world was much more analytical in that it was focused on attempting to identify what YHWH or the gods and goddesses of other nations were doing in the world. Furthermore, the superscription identifies the historical range of the book as the late eighth and early seventh century BCE, the time when the Assyrian Empire took control of both Israel and Judah. This period includes the reigns of the Judean Kings Uzziah (783–742 BCE), Jotham (742–735 BCE), Ahaz (735–715 BCE), and Hezekiah (715–687/86 BCE). Isaiah ben Amoz is therefore portrayed as the ultimate focus of the book, even though some material was written by his disciples (Isa 8:16), and even though those disciples lived hundreds of years later.

The second major component of Isaiah is the sequence of oracles themselves in Isaiah 1:2–31. The passage begins immediately after the superscription in Isaiah 1:1, and it concludes prior to the next superscription in Isaiah 2:1. Some interpreters read Isaiah 1:2–20 as a rhetorical unit that culminates in YHWH's invitation to the people of Israel/Judah to repent from their wrongdoing,[31] or they may read Isaiah 1:2–31 as a whole with similar understandings.[32] But it is best to focus on each of the constituent small sub-units that make up the whole, insofar as they vary so much in form and context.[33] Thus, Isaiah 1:2–3 introduces the sequence with an announcement of YHWH's accusation against Israel that they do not know YHWH. Isaiah 1:4–9 follows with warnings against continued wrongdoing that continues to bring punishment and illness upon the people. Isaiah 1:10–17 is an example of prophetic Torah or instruction that calls upon the people to cease doing what is wrong and start doing what is right so that they might end their own suffering. Isaiah 1:18–20 appeals to the people to go to court with YHWH so that YHWH may offer them restoration, if the people will repent and change their ways. Isaiah 1:21–26 announces

30. Cook, *"Cessation of Prophecy"*; cf. Flannery Dailey, *Dreamers, Scribes, and Priest*.
31. E.g., Gitay, *Isaiah and His Audience*, 14–34.
32. E.g., Blenkinsopp, *Isaiah 1–39*, 176–88.
33. Cf. Williamson, *Isaiah 1–5*, 23.

Zion's restoration following the purification of the people by punishment and purging as one purges ore to produce pure metal. Isaiah 1:27–28 announces Zion's redemption for those who are repentant once the rebels and sinners have been finished. And Isaiah 1:28–31 illustrates the punishment of those who have engaged in idolatry.

The issues taken up in Isaiah 1:2–31 focus on the interplay between punishment for wrongdoing and restoration following the punishment for those who are repentant and do what is right in adhering to YHWH. These same issues appear at the conclusion of the book in Isaiah 65–66, which likewise envisions punishment for wrongdoing and restoration for those who are righteous when YHWH is recognized as King. Although some deny that Isaiah 1 and Isaiah 65–66 form a rhetorical inclusio at the beginning and end of the book, the inclusio view is based on the need to grasp the full dimensions of intertextual exegesis, which focus on *literary function* rather than authorial intention.[34]

B. Isaiah 2–33

Isaiah 2–33 constitutes the core of the first part of the book of Isaiah with a lengthy prophetic instruction concerning YHWH's projected plans to establish worldwide sovereignty in Zion.[35] It includes four major structural elements, viz., Isaiah 2–4, prophetic announcement concerning the preparation of Zion for its role as the center for YHWH's world rule; Isaiah 5–12, prophetic instruction concerning the significance of Assyrian judgment against Israel and Judah culminating in the restoration of righteous Davidic rule; Isaiah 13–27, prophetic announcement concerning the preparation of the nations for YHWH's world rule; and Isaiah 28–33, prophetic instruction concerning YHWH's plans for Jerusalem as the site for the emergence of a royal savior.

1. Isaiah 2–4

Isaiah 2–4 constitutes the first of four textual blocks in Isaiah 2–33 concerned with prophetic instruction regarding YHWH's projected plans to

---

34. Cf. Carr, "Reading Isaiah."
35. Sweeney, *Isaiah 1–39*, 39–51.

Introduction

establish worldwide sovereignty at Zion.[36] As the first textual block in the sequence, Isaiah 2–4 presents a prophetic announcement concerning the preparation of Zion for its role as the center for YHWH's world rule.

Isaiah 2–4 begins with its own superscription in Isaiah 2:1, "The word which Isaiah ben Amoz perceived concerning Judah and Jerusalem." The concern with Judah and Jerusalem continues through Isaiah 4:6. A new sub-unit appears in Isaiah 5:1—12:6, which is concerned with Israel and Judah, albeit without its own superscription.[37] Some might argue that Isaiah 5–12 should also be subsumed under Isaiah 2:1 due to the focus on Davidic kingship, which would be centered in Jerusalem, in Isaiah 9:1–6 and 11:1–16.[38]

The internal structure of Isaiah 2:2—4:6 is complex.[39] It begins with an announcement in Isaiah 2:2-4 concerning the establishment of Zion as the center for YHWH's worldwide rule, insofar as the nations will travel to Zion to learn "instruction" (Hebrew, *tôrâ*) from YHWH so that they will cease to engage in war. Isaiah 2:5—4:6 follows with a sequence of three addresses directed to the House of Jacob (Israel/Judah) concerning the cleansing or purging of Zion so that it might assume this role. The first address appears in Isaiah 2:5–9, which invites the House of Jacob to join the nations in their procession to Zion to learn YHWH's Torah, but it also warns that Jacob is presently unfit to assume this role due to its reliance on foreign nations—and therefore their gods—for support to engage in war. The second address appears in Isaiah 2:10–21 concerning the cleansing or purging of those who are proud and arrogant in the world on the Day of YHWH. The third address appears in Isaiah 3:1—4:6 concerning the cleansing or purging of Jerusalem and Judah, deemed to be overly self-reliant and therefore not sufficient reliant on YHWH (Isa 2:22). Both the men of Jerusalem and Judah (Isa 3:1–15) and the women of Jerusalem and Judah (Isa 3:16—4:1)

---

36. Sweeney, *Isaiah 1–39*, 45–46, 87–121.

37. Sweeney, *Isaiah 1–39*, 46, 121–211.

38. There is a persistent effort to view Isaiah 1–12 as a structural element in Isaiah, as exemplified by Ackroyd, "Presentation of a Prophet"; cf. Blenkinsopp, *Isaiah 1–39*, 173–74; Childs, *Isaiah*, 9–10; but Williamson, *Isaiah 1–5*, 324, for example, maintains that a new section beginning in Isaiah 5:1 is "universally recognized." Wildberger, *Isaiah 1–12*, vii, states, "it is obvious and generally accepted that one comes to a recognizable break in the book of Isaiah at this point," i.e., after Isaiah 1–12. The decision to view Isaiah 1–12 as a major unit actually goes back to Duhm, *Buch Jesaia*, 1892, viii–x; 1968, 10–12. But even as part of Isaiah 1–12, Isaiah 5:1 begins a new sub-unit.

39. See also Wiklander, *Prophecy as Literature*.

will suffer judgment to produce the cleansed or purged remnant of Israel in Jerusalem (Isa 4:2–6). Isaiah 4:2–6 employs the imagery of cloud by day and fire by night known from the exodus and wilderness narratives to portray the protective presence of YHWH in the city, symbolized by the pillar of smoke and fire produced by the altar of the Jerusalem Temple (e.g., Exod 14:19–20, 24; 16:10; 23:23–33; 40:33b–38; Num 10:11–12).

2. Isaiah 5–12

Isaiah 5–12 presents prophetic instruction concerning the significance of Assyrian judgment against Israel, culminating in the anticipated restoration of the Davidic empire.[40] The internal structure of Isaiah 5–12 is even more complex than that of Isaiah 2–4. This is due to heavy editing in these chapters, but in a synchronic analysis, the redactional moves must be set aside in favor of purely literary considerations. Isaiah 5–12 begins with a judicial allegory in which Isaiah portrays Israel and Judah as the vineyard of his friend, who proves to be YHWH. The concern with Israel and Judah continues through the concluding hymn of thanksgiving in Isaiah 12:1–6. A new textual block concerned with the nations appears in Isaiah 13–27, beginning with its own superscription in Isaiah 13:1.

Isaiah 5–12 opens in Isaiah 5:1–30 with an announcement of judgment against Israel and Judah, beginning with a judicial vineyard allegory in Isaiah 5:1–7 and continuing with a sequence of woe oracles that specifically announcement punishment against Israel and Judah by the Assyrian empire in Isaiah 5:8–30.

A complex textual block concerning the explanation for this punishment, viz., that it will result in a restored and righteous Davidic kingdom, follows in Isaiah 6–12.[41] A narrative account of Isaiah oracles of judgment against Israel and Judah by Assyria appears in Isaiah 6:1—8:15, including an account of Isaiah's commission as a prophet (Isa 6:1–13) and an account of YHWH's proposed judgment (Isa 7:1—8:15). A second component concerned with the ultimate downfall of the Assyrian Empire and the restoration of the Davidic monarchy then follows in Isaiah 8:16—12:6. Isaiah 8:16—12:6 expresses Isaiah's frustration while waiting for righteous Davidic kingship (Isa 8:16—9:6). The passage then presents a detailed oracular sequence concerning YHWH's judgment against Assyria that culminates

---

40. Sweeney, *Isaiah 1–39*, 46, 112–211.
41. See also Wieringen, *Implied Reader*.

INTRODUCTION

in a restored David kingdom, portrayed as an act of YHWH akin to the deliverance of Israel in the exodus from Egypt (Isa 9:7—12:6).

3. Isaiah 13–27

The third major component of Isaiah 2–33 appears in Isaiah 13–27, which constitutes a prophetic announcement concerning the preparation of the nations for YHWH's world rule. It includes two major components. The first is the presentation of the pronouncements or oracles concerning the nations in Isaiah 13–23, and the second is a prophetic announcement of YHWH's new world order in the form of a prophecy of salvation or restoration for Zion/Israel.[42]

The pronouncements concerning the nations in Isaiah 13–23 present a sequence of prophetic oracles concerning what YHWH is doing, concerning nine nations in the ancient Near Eastern world. Each of these oracles has its own superscription, and the first superscription in Isaiah 13:1, "The pronouncement of Babylon which Isaiah ben Amoz perceived," serves as an introduction for both the pronouncement concerning Babylon in Isaiah 13:1—14:32 and for the whole sequence of pronouncements in Isaiah 13–23. Like Isaiah 1:1 and 2:1, this superscription identifies Isaiah ben Amoz as the one who "perceived" these oracles.

The sequence includes nine major oracles concerning Babylon (Isa 13:1—14:32), Moab (Isa 15:1—16:14), Damascus (Isa 17:1—18:7), Egypt (Isa 19:1—20:6), the Wilderness of the Sea, often identified with Babylon under the leadership of Merodach-Baladan (Isa 21:1-10), Dumah, often identified with the Arabian Desert and perhaps Edom west of Babylon (Isa 21:11-12), Arabia (Isa 21:13-17), the Valley of Vision, often identified with Jerusalem (Isa 22:1-25), and Tyre (Isa 23:1-18).[43] In the case of the oracle concerning Philistia in Isaiah 14:28-32, it is subsumed structurally under the oracle concerning Babylon in Isaiah 13:1—14:32. It is noteworthy from a diachronic perspective that all of the nations included here were subject to the Achaemenid Persian Empire in the late sixth through the late fourth centuries BCE. This has implications for understanding the interrelationship between the first part of the book in Isaiah 1–33 and the second part

---

42. Sweeney, *Isaiah 1–39*, 39–40, 46.

43. For detailed discussion of these oracles, see Sweeney, *Isaiah 1–39*, 212–311. See also Erlandsson, *Burden of Babylon*; Holt et al., *Concerning the Nations*.

of the book in Isaiah 34–36, which explicitly names King Cyrus of Persia as YHWH's messiah and temple builder in Isaiah 44:28 and 45:1.

The prophetic announcement of YHWH's new world order in Isaiah 24:1—27:13 concludes and contextualizes the pronouncements concerning the nations by identifying the nations as subject to YHWH at Zion.[44] In order to serve this function, Isaiah 24–27 begins in 24:1–23 with a prophetic announcement of YHWH's punishment of the entire earth, which picks up the concerns of the earlier "Day of YHWH" oracle in 2:7–21, which calls for punishment against all those who are proud and arrogant before YHWH. Isaiah 25:1—27:13 then follows up with a prophetic announcement of blessing for the entire earth and its results for Zion/Jerusalem, which entails the return of the exiles of Israel to Zion in language that suggest a second exodus from Egypt and Assyria like the exodus from Egypt portrayed throughout the book of Isaiah as well as the book of Exodus. As part of that restoration, Isaiah 27:1–11 presents a new vineyard song that anticipates restoration for Israel after the judgment portrayed in the earlier vineyard song in Isaiah 5:17.

4. Isaiah 28–33

The fourth and final component of Isaiah 2–33 appears in Isaiah 28–33, a sequence of oracles that together provide prophetic instruction concerning YHWH's plans and purposes for Jerusalem, culminating in the announcement of a royal savior who will preside over Jerusalem on behalf of YHWH. The sequence of oracles is ultimately concerned with the removal of faulty leadership in Israel and Judah that must make way for an ideal leader. Although the prospective leader is understood to be an ideal royal figure who will bring deliverance and restoration to Jerusalem, there is no clear indication that this leader will be a Davidic monarch, which thereby anticipates the emergence of King Cyrus of Persia as YHWH's messiah and temple builder in Isaiah 44:28 and 45:1.

The sequence of oracles in this textual block are primarily "woe" (Hebrew, *hôy*), an exclamation that introduces the oracle with a warning to those addressed of impending disaster or punishment.[45] Within this textual block, the "woe" oracles are directed especially at the leadership of Israel and Judah—and later against an oppressor, understood to be Assyria—of

---

44. Sweeney, *Isaiah 1–39*, 311–53. See also Hays, *Origins of Isaiah 24–27*.
45. Sweeney, *Isaiah 1–39*, 543.

INTRODUCTION

their impending punishment, overthrow, and removal as YHWH takes action against them.

The sequence of oracles includes five major elements. Isaiah 28:1–29 constitutes prophetic instruction concerning YHWH's purpose in bringing Assyrian hegemony. Insofar as it begins with a woe oracle that condemns the drunken leadership of Ephraim, the main power tribe of the northern kingdom of Israel, the oracle functions as a warning of YHWH's impending judgment against the northern kingdom of Israel. Isaiah 29:1–24 constitutes prophetic instruction concerning YHWH's purpose in bringing about assault against Ariel/Zion; it functions as a warning concerning YHWH's intention to take action against the leadership of Judah in Jerusalem. Isaiah 30:1–33 constitutes prophetic instruction concerning YHWH's delay in delivering the people from Assyria. The oracle thereby signals YHWH's intention to bring punishment against the people of Israel and Judah for making diplomatic overtures to Egypt, the traditional enemy of Israel in the exodus and wilderness tradition, to gain support for revolt against Assyria. Such overtures ignore YHWH's promises of protection for Israel and Judah and thereby display a failure to trust in YHWH. Isaiah 31:1–9 constitutes parenesis, a sermonic form that combines admonition or warning and exhortation or encouragement, to convince the people that reliance on Egypt for support against Assyria is a mistake that ignores YHWH's role as the G-d of Israel and Judah. Finally, Isaiah 32:1—33:24 presents prophetic instruction concerning the announcement of a royal savior. The passage comprises two major sub-units. Isaiah 32:1–20, which begins with the exclamation *hēn* ("behold") rather than *hôy* ("woe"), signals a change in the sequence that will anticipate YHWH's act of deliverance on behalf of Israel and Judah. In this case, Isaiah 32:1–20 presents prophetic instruction concerning the announcement of the coming of a royal savior for the people. This royal figure will be known for righteousness and justice, although this monarch is not specifically identified as a Davidic king. The second sub-unit then follows in Isaiah 33:1–24, a text that constitutes the announcement of a royal savior proper. The oracle starts with a "woe" (*hôy*) announcement that is directed against a ravager and betrayer who has oppressed the people of Israel and Judah. It then looks forward to YHWH's actions on behalf of Zion, which will bring about "a king in his beauty" (Isa 33:17), who will act on behalf of YHWH to secure the safety of the city and the people, culminating in their recognition of YHWH as their true king (Isa 33:22). W. A. M. Beuken has produced a brilliant intertextual study that recognizes Isaiah 33 as a "mirror text" or a "bridge text," that links specific texts in Isaiah 1–33 and Isaiah 34–66 to bring the two parts of the book together in an effort to demonstrate that the second part of the book both interests and fulfills the first part of the book of Isaiah.[46]

IV. The Synchronic Internal Structure of Isaiah 34–66

Isaiah 34–66 focuses on the realization of YHWH's plans for worldwide sovereignty at Zion.[47] There are no superscriptions that introduce the various sub-units of this textual block. Rather, the major sub-units are evident due to their distinctive genres (i.e., literary types) and their distinctive concerns.

The first major component of this textual block appears in Isaiah 34–54, which constitutes prophetic instruction concerning the realization of YHWH's worldwide sovereignty.[48] It includes three major sub-units. The first is prophetic instruction concerning YHWH's power to return the redeemed exiles to Zion in Isaiah 34–35.[49] The second is a presentation of royal narratives concerning YHWH's deliverance of Jerusalem and King Hezekiah ben Ahaz in Isaiah 36–39.[50] And the third is prophetic instruction to demonstrate that YHWH is maintaining covenant and restoring Zion in Isaiah 40–54.[51] Isaiah 40–54 includes two major components. Isaiah 40:1–11 presents a renewed prophetic commission to announce YHWH's restoration of Zion.[52] Isaiah 40:12—54:17 presents the prophetic instruction proper to demonstrate YHWH's maintenance of covenant and restoration of Zion. This segment includes five major arguments, viz., (1) YHWH is master of creation in Isaiah 40:12–31;[53] (2) YHWH is master of human events in Isaiah 41:1—42:13;[54] (3) YHWH is redeemer of Israel

---

46. Beuken, "Jesaja 33"; Beuken, *Isaiah 28–39*, 239–77; see also Beuken, *Jesaja 28–39*, 256–97; cf. Sweeney, *Isaiah 1–39*, 420–33.

47. Sweeney, *Isaiah 1–39*, 434–511; Sweeney, *Isaiah 40–66*.

48. Sweeney, *Isaiah 1–39*, 40–41, 46–48; Sweeney, *Isaiah 40–66*, 18–21.

49. Sweeney, *Isaiah 1–39*, 434–54; see also Evans, "Unity"; Steck, *Bereitete Heimkehr*.

50. Sweeney, *Isaiah 1–39*, 454–511; see also Seitz, *Zion's Final Destiny*.

51. Sweeney, *Isaiah 40–66*, 41–231.

52. Sweeney, *Isaiah 40–66*, 41–51; cf. Seitz, "Divine Council"; Seitz, "How Is the Prophet Isaiah Present." See also Poulsen, *Black Hole in Isaiah*.

53. Sweeney, *Isaiah 40–66*, 52–63.

54. Sweeney, *Isaiah 40–66*, 63–81.

Introduction

in Isaiah 42:14—44:23;[55] (4) YHWH will use King Cyrus of Persia for the restoration of Zion in Isaiah 44:24—48:22;[56] and (5) YHWH is restoring Zion in Isaiah 49:1—54:17.[57]

The second major component of Isaiah 34–66 appears in Isaiah 55–66, which constitutes a prophetic exhortation to adhere to YHWH's covenant.[58] Isaiah 55–66 comprises two major textual components. The first is Isaiah 55, which presents the exhortation proper.[59] The second is Isaiah 56–66, which substantiates the prophetic instruction concerning the reconstituted nation in Zion in three parts.[60] The first is prophetic instruction concerning the proper observance of the covenant in Isaiah 56–59.[61] The second is the prophetic announcement of salvation for the reconstituted nation in Isaiah 60–62.[62] And the third is prophetic instruction concerning the reconstituted nation in Isaiah 63–66.[63]

A. Isaiah 34–54

Isaiah 34–54 presents prophetic instruction concerning the realization of YHWH's worldwide sovereignty in Zion, in three major components as described above, viz., Isaiah 34–35; Isaiah 36–39; and Isaiah 40–54.

1. Isaiah 34–35

Isaiah 34–35 presents prophetic instruction concerning YHWH's power to return the redeemed exiles to Zion. It thereby complements Isaiah 1, which presents introductory parenesis concerning YHWH's intention to purify Zion, and Isaiah 2–4, which announces the preparation of Zion for its role as the center for YHWH's world rule over the nations and Israel/Judah.

---

55. Sweeney, *Isaiah 40–66*, 81–108.
56. Sweeney, *Isaiah 40–66*, 108–57.
57. Sweeney, *Isaiah 40–66*, 157–231.
58. Sweeney, *Isaiah 40–66*, 231–385.
59. Sweeney, *Isaiah 40–66*, 231–48.
60. Sweeney, *Isaiah 40–66*, 248–385.
61. Sweeney, *Isaiah 40–66*, 248–96.
62. Sweeney, *Isaiah 40–66*, 297–331.
63. Sweeney, *Isaiah 40–66*, 331–85.

Isaiah 34–35 includes two major sub-units. The first is Isaiah 34, which presents prophetic instruction concerning YHWH's power over the nations, with a focus on Edom.[64] Whereas the ancestor of Israel was the patriarch Jacob, according to Genesis 25–35, the ancestor of Edom was Jacob's fraternal twin brother, Esau, who was always in conflict with Jacob. Just as Jacob is punished and restored to represent Israel/Judah, so Esau is punished and restored to represent the nations. The second major sub-unit of Isaiah 34–35 is Isaiah 35, which constitutes a prophetic oracle of salvation to represent the return of the redeemed exiles to Zion.[65]

2. Isaiah 36–39

Isaiah 36–39 presents royal narratives concerning YHWH's deliverance of Jerusalem and Hezekiah.[66] Isaiah 36–39 also appears in a very similar form in 2 Kings 18–20 and a more developed form in 2 Chronicles 29–32.[67] Isaiah 36–39 is designed to present a contrast between King Ahaz ben Jotham of Judah in Isaiah 7:1—9:6 and King Hezekiah in Isaiah 36–39. When the prophet, Isaiah ben Amoz, meets King Ahaz during the Syro-Ephraimite War at the upper pool by the Fuller's Field while he is inspecting Jerusalem's water supply system, King Ahaz is presented as an unfaithful monarch, who rejects the prophet's advice to turn to YHWH alone, which results in the Assyrian subjugation of Jerusalem and Judah. By contrast, when the Assyrian king, Sennacherib, sends his envoy, the Rab Shakeh, to the upper pool by the Fuller's Field to demand the unconditional surrender of Jerusalem, King Hezekiah shows himself as faithful to YHWH with the result that the city of Jerusalem is saved. In addition, YHWH saves King Hezekiah's life when he falls ill and prays to YHWH for healing, although he is condemned by Isaiah at the end for his alliance with Prince Merodach-Baladan of Babylon, who is Hezekiah's partner in revolt against Assyria. The result is Isaiah's announcement that Hezekiah's sons will be exiled to Babylon, thereby preparing the reader for the following material, beginning with Isaiah 40, which presupposes the Babylonian exile. Second Kings 18–20 ends in a similar manner to anticipate the Babylonian exile as recounted in 2 Kings 25. It is striking that Isaiah 36–39 appears in a slightly different

---

64. Sweeney, *Isaiah 1–39*, 437–47.
65. Sweeney, *Isaiah 1–39*, 447–54.
66. Sweeney, *Isaiah 1–39*, 454–511.
67. Sweeney, *1–2 King*, 397–432; Klein, *2 Chronicles*, 409–70.

INTRODUCTION

form that differs from the similar text in 2 Kings 18-20; whereas 2 Kings 18-20 includes material to indicate that Hezekiah is guilty of submission to Assyrian rule, Isaiah 36-39 omits that material so that it is written to indicate that Hezekiah is completely faithful to YHWH until the very end of the narrative in Isaiah 39.[68]

3. Isaiah 40–54

Isaiah 40:1—54:17 presents a prophetic announcement that YHWH is maintaining the covenant and acting to restore Zion.

The first major sub-unit appears in Isaiah 40:1-11, which most scholars view as a form of renewed call narrative, insofar as the passage depicts unidentified voices that are presumed to represent the angelic figures in YHWH's heavenly court.[69] The passage introduces the second major sub-unit in Isaiah 40:12—54:17. Isaiah 40:1-2, 3-5 focus on the highway by which the exiles will return to Jerusalem as announced in Isaiah 40:12—48:22, and Isaiah 40:6-11 announce instructions to the Herald of Zion/Jerusalem, which is the concern of Isaiah 49:1—54:17.

The second major sub-unit of Isaiah 40–54 appears in Isaiah 40:12—54:17, which constitute prophetic instruction to demonstrate that YHWH is maintaining the covenant and restoring Zion.[70] Some maintain that Isaiah 40:12—48:22 and Isaiah 49–54 constitute two discrete compositions due to their differing contents and literary styles, but in a synchronic analysis of the text they function together, insofar as the arguments offered in Isaiah 40:12—48:22 are designed to lead to the conclusion in Isaiah 49:1—54:17 that YHWH is restoring Zion, here portrayed as YHWH's abandoned bride and the mother of the tribes of Israel. Indeed, Isaiah 40:12—54:17 indicates a combination of two major Israelite traditions or concerns in one sustained argument, i.e., the exodus from Egypt, now concerned with Babylon, and the restoration of Zion as YHWH's bride, so well-known from the prophetic tradition concerning Israel or Jerusalem as YHWH's bride.[71]

---

68. For a convenient and graphic portrayal of the differences between Isaiah 36-39 and 2 Kings 18-20, see Wildberger, *Isaiah 28-39*, 481-93.

69. Sweeney, *Isaiah 40-66*, 41-51; see also Cross, "Council of YHWH"; Seitz, "Divine Council."

70. Sweeney, *Isaiah 40-66*, 52-231.

71. Cf. Anderson, "Exodus and Covenant"; Kiesow, *Exodustexte im Jesajabuch*; Baumann, *Love and Violence*, 175-202.

Altogether, Isaiah 40:12—54:17 presents a sequence of consecutive arguments to support the conclusion that YHWH is keeping covenant and restoring Zion. Isaiah 40:12-31 argues that YHWH is the master of creation and therefore plays a key role in the events of creation.[72] Isaiah 41:1—42:13 argues that YHWH is the master of human events, and therefore plays a key role in the events of the human world.[73] Isaiah 42:14—44:23 argues that YHWH is the redeemer of Israel, especially as exemplified in the exodus and wilderness tradition by which YHWH freed Israel from Egyptian exile and led them back to the promised land of Israel.[74] Isaiah 44:24—48:22 argues that YHWH will employ King Cyrus of Persia as messiah and temple builder to restore Zion, thereby setting the stage for the displacement of the Davidic monarchy and the contention that YHWH supports the Achaemenid Persian monarchy.[75] Isaiah 49:1—54:17 then presents a lengthy argument that YHWH is restoring Bat-Zion, Zion/Jerusalem metaphorically portrayed as YHWH's bride, so that her sons, the tribes of Israel, can return to their homeland from Babylonian exile much as their ancestors returned to the land of Israel from Egyptian exile and slavery.[76]

B. Isaiah 55–66

Isaiah 55:1—66:24 constitutes a prophetic exhortation to adhere to YHWH's covenant.[77] Although most scholars correctly maintain on diachronic grounds that Isaiah 55 concludes the work of Deutero-Isaiah,[78] a synchronic reading of the text on purely literary grounds recognizes that Isaiah 55, which constitutes the exhortation proper, looks forward in anticipation that YHWH's covenant with Israel/Judah will be accepted and implemented by the people of Israel/Judah at large.[79] Consequently, the exhortation proper in Isaiah 55:1-13 both redefines the eternal covenant with the House of David to be an eternal covenant with Israel/Judah and

---

72. Sweeney, *Isaiah 40–66*, 52–63.
73. Sweeney, *Isaiah 40–66*, 63–81.
74. Sweeney, *Isaiah 40–66*, 81–108.
75. Sweeney, *Isaiah 40–66*, 108–57; cf. Kratz, *Kyros im Deuterojesaja Buch*.
76. Sweeney, *Isaiah 40–66*, 157–231.
77. Sweeney, *Isaiah 40–66*, 11, 20–21.
78. E.g., Childs, *Isaiah*, 431–38; Blenkinsopp, *Isaiah 40–55*, 366–73.
79. Sweeney, *Isaiah 1–4*, 87–92; Sweeney, *Isaiah 40–66*, 231–48; cf. Berges, *Jesaja 55–66*, 29–92, 94–168.

introduces the following material in Isaiah 56:1—66:24, which provides substantiation, i.e., prophetic instruction, concerning what the covenant with YHWH entails.

Isaiah 56:1—66:24 thereby contains prophetic instruction concerning the reconstituted nation in Zion.[80] It includes three major components. The first is Isaiah 56:1—59:21, which presents prophetic instruction concerning the proper observance of the covenant.[81] This section envisions that people from the nations can become part of the covenant, provided that they observe its requirements. This would include observance of the Shabbat as well as the other requirements of the covenant as expressed in YHWH's Torah, "Instruction," to Israel. Such observance entails an early form of conversion to Judaism. The second component appears in Isaiah 60:1—62:12, which presents a prophetic announcement of salvation or restoration for the reconstituted nation at Jerusalem/Zion.[82] The third component appears in Isaiah 63:1—66:24, which constitutes prophetic instruction concerning the selection of those who will be part of the reconstituted nation.[83] Those selected are considered righteous, especially because they recognize that YHWH is the true king of Israel/Judah and creation at large.

V. Conclusion

Altogether, the final, synchronic form of the entire book of Isaiah indicates that it is a prophetic reflection on YHWH's purpose in bringing both punishment and restoration on Israel and Judah from the time of the prophet, Isaiah ben Amoz, who lived during the latter part of the eighth century BCE through some four centuries or more of the experience of Israel and Judah during the periods of Aramean, Assyrian, Babylonian, and Achaemenid Persian dominance. Isaiah ben Amoz, himself, appears only in Isaiah 1–39, but his tradents (i.e., disciples who passed on his work and developed it; Isa 8:16) continued to write and ultimately produced the final form of the book as a testimony to the vision of the prophet. Although the first part of the book through Isaiah 39 affirms a future in which righteous Davidic kingship will emerge, the Davidic promise is transferred to the people of Israel and Judah at large in Isaiah 55. The motif of YHWH's deliverance of Israel

---

80. Sweeney, *Isaiah 40–66*, 11, 21.
81. Sweeney, *Isaiah 40–66*, 248–96.
82. Sweeney, *Isaiah 40–66*, 297–331.
83. Sweeney, *Isaiah 40–66*, 331–85.

An Introduction to Isaiah 1–39

from Egyptian bondage and exile in the exodus tradition and YHWH's guidance of Israel through the wilderness from Egypt to the promised land of Israel informs the entire book of Isaiah, in which the exodus and wilderness motifs are applied to the later Assyrian, Babylonian, and Achaemenid Persian periods.[84]

VI. Appendix: Structure Diagram of the Book of Isaiah

The Vision of Isaiah ben Amoz:
Prophetic Exhortation to Jerusalem/Judah to Adhere to YHWH[85]

Isaiah 1–66
I. Concerning YHWH's Plans for Worldwide Sovereignty at Zion (1–33)
  A. Prologue to the book of Isaiah: introductory parenesis concerning YHWH's intention to purify Jerusalem (1)
  B. Prophetic instruction concerning YHWH's projected plans to establish worldwide sovereignty at Zion: announcement of the Day of YHWH (2–33)
      1. Prophetic announcement concerning the preparation of Zion for its role as the center for YHWH's world rule (2–4)
      2. Prophetic instruction concerning the significance of Assyrian judgment against Jacob/Israel: restoration of Davidic rule (5–12)
      3. Prophetic announcement concerning the preparation of the nations for YHWH's world rule (13–27)
          a. Pronouncements concerning the nations (13–23)
          b. Prophetic announcement of YHWH's new world order: prophecy of salvation for Zion/Israel (24–27)
      4. Prophetic instruction concerning YHWH's plans for Jerusalem: announcement of a royal savior (28–33)

II. Concerning the Realization of YHWH's Plans for Worldwide Sovereignty at Zion (34–66)
  A. Prophetic instruction concerning the realization of YHWH's worldwide sovereignty at Zion (34–54)

---

84. See now Sweeney, "Reading the Final Form of Isaiah"; Sweeney, "Synchronic, Diachronic, and Intertextual Dimensions."

85. Cf. Sweeney, *Isaiah 1–39*, 39–41; Sweeney, *Isaiah 40–66*, 10–11.

INTRODUCTION

1. Prophetic instruction concerning YHWH's power to return the redeemed exiles to Zion (34–35)
2. Royal narratives concerning YHWH's deliverance of Jerusalem and Hezekiah (36–39)
3. Prophetic instruction that YHWH is maintaining covenant and restoring Zion (40–54)
    a. Renewed prophetic commission to announce YHWH's restoration of Zion (40:1–11)
    b. Instruction proper: YHWH is maintaining covenant and restoring Zion (40:12—54:17)
        1) Contention: YHWH is master of creation (40:12–31)
        2) Contention: YHWH is master of human events (41:1—42:13)
        3) Contention: YHWH is redeemer of Israel (42:14—44:23)
        4) Contention: YHWH will use Cyrus for restoration of Zion (44:24—48:22)
        5) Contention: YHWH is restoring Zion (49:1—54:17)

B. Prophetic exhortation to adhere to YHWH's covenant (55–66)
   1. Exhortation proper (55)
   2. Substantiation: prophetic instruction concerning the reconstituted nation in Zion (56–66)
       a. Prophetic instruction concerning proper observance of covenant (56–59)
       b. Prophetic announcement of salvation for the reconstituted nation (60–62)
       c. Prophetic instruction concerning the reconstituted nation (63–66)

2

Isaiah 1–12

I. Overview

THE STUDY OF ISAIAH 1–12—and indeed, the study of Isaiah 1–39—was revolutionized by the redaction-critical study of the book of Isaiah. Key among the many important studies that appeared during this period were the first volume of the Isaiah 1–39 commentary by Hans Wildberger, published in 1972 in the German Biblischer Kommentar series,[1] and the plenary paper by Peter R. Ackroyd on Isaiah 1–12, presented at the Congress of the International Organization for the Study of the Old Testament, held in Göttingen, Germany, in 1978.[2]

Wildberger's commentary was especially important because it was the most detailed, thorough-going, and up-to-date commentary on Isaiah 1–12 at the time, and it continues to be an authoritative commentary today. His work focused especially on the analysis of the short, self-contained oracular and narrative sub-units that constituted Isaiah 1–12, and in his later volumes he would develop a model of the formation of Isaiah 1–39.[3] Wildberger passed away in 1986, some four years after publishing his concluding volume on Isaiah 28–39, so he took little notice of the growing discussion of the formation of the book of Isaiah as a whole, although his

---

1. Wildberger, *Jesaja 1–12*; ET, *Isaiah 1–12*.
2. Ackroyd, "Isaiah 1–12."
3. Wildberger, *Jesaja 13–27*; ET, *Isaiah 13–27*; *Jesaja 28–39*; ET, *Isaiah 28–39*.

commentary proved to be the foundation on which many scholars concerned with the formation of the book worked.

Ackroyd's paper is especially important because it signaled the shift in the redaction-critical study of Isaiah, not simply in relation to the formation of Isaiah 1–39, but in relation to the formation of the book of Isaiah as a whole, as scholars began to realize that we have no manuscript evidence that Isaiah 1–39 ever circulated as a stand-alone text. Whereas Wildberger's commentary was especially concerned with the reconstructing the "original" meaning of the text in the time of Isaiah ben Amoz as well as its preservation and expansion by Isaiah's tradents in later period, Ackroyd's study was primarily concerned with the role played by Isaiah's tradents, not only in the time of Isaiah himself, but in later times, such as the periods of the Babylonian exile and the post-exilic restoration in the Persian period. Such work was inspired especially by the publications of Sigmund Mowinckel, whose earlier studies had focused on Isaiah's tradents,[4] as well as by the above-noted work of scholars such as Georg Fohrer and others.[5] Although Ackroyd lived until 2005, a combination of focus on other projects, such as Chronicles, and ill health prevented him from concentrating on Isaiah in his later years.[6] Nevertheless, his work was very influential in early discussion concerning the unit of the book of Isaiah.

With the emerging interest in the formation of the entire book of Isaiah, three major textual blocks emerged as foci for study, viz., Isaiah 1:1–31; Isaiah 2:1—4:6; and Isaiah 5:1—12:6.

II. Isaiah 1

Georg Fohrer identified Isaiah 1 as the Prologue for Isaiah 1–39, but as the prior discussion of the synchronic form of the book indicates, Isaiah 1 serves as the Prologue for the final, synchronic form of the *entire* book of Isaiah.[7] Nevertheless, diachronic analysis of the chapter demonstrates that most of its sub-units appear to presuppose the work of the late eighth-century BCE

---

4. Mowinckel, *Spirit and the Word*, a republication of Mowinckel, *Prophecy and Tradition*; see also Mowinckel, *Jesaja-Disiplene*.

5. Fohrer, "Jesaja 1."

6. In the mid-1980s, the author contacted Ackroyd to invite him to join the new Society of Biblical Literature seminar on "The Formation of the Book of Isaiah." Ackroyd declined due to poor health. May his memory be a blessing.

7. Fohrer, "Jesaja 1"; cf. Sweeney, *Isaiah 1–39*, 63–71.

prophet Isaiah ben Amoz. The chapter therefore represents a redactional or editorial combination of a number of smaller units to construct the present form of the text.[8] Insofar as Isaiah 1 constitutes parenesis, i.e., a form of exposition that emphasizes both the exhortational and the judgmental elements of the passage, the final form of this text lends itself easily to the late fifth- or early fourth-century edition of the final form of the book of Isaiah, which presupposes the work of Nehemiah and Ezra in reconstituting the post-exilic Jewish community in Jerusalem during the period of Achaemenid Persian rule. A number of interpreters note lexical and thematic links with Isaiah 65–66, which indicates that Isaiah 1 functions together with Isaiah 65–66 as a redactional or editorial envelope for the final form of the book of Isaiah.[9]

Isaiah 1:1–31 comprises a number of small sub-units that, when placed together, produce the final form of the text.

Isaiah 1:1 is the superscription of the book, which identifies it as "the vision of Isaiah ben Amoz which he saw concerning Judah and Jerusalem in the days of Uzziah, Jotham, Ahaz, and Hezekiah, kings of Judah."[10] We have already noted that the term *ḥāzôn* ("vision") and the verb *ḥāzâ* ("he saw") both presuppose a Hebrew/Aramaic root that means "to perceive," which refers to both visual and auditory perception.[11] The terms therefore indicate both visual revelation, such as the vision of YHWH in the Jerusalem Temple in Isaiah 6, and the many oracular and narrative passage that appear throughout the book. The reference to "Judah and Jerusalem" employs a formula that was characteristic for the Persian-period Jewish community that was based in Judah and Jerusalem following the return of exiles after the Babylonian exile.[12] Such a phrase indicates a primary concern with Judah and Jerusalem even though the book as a whole shows a great deal of interest in Israel—both as the northern kingdom of Israel and the Israelite nation as a whole—and the nations of the world at large. The enumeration of the Judean kings presents those who ruled during the eighth century BCE and the early seventh century. According to the chronology adopted by the American Albrightian school, their reigns include

---

8. Sweeney, *Isaiah 1–39*, 71–96.

9. E.g., Lack, *Symbolique*, 139–41; Williamson, *Isaiah 1–5*, 7–11; cf. Conrad, *Reading Isaiah*, 83–116. See also the critique of Carr, "Reaching for Unity."

10. Sweeney, *Isaiah 1–39*, 71–73.

11. For detailed discussion, see Jepsen, "*Ḥāzâ*."

12. Cf. Williamson, *Isaiah 1–5*, 20.

Uzziah (783–742 BCE); Jotham (742–735 BCE); Ahaz (735–715 BCE); and Hezekiah (715–687/6 BCE).

Uzziah's reign was relatively peaceful, although Judah was a vassal of northern Israel during his reign, and Uzziah—sometimes identified as Azariah—suffered from a form of leprosy, which required his son, Jotham, to act as regent (2 Kgs 15:1–7).[13] Toward the end of Uzziah's reign, northern Israel initiated a revolt against the Assyrian Empire—which both Israel and Judah served as vassals—that would lead to the Syro-Ephraimitic War (735–732 BCE). Israel, under King Pekah ben Remaliah, who had overthrown King Pekahiah ben Menahem of Israel, allied with King Rezin of Aram to revolt against Assyria.[14] Prior to the revolt, the combined forces of Israel and Aram attacked Judah in an effort to overthrow King Jotham ben Uzziah and replace him with a Trans-Jordanian figure named ben Tabeel, in order to force Judah into their anti-Assyrian alliance. Although Jotham appears to have died, his twenty-year-old son, Ahaz, ascended to the throne of Judah and was forced to meet the attack. Ahaz ignored Isaiah's advice simply to hold out against the invasion, based on the insight that the Syro-Ephraimitic coalition did not have time for a protracted siege of Jerusalem because the Assyrian army would invade Aram due to the revolt (see Isa 7). Ahaz rashly appealed to Assyria for help, not understanding that Assyria would invade anyway to put down the revolt. Indeed, Tiglath Pileser III of Assyria invaded Aram, destroyed Damascus, and stripped Israel of its Galilean, Trans-Jordanian, and northwestern tribal territories situated along the Mediterranean (see 2 Kgs 16).[15] Ahaz was left indebted to Assyria for saving his own life and his kingdom, and Tiglath Pileser, rather than recognizing Ahaz's loyalty, imposed a heavier tribute to be paid by Judah.

The failed Syro-Ephraimitic attempt led to further revolt. In 724–722 BCE, Israel revolted again, and the Assyrian army under Shalmaneser V and Sargon II invaded Israel, destroyed Samaria, and exiled major elements of the Israelite upper classes.[16] Following the death of Sargon II in battle in 705 BCE, King Hezekiah of Judah allied with Prince Merodach-Baladan of Babylon to initiate a two-pronged revolt against Assyria, now ruled by

---

13. For detailed discussion of Uzziah's reign, see Sweeney, *1–2 Kings*, 369–71; Klein, *2 Chronicles*, 367–83.

14. For discussion of King Pekah of Israel and the turmoil that engulfed Israel leading up to the Syro-Ephraimitic War, see Sweeney, *1–2 Kings*, 371–77.

15. Sweeney, *1–2 Kings*, 378–86.

16. Sweeney, *1–2 Kings*, 386–96.

An Introduction to Isaiah 1–39

Sennacherib. Sennacherib surprised everyone and proved to be a very able military commander.[17] He overran much of Judah in 701 BCE, and forced Hezekiah to capitulate, although he did not actually take Jerusalem due to his need to put down revolt in Babylon. Although Judah was devastated, Hezekiah survived and claimed victory. Judah nevertheless remained under Assyrian control for most of the seventh century BCE until the reign of King Josiah ben Amon of Judah, who joined Nebopolassar of Babylon in a revolt against Assyria.[18] Although Nebopolassar defeated Assyria and brought the Assyrian Empire to an end in 609 BCE, King Josiah was killed by the Egyptians at Megiddo in a failed attempt to stop Pharaoh Necho of Egypt from advancing to Haran to support his Assyrian ally. In the aftermath of Josiah's death, Babylon, under King Nebuchadnezzar, ultimately took control of Judah in 605 BCE and treated it as a conquered enemy. This led to three Judean revolts against Babylon in 598–597 BCE, 588–586 BCE, and 582 BCE, which saw the destruction of Jerusalem and Solomon's Temple in 586 BCE and the beginning of the Babylonian exile.[19]

It was only in 539 BCE that the prospects for a Judean restoration became clear when King Cyrus of Persia conquered Babylon and decreed that Jews could return to Jerusalem and rebuild the Temple.[20] Construction of the Temple was completed in 520–515 BCE during the reign of King Darius of Persia, and full restoration occurred during the late fifth and early fourth centuries BCE under the leadership of Nehemiah and Ezra during the reign of King Artaxerxes II (405–359 BCE), although Judah and Jerusalem remained subject to Achaemenid Persia. This period is the most likely time for the final composition of the book of Isaiah and the editing of Isaiah 1 as the Prologue for the book.

As noted in the introduction, a superscription stands apart structurally from the material it introduces.[21] In the present case, Isaiah 1:1 introduces either the entire book of Isaiah or Isaiah 1:2–31.[22]

Isaiah 1:2–31 includes a number of sub-units, viz., verses 2–3, 4–9, 10–17, 21–26, 27–28, and 29–31.[23] Although they are assembled into one

17. Sweeney, *1–2 Kings*, 397–424.
18. Sweeney, *1–2 Kings*, 424–50.
19. Sweeney, *1–2 Kings*, 450–70.
20. Sweeney, *Tanak*, 459–69.
21. Tucker, "Prophetic Superscriptions."
22. Sweeney, *Isaiah 1–39*, 72; Williamson, *Isaiah 1–5*, 15.
23. Sweeney, *Isaiah 1–39*, 63–87.

full chapter in the present form of the book, their individual characteristics indicate different origins for each, some of which were redactional and some of which may once have stood as independent oracles.

Isaiah 1:2–3 is a very short oracular statement that announces YHWH's accusation against Israel.[24] The oracle begins with courtroom language in which the heavens and the earth are summoned as witnesses to YHWH's declaration that YHWH had raised children—in this case, Israel—but that the children had rebelled. The announcement then indicates that animals such as bulls and asses know their owners and their masters' cribs, a reference to feeding troughs, but Israel does not know YHWH, who is Israel's "owner" and "master." The reference to Israel may indicate the northern kingdom of Israel or the Israelite people as a whole, but the present context does not provide enough information for us to know which. The oracle itself is very brief, which makes it difficult to understand why the prophet might have blurted out such a statement, unless something was meant to follow that would explain the specific intention of the oracle. Consequently, interpreters suggest that Isaiah 1:2–3 extends through Isaiah 1:20 or even 1:31. But the later material in Isaiah 1:4–9 and 1:10–17 can stand independently, so Isaiah 1:2–3 may have been composed as a redactional introduction to a larger unit in Isaiah 1:2–20 or 1:2–31.[25] Nevertheless, the tensions within Isaiah 1 suggest that it is a redactional unit.

Isaiah 1:4–9 constitutes an admonition, i.e., a warning, against continued wrong-doing.[26] It is written in the form of a "woe" oracle, introduced with the Hebrew particle *hôy* ("woe!"), which warns its audience, here portrayed as "the sinful nation," etc., of impending danger.[27] In this case, the impending danger is the threat of destruction brought about by an enemy that has severely wounded the nation. The nation in question appears to be Judah, although the oracle itself indicates that the G-d of the nation is "the Holy One of Israel," but interpreters recognize that in the book of Isaiah Judah represents the "remnant (Hebrew, *šě'ar*) of Israel" in the aftermath of the Assyrian destruction of northern Israel in 722–721 BCE (e.g., Isa 10:20; cf. 10:21).[28] The context presumes rebellion against G-d, as Isaiah 1:2–3 might suggest, insofar as the wounds of the people are

24. Sweeney, *Isaiah 1–39*, 73–75.
25. E.g., Gitay, "Reflections"; Fohrer, "Jesaja 1."
26. Sweeney, *Isaiah 1–39*, 75–78.
27. Sweeney, *Isaiah 1–39*, 543.
28. See esp. Hasel, *Remnant*, 216–372.

indications of divine punishment for allegedly forsaking YHWH. Although many of the translations employ language indicating illness of some sort to describe metaphorically the wounds of the nation (e.g., NRSV; NJPS), the context refers specifically to wounds received from a beating, such as one would receive from a taskmaster or from an enemy in combat. The portrayal of wounds that must be pressed, softened with oil, and bound up indicates broken skin, from a whip, a sword, a spear, or an arrow, that must be cleaned and disinfected as best as one is able and then bound up in some sort of bandage so that it might heal. The portrayal of a devastated land aids in determining the context, and daughter Zion (i.e., Jerusalem portrayed metaphorically as the bride of YHWH) as left alone like a *sukkah* or booth in a vineyard or a cucumber field during harvest time further indicates historical context. Sennacherib's 701 BCE invasion of Judah left the land devastated, as indicated by archaeological excavations throughout late eighth-century Judah.[29] The population moved south into the Negev and east into the Judean hill country to escape the Assyrian occupation of the Shephelah region in western Judah. The Assyrians then developed an olive oil industry extensive enough to supply the needs of their empire.[30] Only Jerusalem was left intact, insofar as Sennacherib could not tarry for a prolonged siege due to his need to put down the Babylonian revolt led by Merodach-Baladan. Consequently, Sennacherib did not destroy Jerusalem, but took extensive tribute and captives while leaving Hezekiah on the throne to claim victory.[31] The oracle compares the devastation of the land to the destruction of Sodom and Gomorrah, presumably as recounted in the E-stratum of the Pentateuch (Genesis 19), a tale which would have been brought south from northern Israel to Judah in the aftermath of the Assyrian destruction of Samaria in 722–721 BCE.[32]

Isaiah 1:10–17 then follows with a prophetic Torah (i.e., instruction) on what YHWH requires from the people.[33] Some have tried to argue that this oracle represents a rejection of ritual service to G-d, i.e., the offerings of animal sacrifices and the observance of the New Moon, the Shabbat,

---

29. Finkelstein, "Archaeology"; cf. Mazar, *Archaeology*, 416–63.

30. Gitin, "Tel Miqne-Ekron"; Gitin, "Seventh Century B.C.E."; Dothan and Gitin, "Tel Miqne (Ekron)."

31. For Sennacherib's account of the siege of Jerusalem, see Pritchard, *ANET*, 287–88. Cf. Isa 36–39; 2 Kgs 18–20.

32. For discussion of Pentateuchal sources, see Sweeney, *Pentateuch*, esp. xvii–xxix.

33. Sweeney, *Isaiah 1–39*, 78–81.

and others, but such an argument misses the point. The passage does not reject such service per se; instead, it rejects such service without the appropriate action to implement what the ritual of the liturgy celebrates, as stated in Isaiah 1:16–17, rejecting evil and engaging in righteous and just action, helping those who are oppressed together with widow and orphan who have no support. Such ritual acknowledges the sanctity of G-d and G-d's divine expectations of the people. Only then does ritual action, which reminds us of our obligations to those in need, make sense. Others claim that the passage must be late because it refers to the observance of the "new moon" and the "Shabbat," but such arguments overlook the fact that issues such as observance of the Shabbat and care for the poor appear very clearly in the Covenant Code of Exodus 20–24, which is cited by mid-eighth-century prophets, such as Hosea and Amos, and which apparently served as the primary law code of the northern kingdom of Israel prior to its destruction.[34] It is striking that the oracle begins with references to the leadership of the people as officials of Sodom and Gomorrah, which picks up the motif from the preceding oracle in Isaiah 1:4–9, even though 1:4–9 and 1:10–17 can stand on their own as oracular statements made by the prophet in the late eighth century BCE. It is also striking that the oracle portrays the hands of the people as "filled with blood," presumably as a result of making the offerings of animal sacrifice to YHWH. Such an image then lends itself to a charge of wrongdoing when such ritual is undertaken without the principles stated in Isaiah 1:16–17.

Isaiah 1:18–20 then follows with an appeal to the people to engage in a legal proceeding with YHWH.[35] The courtroom setting then reprises the motif from Isaiah 1:2–3. In the present case, YHWH, speaking through the prophet, appeals to the people to engage in legal arbitration, Hebrew, *wĕniwwākĕḥāh*, "and let us arbitrate," in verse 18. YHWH's offer builds upon the portrayal of blood-stained hands in Isaiah 1:15, i.e., if the people engage in arbitration, their red, blood-stained hands can be cleansed so that they will appear as white as the wool of sheep. If the people come to YHWH and agree, all will be well, and they will eat the goodness of the earth's produce. But if they refuse to come to YHWH and continue in their alleged rebellion,

---

34. For discussion of Hosea 4 and Amos 2:6–16, both of which cite elements of the Covenant Code, see Sweeney, *Twelve Prophets*, 1:40–51, 1:214–18; see also Sweeney, *Exodus*, forthcoming.

35. Sweeney, *Isaiah 1–39*, 81–84.

they will be devoured by the sword. The YHWH speech formula at the end of verse 20 confirms this statement as a declaration by YHWH.

Isaiah 1:21–26 presents a prophetic announcement of Zion's rehabilitation.[36] The passage is based on the genre of the prophetic judgment speech,[37] insofar as it presents an indictment of Jerusalem's leaders in verses 21–23 and an announcement of cleansing judgment in verses 24–26. Indeed, the announcement of judgment employs the "woe" (Hebrew, *hôy*) formula in verse 24 to warn of YHWH's impending judgment against YHWH's enemies.[38] The metaphor employed to represent the cleansing or purging of Jerusalem is one of refining raw metal ore—in this case, silver, as noted in verse 22—by heating it up and melting in down repeatedly to produce the purified metal by progressively removing its impurities or dross.[39] Although the oracle begins with a reference to "murderers" in verse 22—which is suggestive of the motif of blood-stained hands in verses 15 and 18, the shift in motif from sacrificial religious observance to the smelting of silver indicates that Isaiah 1:21–26 was not originally a part of the oracular sequence in Isaiah 1:2–20. The closing YHWH speech formula in verse 20 and the fact that Isaiah 1:21–26 can stand on its own as a prophetic judgment speech likewise indicates the independent character of the passage. The use of fire imagery for smelting might link to the motif of sacrificial offerings by fire in Isaiah 1:10–17, but it more readily lends itself to the motif of invasion by an enemy and the potential destruction of the city that such invasion entails. Although Sennacherib's 701 BCE invasion succeeded in destroying many Judean cities and towns, particularly Lachish, Sennacherib failed to take and destroy Jerusalem. The Assyrian failure to destroy the city then aids in understanding why this oracle was placed into its present position, even though it relates to the preceding oracular sequence only in relation to the very general concern with Jerusalem's punishment. It thereby signals Jerusalem's destruction in much later periods, i.e., the destruction of Jerusalem by the Babylonians in 586 BCE and the later destruction of Jerusalem by the Romans in 70 CE. Such a phenomenon helps in explaining

---

36. Sweeney, *Isaiah 1–39*, 86.
37. See also Sweeney, *Isaiah 1–39*, 533–34.
38. Sweeney, *Isaiah 1–39*, 543.

39. I worked in various capacities as a foundryman in the summers of 1972, 1973, and 1974. At the Wagner Casting Company, Decatur, Illinois, I was a laborer, a spruer, and a heat-treat furnace operator. At the Mueller Iron Foundry, Decatur, Illinois, I was a ladleman. Such work helped immensely in paying my college expenses and providing me with the incentive to complete my education.

how Isaiah is read in relation to much later periods when Jerusalem was actually destroyed, even though the final form of the book of Isaiah itself lacks any clear depiction of the event, leaving interpreters to posit a "black hole" in the book of Isaiah concerning the destruction of the city.[40] The motif therefore signals the role of Isaiah 1:1–31 as the introduction to the entire book of Isaiah, not simply Isaiah 1–39 or any posited edition of the late eighth-century oracles of Isaiah ben Amoz.

Isaiah 1:27–31 presents a prophetic announcement of Zion's redemption.[41] The passage has two very distinctive components. Isaiah 1:27–28 constitutes an announcement of redemption for Zion and those within her who repent. These verses play a key role in organizing the presentation of Isaiah 1:2–31 by highlighting the pending redemption of those who adhere to YHWH, as signaled in Isaiah 1:2–3 and anticipating the destruction of those who have abandoned YHWH, again as signaled in Isaiah 1:2–3 and illustrated throughout the chapter. Isaiah 1:27–28 therefore appears to be product of the final redaction of the book and its prologue in the late fifth or early fourth century BCE. The following announcement of annihilation for those who continue to sin against YHWH by engaging in the worship of foreign gods in Isaiah 1:29–31 then illustrates the fate of those who do not heed the prophet's warning. The imagery employed here is that of a sacred tree or terebinth in the midst of a garden. Such trees were often understood to symbolize the Canaanite fertility goddess, such as Asherah, the consort of the Canaanite creator god, El,[42] or Hathor/Kadesha, an Egyptian/Canaanite goddess who stands nude between Resheph, the god of plague and death, and Min, the god of male fertility.[43] Asherah is frequently symbolized by a sacred tree, named after her as Asherah, and Hathor/Kadesha apparently stands behind the depiction of Eve, who eats from the tree of knowledge of good and evil in the Garden of Eden in Genesis 3. As noted above, the image of the tree is preserved in the Jerusalem Temple with the seven-branched Menorah or candelabrum, which supplies light in the Temple and is structured as a tree with seven branches.[44] The tree plays a key role in Isaiah;[45] here it symbolizes the demise of those who

40. Poulsen, *Black Hole in Isaiah*.
41. Sweeney, *Isaiah 1–39*, 36–37.
42. Merlo, "Asherah."
43. Goelt, "Hathor." For depictions of Hathor/Kadesha, see Pritchard, *ANEP*, 469–74.
44. Meyers, *Tabernacle Menorah*.
45. Nielsen, *There Is Hope for a Tree*, 201–15.

fail to adhere to YHWH, insofar as its leaves will fade and it will eventually die for lack of water provided by YHWH. As a result, the tree will burn (cf. Isa 6:13). This imagery appears to go back to Isaiah, who is well versed in the care of trees, vineyards, and other agricultural products, and frequently employs them as metaphors for understanding divine action in the world.

III. Isaiah 2–4

Isaiah 2–4 constitutes a discrete formal unit within the larger structure of the book of Isaiah. Although some, such as Ackroyd, view it as a sub-unit of Isaiah 1–12, it functions more like Isaiah 1 in that it introduces concern with Judah and Jerusalem within the larger structure of the book of Isaiah. It is demarcated at the beginning by the superscription in Isaiah 2:1, which is formulated somewhat similarly to Isaiah 1:1, although it is identified generically as "the word" (Hebrew, *haddābār*) that Isaiah "perceived" (Hebrew, *ḥāzâ*) "concerning Judah and Jerusalem." It is therefore also much shorter than the superscription in Isaiah 1:1 in that it does not make reference to the kings of Judah. The following unit in Isaiah 5–12 does not include a superscription to demarcate its beginning. Instead, it shifts the topic very noticeably by focusing on both Israel and Judah in relation to Jerusalem as indicated by the references in the opening vineyard allegory in Isaiah 5:1–7 (esp. vv. 3, 7). Consequently, Isaiah 2–4 concludes with the prophetic announcement of salvation or restoration for the cleansed or purified remnant of Israel (Judah) in Jerusalem in 4:2–6. Isaiah 4:2–6 conveys this concern with a portrayal of Jerusalem restored with a pillar of cloud by day and a pillar of flaming fire at night metaphorically to form a productive umbrella over the city and its people.

Although some interpreters have attempted to define the unit as Isaiah 1:1—2:5, the presence of the two superscriptions in Isaiah 1:1 and 2:1 and the overriding concern with Judah and Jerusalem in Isaiah 2–4 indicate that Isaiah 2–4 defines the synchronic and diachronic form of the unit.[46]

Considered from a diachronic perspective, Isaiah 2–4 would have been edited into its present form as part of the sixth-century BCE edition of the book of Isaiah, although some elements appear to have been added during the final fifth-/fourth-century edition of Isaiah completed in the

---

46. See Duhm, *Jesaia*, 1892, 14–33; Duhm, *Jesaia*, 1968, 36–54; Wiklander, *Prophecy as Literature*; Sweeney, *Isaiah 1–39*, 87–112.

time of Nehemiah and Ezra.⁴⁷ It is clear that much of the oracular material in Isaiah 2:6–30 and 3:1—4:1 may be traced back to Isaiah himself, but the oracular material in Isaiah 2:2–4, 5, and 4:2–6 appears to be later. In the case of Isaiah 2:1, the superscription would have been composed at the time when the basic form of the sub-unit would have been composed, i.e., in the late sixth century BCE. Like all superscriptions, it stands apart structurally from the material that it introduces and interprets.⁴⁸ The late sixth-century dating is evident from the portrayal of the pilgrimage of the nations to Zion to learn YHWH's Torah ("instruction") in Isaiah 2:2–4. Isaiah ben Amoz never looks forward to the pilgrimage of the nations to Zion to learn cessation of war from YHWH; that appears to be the concern of Deutero-Isaiah, the anonymous prophet of the late Babylonian exile during the late sixth century BCE when King Cyrus of Persia was advancing against Babylon in Isaiah 51:4–5. Isaiah ben Amoz himself looked forward to the punishment of the arrogant among the nations (Isa 2:6–21), the downfall of the arrogant Assyrian king (Isa 10:5–34; 14:3–27), and the emergence of the ideal Davidic king (Isa 9:1–6). Furthermore, the portrayal of the restoration of the Temple in Isaiah 4:2–6 presupposes the restoration of the Temple under the Persian King Darius in the late sixth century BCE and the restoration of the rebuilt Jerusalem Temple as the holy center of Jewish life in the late fifth and early fourth century BCE.

Isaiah 2:2–4 does not mention the threats against Jerusalem—by Assyria or anyone else—evident in the work of Isaiah ben Amoz, nor the portrayal of an ideal Davidic king, nor the punishment of the nations that threaten Jerusalem. The scenario of the recognition of YHWH by the nations and the end of warfare appears to be the concern of the late sixth century BCE when King Cyrus of Persia entered Babylon peaceably and was crowned as king of Babylonia with the approval of the Babylonian priesthood. Cyrus's ascension to the Babylonian throne in 539 BCE marked the end—at least for a while—of warfare among the nations in the late sixth century BCE. Clements recognized that Isaiah 2–4 pointed to the restoration of Jerusalem following the defeat of Babylon. Sweeney argues that Isaiah 2–4 was edited by a late sixth-century editor, likely from among the disciples of Isaiah, who sought to join the work of Isaiah ben Amoz with the work of Deutero-Isaiah.⁴⁹ Williamson argues that the editor was

---

47. Sweeney, *Isaiah 1–39*, 31–62, 87–112;
48. Tucker, "Prophetic Superscriptions."
49. Sweeney, *Isaiah 1–39*, 92–95.

Deutero-Isaiah himself.[50] Roberts attempts to claim that Isaiah ben Amoz is the author of the passage, due in part to his own ill-informed rejection of redaction-criticism in principle and his failure to recognize that the issues noted above pertain to Deutero-Isaiah and the late sixth century BCE and not to Isaiah ben Amoz and the late eighth century BCE.[51]

Some interpreters view Isaiah 2:2–4 as an eschatological prophecy, but this is based on the Greek Septuagint reading of the text, which reads, *hoti estai en tais eschatais hēmeris*, "for it shall come to pass in the end of days." The Hebrew temporal formula, *wěhāyâ běʾaḥărît hayyāmîm* ("and it shall happen in the later days"), is simply a reference to a future time without reference to the end of time.[52] The phrase is akin to Akkadian, *ina aḥrât ūmi*, which also refers to a future time.[53] The eschatological meaning is derived from the Greek rendition of the texts, which is an interpretative reading, and Christian theology, which looks forward to the second coming of Christ at the end of time (see below).

The following sets of oracles in Isaiah 2:5–21 and 2:22—4:1 appear to be oracles that may be attributed to Isaiah ben Amoz himself, but they have been edited so that they will be contextualized in relation to the prophetic announcement concerning Zion's role as the center for YHWH's world rule in Isaiah 2:2–4 and the prophetic announcement of the oracle of salvation or restoration for the purified remnant of Israel in Isaiah 4:2–6.

The portrayal of the nations "flowing" to Mt. Zion to learn YHWH's Torah, "instruction," employs the verb *wěnāhărû* ("and they shall flow"), which may be used to portray the "flow" of water up the mountain or the "streaming" of light.[54] As previously mentioned, the Hebrew word *tôrâ* is often mistranslated as "law," due in large measure to the Septuagint and the New Testament. The Hebrew term is derived from a Hiphil (causative) form of the verb root *yrh*, which means "to guide." The Hebrew word for "law" is *mišpāṭ*, often translated as "justice."

Isaiah 2:5–21 constitutes a prophetic announcement of the punishment of Jacob and humankind at large on the Day of YHWH. Within the synchronic form of Isaiah 2–4, Isaiah 2:5–21 anticipates a day when YHWH will punish or bring judgment against the arrogant among both

50. Williamson, *Book Called Isaiah*.
51. Roberts, *First Isaiah*, 1–8.
52. De Vries, *From Old Revelation to New*, 89–95.
53. Wildberger, *Isaiah 1–12*, 87–89.
54. Williamson, *Isaiah 1–5*, 169.

Jacob and the nations at large. This passage is frequently interpreted as an eschatological text due to the repeated references to the punishment taking place "in that day" (Hebrew, *bayyôm hahû'*), which has been understood to be a reference to the eschatological final judgment of the future. But the understanding of the formula *bayyôm hahû'* has changed markedly. De Vries has demonstrated in a very careful study of the *bayyôm hahû'* formula that it is not an eschatological formula; it is simply a reference to the future, i.e., some unspecified time in the future.[55] The eschatological dimensions of the formula have been unduly influenced by Christianity's understanding of the end time when the second coming of Jesus will take place and the wicked of the world will suffer punishment while the righteous enjoy eternal life in heaven with G-d and Christ. The concept of the Day of the L-rd as an eschatological event is well ensconced in the New Testament, for example, Acts 2:17–21, which cites Joel 2:28–32 (ET; Hebrew, Joel 3:1–5) to portray the Day of the L-rd/YHWH as a day when the sun will turn to darkness and the moon will turn to blood. Although this language is often understood to be eschatological, it actually portrays nothing more than the time of the sirocco winds, known in Arabic as the *Ḥamsin*, in Hebrew as the *Sharav*, and in the American Southwest as the Santa Ana winds.[56] The sirocco is a natural weather pattern that occurs during the annual transition from dry to rainy season and vice versa in the eastern Mediterranean and the American Southwest when a high weather system lingers over the hot desert, pushing the winds to move from east to west, and thereby blowing considerable quantities of dust into the atmosphere, which darkens the sun and causes the moon to appear blood red. Acts 2:17–21 interprets the effects of the sirocco as an eschatological event, but it is nothing more than a natural weather phenomenon. Other New Testament texts follow suit. First Thessalonians 5:2 understands the Day of the L-rd to be an eschatological event that will occur suddenly, and 2 Corinthians 1:14 understands the Day of the L-rd to be the day of Jesus's return. The book of Revelation also draws on Joel 3:1–5, Isaiah 2:6–21, and other texts to depict the day as one of divine wrath in which the wicked are punished when Christ returns to earth. But the New Testament imposes its eschatological vision of the return of Christ on the Day of YHWH texts in the Hebrew Bible.

In the Hebrew Bible, these texts do not function eschatologically; they do not concern "the end time" when YHWH will return to judge the

---

55. De Vries, *From Old Revelation to New*, 38–63.
56. Fitzgerald, *L-rd of the East Wind*.

wicked; they simply refer to the future when YHWH will punish the wicked in *any* future time. In the case of Isaiah ben Amoz, Isaiah 2:5–21 refers to a time when YHWH will punish the Assyrian Empire and Israelites or Judeans who enabled Assyria to oppress Israel and Judah. In the late sixth century, the Day of YHWH refers to YHWH's punishment of Babylon (Isa 13:1—14:2). In the late fifth to early fourth century, the Day of YHWH refers to a day when YHWH will punish those who attempt to resist YHWH's plan to use the Persian monarchy to rule Jerusalem and Judah (cf. Isa 66). And later readers will understand these texts to refer to the punishment of other wicked parties, e.g., the Romans, who committed genocide against the Jewish people in the Bar Kochba Revolt in 132–35 CE; the Muslims, who subjugated Jews to Dhimmi status throughout lands under their rule, beginning in the seventh century CE; the Crusaders, who massacred Jews on the way to conquer Muslim Palestine in 196–98 CE and beyond; the Nazis, who also committed genocide against the Jewish people in World War II; Hamas, who attempted to commit genocide against Israel on October 7, 2023, and beyond; and all anti-Semites who oppress and defame the Jewish people.

The oracle of Isaiah ben Amoz appears in Isaiah 2:6–21. Isaiah 2:5 is an editorial statement that is made to connect Isaiah's Day of YHWH oracle (Isa 2:6–21) to the preceding oracle concerning the nations' procession to Zion to learn YHWH's Torah/"instruction" and thereby to end war among humankind (Isa 2:1–4).[57]

Isaiah 2:22 is also an editorial addition, lacking in the LXX form of Isaiah, that calls upon YHWH to cease punishment against humankind.[58] The date of this addition is uncertain because a wisdom saying designed to call on YHWH to cease punishment could have come from Isaiah himself, a sixth-century BCE writer, or a fifth-century BCE writer. Although most interpreters view Isaiah 2:22 as a concluding statement for Isaiah 2:5–21, its second-person plural address form, directed to YHWH, marks the beginning of a new address that appeals to YHWH to cease punishing humans, such as the men and women portrayed in Isaiah 3:1—4:1.

Within the address concerning the process of cleansing or purging Jerusalem and Judah in Isaiah 2:22—4:6, Isaiah 2:22 introduces the unit with a plea to desist from human self-reliance, which would entail a plea to rely on YHWH. Isaiah 3:1—4:6 then presents an explanation of this concern as

57. Sweeney, *Isaiah 1–39*, 90, 93–94.
58. Sweeney, *Isaiah 1–39*, 100–101, 105, 109.

applied to Jerusalem and Judah. This text is formulated on the model of the prophetic judgment speech, which typically includes an explanation for the judgment or an accusation against those who are to be judged followed by an announcement of judgment.[59] Isaiah 3:1—4:1 focuses on the explanation of the judgment, i.e., the accusations made against the male leadership of Jerusalem in Isaiah 3:1–11, and Isaiah 3:12—4:1 announces the judgment that will be imposed on the leaders and women of Jerusalem as a result of the accusations. The oracle concerning the leadership of Jerusalem in Isaiah 3:1–11 contains the accusations made against the leaders of Jerusalem, defined as a combination of skilled men and military men, who demonstrate their incompetence like children and babies who are appointed to positions of authority. The leaders are accused of ignoring YHWH in word and deed and thereby acting like the people of Sodom and Gomorrah as portrayed in Genesis 18–20. More specific causes of judgment will be outlined in Isaiah 5 and elsewhere. Noteworthy among them is a capacity to defraud the poor in Isaiah 5:1–30 and to rely on alliances with foreign nations and their gods (e.g., Isa 2:6–9; 7; 28–32). Isaiah 3:12—4:1 then turns to the announcement of judgment against the leaders and the women of Jerusalem and Judah. Isaiah 3:12–15 announces punishment against the (male) leaders, who are incompetent and act like babies and women (who in the ancient world were not considered competent to rule). Isaiah 3:16—4:1 then focuses on the announcement of judgment against the women of Jerusalem and Judah, who will suffer as a result of the incompetence of the men and their own arrogance. The women are portrayed as obsessed with clothing, jewelry, and hair styles, but when judgment comes in the form of the Assyrian Empire, all of this will change as the women lose their finery and find themselves without husbands, who have been killed in battle or led away into exile. At that point, desperate women will agree to be married, seven women to one man, to secure standing in society and support by their husbands. Such a portrayal presupposes that men—and not women—owned land and therefore controlled wealth. In modern times, women have obtained greater rights, though women's earnings and ownership of property continue to lag behind those of men.

All elements of Isaiah 3:1—4:1 appear to presuppose the late eighth century BCE when the Assyrian Empire invaded Israel during the

---

59. Sweeney, *Isaiah 1–39*, 105–12, 533–34.

Syro-Ephraimitic War in 735–732 BCE and the northern Israelite revolt in 724–721 BCE and Sennacherib's invasion of Judah in 701 BCE.[60]

Isaiah 4:2–6 follows with a prophetic announcement of salvation or restoration for the purified remnant of Israel at Zion. As previously mentioned, the formula *bayyôm hahû'* ("in that day") is nothing more than a reference to the future. Although the use of the phrase *ṣemaḥ yhwh* ("branch of YHWH") has clear messianic connotations (Jer 23:5; 33:15; Zech 3:8; 6:12),[61] it also has priestly connotations that apply to the high priest, who was also anointed with oil like the king (cf. Zech 4), and it points to the tree imagery that also plays a role in portraying the protective canopy over the Jerusalem Temple (see below). The passage presupposes the conceptualization of a Temple restoration in which the Temple is purged of its "sins" (i.e., improper practice that was undertaken in the past) and re-sanctified so that it can once again serve as the holy center of creation. Such a conceptualization underlies Temple reforms in the history of Judah, such as those of King Hezekiah ben Ahaz (2 Kgs 18–20) and King Josiah ben Amon (2 Kgs 22–23). The passage presupposes the understanding of Isaiah ben Amoz that Jerusalem and Judah will constitute the remnant of Israel.[62] It also presupposes the identity of Zion—and the Temple—as YHWH's bride, Bat Zion or Bat Jerusalem, "Daughter Zion" or "Daughter Jerusalem," particularly since the language associated with the Holy of Holies of the Temple—where the ark of YHWH resides to signify the presence of YHWH in the Temple—is explicitly sexual (i.e., the Hebrew, *yarkĕtê hāʿôlām*, often translated as "the farthest reaches of universe" means literally "the thighs of creation"). The sexual conceptualization of the relationship between YHWH and the Jerusalem Temple then explains the metaphorical reference in verse 4 to the menstrual cleansing of the daughters of Zion and the blood of Jerusalem, insofar as they would then personify the feminine character of Zion/Jerusalem as the bride of YHWH. The reference to Mt. Zion as the site where the cloud of smoke appears by day and the blazing fire appears at night draws upon the imagery of the presence of YHWH and YHWH's angel who guides Israel out of Egypt and through the wilderness to the land of Israel in the exodus and wilderness narratives (e.g., Exod 14:19–20; 23:23–33; 40:33b–38; Num 10:11–12).[63] The portrayal of this cloud and fire as a pro-

---

60. Sweeney, *Isaiah 1–39*, 109–10.
61. Williamson, *Isaiah 1–5*, 307.
62. See, e.g., Isaiah 7:1–9; 10:21; Hasel, *Remnant*, 216–372.
63. See Anderson, "Exodus Typology in Second Isaiah"; Anderson, "Exodus and

tective "canopy" (Hebrew, *ḥuppâ*) and a "booth" (Hebrew, *sukkâ*) reiterates the marriage metaphor in that Jewish weddings take place under the *ḥuppâ*, "canopy" (cf. Ps 19:6; Joel 2:16).[64] The role of the Temple as the holy center of creation is signaled by the metaphorical use of the *sukkâ* ("booth"), a structure employed by ancient Israelite farmers as a shelter for their work in the orchards, vineyards, and fields to bring in the final fruit harvest of the fall before the fall rains begin. In this respect, the use of the Hebrew term *tip'eret* ("beauty") in verse 2 is also significant in that the term relates to the portrayal of the canopy of a fruit tree, such as an olive tree, from which the fruit harvest is grown. (See Isaiah 10:33, which employs the Hebrew term *pĕ'urâ*, derived from the same root as *tip'eret*, to portray the canopy of an olive tree that needs to be beaten to bring in the olive harvest.)

Isaiah 4:2-6 appears to be a composite text when considered diachronically.[65] The initial statement in verse 2 makes reference to "the escaped of Israel," which may have been written in reference to the refugees of northern Israel in the aftermath of the destruction of Samaria by the Assyrian Empire in 724-721 BCE. But verses 3-6 employ the priestly language of purification in relation to the remnant of Israel in Zion and Jerusalem which appears to presuppose the restoration of the Jerusalem Temple in 620-615 BCE and the reforms of Nehemiah and Ezra in the late fifth and early fourth centuries BCE to purge and purify the Temple and the Jewish community of Jerusalem and Judah so that the Temple might best serve its role as the holy center of creation in Persian-period Judean thought.

IV. Isaiah 5-12

Isaiah 5-12 constitutes the discrete block of material that presents prophetic instruction concerning the significance of Assyrian judgment against Israel, which will result in the restoration of the Davidic Empire.[66] The block lacks its own superscription, suggesting that it bears some relation to the preceding block in Isaiah 2-4, which is explicitly concerned with Judah and Jerusalem. Isaiah 5-12 ultimately points to the rise of a just and righteous Davidic monarch in Isaiah 9:1-6 and 11:1-16 who will rule in Jerusalem and restore the combined kingdoms of Judah and Israel. Isaiah 5-12 might

---

Covenant," 339-60; Kiesow, *Exodustexte im Jesajabuches*.

64. Contra Williamson, *Isaiah 1-5*, 115.
65. Sweeney, *Isaiah 1-39*, 105-12, esp. 110-11.
66. Sweeney, *Isaiah 1-39*, 112-21.

therefore be viewed as explaining how Israel and Judah will suffer punishment at the hands of the Assyrian Empire, which will lead ultimately to recognition of Zion/Jerusalem as the locus of YHWH's worldwide rule, beginning with Judah and Israel.

Isaiah 6–12 then provides a lengthy oracular and narrative explanation of how Assyrian judgment of Israel and Judah will lead to the restoration of the united Davidic kingdom. Isaiah 6:1—8:15 presents an account of the basis for the punishment of Israel and Judah by Assyria, including Isaiah's commissioning account in Isaiah 6:1–13 and an account of Isaiah's signs concerning the punishment of the House of David and the punishment of Judah in Isaiah 7:1—8:15. Isaiah 8:16—12:6 then presents an account of the fall of Assyria and the Assyrian king and the subsequent restoration of the Davidic Empire, including Isaiah's instruction concerning YHWH's signs to Israel and the House of David in Isaiah 8:16—9:6 (9:7 ET) and a prophetic announcement concerning the fulfillment of those signs in Isaiah 9:7—12:6 (9:8—12:6 ET).

Isaiah 5–12 comprises two major components. The first is an announcement of judgment against Israel and Judah in Isaiah 5:1–30.[67] Isaiah 5:1–30 begins with an allegorical text in Isaiah 5:1–7, which depicts Israel and Judah as a failed vineyard tended by Isaiah's "friend," who turns out to be YHWH. When the vineyard produces sour grapes despite the "friend's" efforts, the "friend" decides to destroy the vineyard in frustration. The "friend's" action in commanding the clouds to allow no rain to fall upon the vineyard reveals that the "friend" is indeed YHWH and that the vineyard is Israel and Judah, which have failed to produce the justice and righteousness that YHWH expects. The announcement in verse 7 employs puns in Hebrew to make its point, i.e., the failure to produce *mišpāṭ* ("justice") produces *mišpāḥ* ("murder") and the failure to produce *ṣĕdāqâ* ("righteousness") produces *ṣĕʿāqâ* ("outcry").

The vineyard allegory is followed by two sequences of "woe" (*hôy*) oracles that warn the addressees of coming punishment due to their wrong behavior.[68] Each of these sequences of "woe" oracles results in consequences. The first sequence appears in Isaiah 5:8–17, which includes woe oracles concerning the seizure of the property of the poor by the rich (vv. 8–10) and the drunkenness of the rich, who do not perceive the actions of YHWH (vv. 11–12). Isaiah 5:13–17, which begins with the particle, "therefore" (*lākēn*),

---

67. Sweeney, *Isaiah 1–39*, 121–31.
68. Sweeney, *Isaiah 1–39*, 543.

states the consequences, i.e., that the people will go into exile and to the underworld of death, leaving only flocks and cattle to graze on the land. The second "woe" sequence with consequences then follows in Isaiah 5:18–24. There are four woe oracles concerning the pursuit of falsehood (vv. 18–19), deceit (v. 20), self-aggrandizement (v. 21), and drunkenness, which results in the perversion of justice in the law courts (vv. 22–23). Isaiah 5:24, which also begins with "therefore" (*lākēn*), then states the consequences for these actions, i.e., the people will face destruction for ignoring YHWH's instructions.

Isaiah 5:25–30, introduced by *ʿal-kēn* ("therefore" or "consequently," a stronger term than *lākēn*), then explains how the punishment announced in the "woe" oracles will be administered. YHWH will stretch out YHWH's hand, much as YHWH had done during the plagues of the exodus to punish the Egyptians. But instead of delivering Israel and Judah from oppression, YHWH's gesture will summon the Assyrian army to administer the punishment in a reversal of the exodus motif. Assyria's role as the agent of YHWH's punishment appears to presuppose the Syro-Ephraimitic War of 735–732 BCE, in which Israel and Aram allied to attack Judah in an effort to force it to join their revolt against Assyria. Instead of trusting in YHWH to defend Jerusalem and Judah, King Ahaz of Judah called on the Assyrians to save him (see Isa 7:1—8:15; 2 Kgs 16), which only resulted in greater Assyrian oppression of Jerusalem and Judah.

Isaiah 6:1—8:15 presents an account of the basis for YHWH's punishment of Israel and Judah by Assyria as part of the explanation for the judgment of Israel and Judah leading to a righteous Davidic monarchy in Isaiah 6:1—12:6.[69] Many interpreters follow Karl Budde's 1928 hypothesis that these chapters constitute Isaiah's "memoir" (German "*Denkschrift*") of YHWH's decision to punish Israel and Judah,[70] but Budde's understanding of this passage is mistaken. In order for it to be Isaiah's "memoir," the entire passage would have to be written in first-person narrative form. This may be the case for Isaiah 6:1–13 and Isaiah 8:1–15; Isaiah 8:16—9:6, but Isaiah 7:1–25 is written in third-person narrative form, which means that they cannot constitute a part of the prophet's memoir. Interpreters presuppose, perhaps, that a later editor has changed the narrative form from a first- to

---

69. Sweeney, *Isaiah 1–39*, 112–21.

70. Budde, *Jesajas Erleben*. See, e.g., Wildberger, *Isaiah 1–12*, 252; Childs, *Isaiah*, 51–54; Kaiser, *Isaiah 1–12*, 114–17; Blenkinsopp, *Isaiah 1–39*, 223–24.

a third-person account,[71] but the thesis is based on a diachronic reconstruction of an underlying narrative for which there is no demonstrable evidence. Instead, Isaiah 6:1—8:15 must be constructed as a sequence of sub-units that include both first- and third-person narratives that reflect upon the role of the Syro-Ephraimitic War that is understood as YHWH's punishment of Israel and Judah.[72] Isaiah 8:16—9:6 begins a sequence of oracles concerned with the downfall of Assyria and the restoration of the House of David in Isaiah 8:16—12:6.

The first sub-unit is the account of Isaiah's commission as a prophet of YHWH in Isaiah 6:1–13.[73] The account is formulated as a first-person narrative for which Isaiah is presumed to be the author. According to Isaiah 6:1a, the narrative is set in the year of the death of King Uzziah (also known as Azariah) ben Amaziah in 742 BCE, which marked the end of a period of relative prosperity and security for Israel and Judah. It portrays Isaiah's vision of YHWH in the Jerusalem Temple, perhaps on Yom Kippur, the Day of Atonement, given its focus on YHWH's intention to punish Israel and Judah.

The vision account presupposes that Isaiah is standing at the entrance to the Temple by the two columns, Boaz and Jachin, which form the entrance to the *Ulam*, "Porch, Entryway," by which one enters the Temple building. This is the location where the king stands (2 Kgs 11:14; 23:3) because he is not a priest and therefore does not enter into the Temple structure. Insofar as Isaiah functions as a royal advisor, he stands with the king. From this vantage point, one can see into the *Ulam* and the *Heikhal*, "Main Hall," of the Temple structure, to the *D'vir*, "the Holy of Holies," where the ark of the covenant resides behind its curtain embroidered with a cherub. Insofar as the Temple is modeled on the structure of a royal palace, the *D'vir*, with ark, is YHWH's throne room.[74]

The imagery in Isaiah's vision is drawn from the furnishings of the *Heikhal* (Temple). The portrayal of the skirts of YHWH's robe that fills the Temple is drawn from the imagery of the incense smoke from the ten incense altars in the *Heikhal*. The portrayal of the angelic figures known as *seraphs*—a Hebrew term that means "burning"—is drawn from the imagery of the ten candelabra, each of which have seven oil lamps, burning

---

71. E.g., Gitay, *Isaiah and His Audience*.
72. Sweeney, *Isaiah 1–39*, 112–20.
73. Sweeney, *Isaiah 1–39*, 132–42.
74. Halpern, *First Historians*, 46–54; Sweeney, *1-2 Kings*, 110.

within the incense smoke in the *Heikhal*. The singing, "Holy, holy, holy is the L-rd of Hosts; the whole earth is full of His glory," is based on the Levitical singers in the Temple. The shaking doorposts presupposes the heavy wooden doors of the Temple opening to the east at sunrise. Isaiah's cry that his lips are impure and the application of a hot coal to his lips presupposes a typical mouth-purification ceremony undergone by oracular prophets who would speak on behalf of their gods in the ancient world.[75]

Isaiah's mouth purification enables him to hear YHWH's request for a prophet and to offer own response, "send me!" But YHWH's commission to Isaiah—i.e., that he is rendering the people deaf, blind, and unable to speak—is an oracle of judgment that will ensure that the people will suffer judgment without the ability to repent. Such an oracle presents a moral problem in that it represents teleological ethics, i.e., that the end result of an act represents a moral goal that justifies the means necessary to achieve the goal. In this case, it is the suffering of generations that are unable to repent. It differs from ontological ethics, in which a moral action is justified in its own right. In this case, the goal is the recognition of YHWH as the true G-d throughout all the world.

When Isaiah asks, "How long, my L-rd?" he does not tell YHWH that YHWH's action is wrong. There are a number of cases in which human figures challenged YHWH's intentions to bring punishment, e.g., Abraham told YHWH that the deaths of even ten righteous people in Sodom and Gomorrah would be wrong (Gen 18); Moses told YHWH that killing the people of Israel to make a new nation out of his own descendants would be wrong (Exod 32–34; Num 13–14); and Job told YHWH that his own suffering was wrong. In all cases, YHWH agreed and relented. But Isaiah did not do this, and the book of Isaiah therefore ends in Isaiah 66 with a vision of the dead bodies of the wicked scattered about. YHWH's response to Isaiah, "until cities are *laid waste* without inhabitant" (Isa 6:11), employs the Hebrew verb *šā'û* ("[they] are laid waste") and "and the ground is *laid waste* and desolate" employs the Hebrew verb *tiššā'eh* ("[it] is laid waste"). Both employ the same verbal root that stands behind the Hebrew word *Shoah*, "destruction," which is used to describe the Holocaust.[76] YHWH's use of the imagery of a fallen terebinth and oak tree trunk that burns until only a tenth of it remains employs the imagery of a fallen tree that is burned down to its trunk to represent those who will survive the destruction. The

---

75. Hurowitz, "Isaiah's Impure Lips."
76. Sweeney, *Reading the Hebrew Bible After the Holocaust*, 84–103.

portrayal of the one-tenth of the population that survives is then employed in Ezra 9:2 to describe those who would return to repopulate Jerusalem in the aftermath of the Babylonian exile during the early Persian period in fifth and fourth centuries BCE.

Isaiah 7:1—8:15 follows with an account concerning Isaiah's signs of YHWH's judgment against the House of David and Judah. The account includes two major segments. Isaiah 7:1–25 recounts Isaiah's dialogue with King Ahaz of Judah as he inspects the defenses of Jerusalem at the outset of the Syro-Ephraimitic War, and Isaiah 8:1–15 is an autobiographical account of the Maher-Shalal-Hash-Baz sign concerning YHWH's judgment against Judah.

Isaiah 7:1–25 is a third-person narrative concerning Isaiah's dialogue with King Ahaz ben Jotham of Judah as he inspects the defenses of Jerusalem at the outbreak of the Syro-Ephraimitic War. Although many interpreters consider this narrative to be part of the so-called Isaiah "memoir" or "*Denkschrift*," its third-person narrative form distinguishes it from the first-person autobiographical form in Isaiah 6:1–13 and Isaiah 8:1–15 and 8:16—9:6.[77]

Isaiah 7:1–25 begins with a notice in 7:1 concerning the alliance between King Rezin of Aram and King Pekah ben Remaliah of Israel to attack Judah during the reign of King Ahaz. The purpose of the alliance was to force Judah to join the Syro-Ephraimitic coalition that was preparing to revolt against the Assyrian Empire, which had controlled Aram and Israel since the reign of King Jehu ben Jehoshaphat ben Nimshi (842–815 BCE).[78]

---

77. See note 70 above.

78. For the account of King Jehu's revolt against the House of Omri and his reign over Israel, see 2 Kings 8:1—13:25. Although 2 Kings does not mention Jehu's submission to the Assyrian Empire, the Black Obelisk of King Shalmaneser III of Assyria portrays Jehu bowing in submission at the feet of Shalmaneser (Pritchard, *ANEP*, 351, 355). Israel's alliance with Assyria during the reign of the House of Jehu (842–746 BCE) secured Israel against attack by Aram and ensured peace throughout the reign of the Jehu kings. But with the assassination of King Zechariah ben Jeroboam in 746 BCE by pro-Aramean forces, Israel descended into a period of conflict during 746–737 BCE, which saw the throne exchange hands repeatedly until the emergence of King Pekah ben Remaliah, a pro-Aramean usurper of the throne, who allied with King Rezin of Aram to revolt against Assyria. Pekah and Rezin knew they could not revolt safely against Assyria unless Judah was a part of their alliance. They therefore attacked Jerusalem in 735 BCE in an effort to depose the Davidic king (Ahaz) and replace him with a man named ben Tabeel from the Trans-Jordan region of Israel to ensure the success of their revolt. For discussion of the reigns of the Israelite and Judean kings during this period, see Sweeney, *1–2 Kings*, 314–86.

The narrative indicates the fear of the House of David, specifically the twenty-year-old King Ahaz, who had just ascended the throne on the death of his father, Jotham, in 735 BCE, upon hearing the report of the Syro-Ephraimitic alliance and its plans to attack Jerusalem to depose him. The narrative recounts Ahaz's inspection of Jerusalem's water system at the end of the conduit of the Upper Pool by the road of the Fuller's Field, where Isaiah ben Amoz, accompanied by his son Shear Jashub, met him. The conduit of the Upper Pool by the road of the Fuller's Field was the point where the Gihon spring, the major water source for ancient Jerusalem, flowed closest to the walls of the city. The inhabitants of Jerusalem could descend through Warren's shaft, cut through solid rock from Canaanite times to draw water from behind the defensive walls of Jerusalem. The Fuller's Field was the site in Jerusalem where people did their laundry, insofar as the English word "fuller" refers to one who does laundry. Access to water was key to Jerusalem's survival, and the source of the water had to be well hidden and well protected to ensure the safety of the city. Indeed, David had conquered Jerusalem in the late tenth century BCE by sending his army commander up the water shaft, thereby enabling him to take the city without a full-scale attack against its defensive walls (see 2 Sam 5:4–10; 1 Chr 8:4–6).[79]

Isaiah met Ahaz at this location with his son, symbolically named Shear Jashub (Hebrew, *šĕ'ār yāšûb*), which means "a remnant shall return," i.e., a remnant of the people will survive to return to the city. The boy's symbolic name indicated that many in Jerusalem would likely die during the Syro-Ephraimitic invasion, but they and Jerusalem would ultimately survive (see Isa 6:12–13). Isaiah assured Ahaz with a speech introduced by the "reassurance formula" "do not fear" (Hebrew, *'al-tîrā'*), beginning in verse 4,[80] and concluded with a statement based on a pun with the Hebrew root *'āmēn*: *'im-lō' ta'ămînû* ("if you do not believe") *kî lō' tē'āmēnû* ("you will not be secured"). The pun was intended to illustrate the threat to the security of Ahaz and Jerusalem if he does not follow Isaiah's advice.

Ahaz's response in Isaiah 7:10–17 demands attention. When Isaiah told Ahaz to ask for a sign from YHWH, Ahaz responded in verse 12 with the statement, "I will not ask, and I will not test YHWH," which is taken in the narrative to indicate Ahaz's rejection of Isaiah's advice. In fact, Ahaz's statement is an expression of Ahaz's piety with regard to YHWH. Isaiah responds with exasperation and announces that YHWH will give Ahaz a

79. Sweeney, *1–2 Samuel*, 211–13.
80. Sweeney, *Isaiah 1–39*, 547.

sign with the birth of a son, to be named Emmanuel (Hebrew, ʿimmānû ēl), "G-d is with us," to a young woman (Hebrew, ʿalmâ). Although the Hebrew word ʿalmâ refers to a young woman of child-bearing age, the New Testament, following the Greek translation of the Septuagint, uses the word *parthenos*, "virgin," and sees in it a reference to Jesus's birth (Matt 1:23). The Hebrew term for virgin is bĕtûlâ. In the aftermath of Ahaz's presumed rejection of Isaiah's advice, the prophet portrays the coming judgment against Jerusalem and Judah at the hands of the Assyrian Empire in Isaiah 7:17–25.

This narrative appears to be the product of a later narrator, likely during the reign of King Josiah ben Amon of Judah, who intended to contrast Ahaz's unwillingness to follow Isaiah's advice with the piety of his son, King Hezekiah ben Ahaz, who followed Isaiah's advice and turned to YHWH at the time of the invasion of Judah and siege of Jerusalem by King Sennacherib of Assyria in 701 BCE, according to Isaiah 36–37. The relationship between the two narratives is clear, insofar as each is set by the Upper Pool of the Fuller's Field, where the Assyrian Rab Shakeh, "Chief Cup Bearer," stood to demand Hezekiah's unconditional surrender of the city. But Isaiah 36–37 is written well after the 701 BCE Assyrian invasion of Judah and after Sennacherib's assassination by his own sons in 681 BCE. The purpose was to show that Hezekiah, the presumed righteous monarch portrayed in Isaiah 7:14 and 9:1–6, was delivered from Assyria by the power of YHWH and that Ahaz was condemned for his presumed refusal to follow Isaiah's advice. As the discussion of Isaiah 36–39 below shows, Isaiah 36–37 was likely written during the reign of King Josiah (642–649 BCE).

Isaiah 8:1–15 presents a first-person, autobiographical account of Isaiah's presentation of the Mahar-Shalal-Hash-Baz sign of YHWH's judgment against Judah.[81] The passage follows the third-person narrative in Isaiah 7:1–25 concerning YHWH's judgment against the House of David, and the two narratives together form Isaiah 7:1—8:15, which concludes Isaiah 6:1—8:15, which is concerned with the punishment of Israel and Judah by the Assyrian Empire.

The passage begins with Isaiah 8:1–4, which recounts YHWH's instructions to Isaiah concerning the birth of his son, Mahar-Shalal-Hash-Baz. The name means "the spoil speeds; the prey hastens," and it will function as a sign of YHWH's judgment against Judah. YHWH instructs Isaiah to prepare a document in which two men, Uriah the priest and Zechariah ben Jeberechiah, will serve as witnesses to the birth and naming of the

---

81. Sweeney, *Isaiah 1–39*, 165–75.

child. The second witness, Zechariah ben Jeberechiah, will later prove to be a factor in identifying the prophet Zechariah ben Berechiah ben Iddo, in the book of the Twelve Prophets, who is presented as a figure who confirms the prophecies of Isaiah and the other prophets at the time of the building of the Second Temple in the early Persian period.[82]

Isaiah 8:5–15 then presents an account of YHWH's disputation speech to Isaiah in which YHWH explains the significance of the sign. The speech begins with YHWH's argument that the people have rejected "the Waters of Siloam," a metaphor for YHWH's provision of the Gihon Spring to supply Jerusalem with water and thereby to ensure the welfare and safety of the people. Such a statement functions metaphorically as a claim that Judah has rejected YHWH's protection. Instead, they have chosen the water of the Euphrates River, a metaphorically expressed claim that Judah has chosen the Assyrian Empire, located across the Euphrates River in Mesopotamia, as indicated by King Ahaz's decision to appeal to King Tiglath Pileser III of Assyria for deliverance from the Syro-Ephraimitic attack (2 Kgs 16). YHWH depicts the Euphrates River as a mighty flood that will inundate Judah. As part of the argument, YHWH portrays the Assyrian king spreading his wings over Judah and flooding the land with water. The imagery of spreading one's wings functions as metaphor for rape in this instance. In Ruth 3:9 where Ruth asks Boaz to spread his wings over her, she is metaphorically asking him to engage in sexual intercourse with her as part of a Levirate marriage in which Boaz will father a child with Ruth to serve as a son for her now dead husband (cf. Deut 25:5–10). The image of filling the land with water also constitutes a metaphorical portrayal of the sexual act, in this case a rape. The land of Judah is considered to be feminine and the bride of YHWH, a theme that is revisited in Isaiah 54, which portrays YHWH's return to Bat Zion/Daughter Zion (Jerusalem), YHWH's bride, who awaits the return of her husband (YHWH) and her sons (the tribes of Israel) after she had been raped by the unclean (Isa 52:1).[83] The balance of the oracle calls upon the people to recognize YHWH as their true G-d and deliverer.

Insofar as Isaiah 8:1–15 is written in first-person autobiographical form, it may well have formed part of the presumed "memoir" together with Isaiah 6:1–13 and 8:16—9:6.

Isaiah 8:16—12:6 then forms a lengthy sequence of oracles that constitute a prophetic announcement of the fall of Assyria and the restoration of

---

82. Sweeney, *Twelve Prophets*, 2:561–73; Sweeney, "Political Perspective."
83. Sweeney, "Where Were You?"

the Davidic Empire.[84] The oracular sequence includes Isaiah 8:16—9:6 (ET 9:7), which presents prophetic instruction concerning YHWH's signs for restoration to Israel and the House of David, and Isaiah 9:7—12:6, which presents a series of oracles concerning the fulfillment of YHWH's signs.

The first element in this sequence is Isaiah 8:16—9:6, which records prophetic instruction regarding YHWH's signs to Israel and the House of David.[85] The passage is written in first-person autobiographical form. The instruction begins in Isaiah 8:16-17 with an expression of Isaiah's frustration as he calls for his testimony and his instruction (*tôrâ*) to be bound up and sealed among his teaching/disciples. The Hebrew word *limmudāy* is confusing here, insofar as it can refer to "my teachings" (i.e., "those things/ideas that are taught") or "my disciples" (i.e., "those persons/students who are taught"). The presence of the writings and teachings of later prophets who develop the ideas of Isaiah ben Amoz in Isaiah 40-66 suggests that both understandings are operative within the book of Isaiah. The prophet states in verse 17 that he will wait for YHWH, who is currently hiding the divine face from the House of Jacob.

Isaiah 8:18—9:6 follows with an announcement of the significance of YHWH's signs for the restoration of Israel and the House of David. Isaiah 8:18 asserts that Isaiah and his children are to serve as signs for the restoration. Isaiah 8:19—9:6 then serves as a disputation speech in which YHWH argues that the people will suffer through a period of darkness and suffering until they come upon a great light (Isa 9:1-6), i.e., a new Davidic king who will serve as a mighty counsellor on behalf of YHWH and a prince of peace who will establish the Davidic throne as the basis for justice and righteousness throughout the land. Most interpreters maintain that this oracle was written in relation to the birth or accession to the throne of King Hezekiah ben Ahaz, who would lead Judah in revolt against the Assyrian Empire in 701 BCE. Later generations considered this king to be King Josiah, Jesus, Rabbi Hillel, Shimon Bar Kochba, Shabbetai Zvi, Shukr Kuhayl II, the Baal Shem Tov, and others.[86]

Isaiah 9:7—12:6 (ET 9:8—12:6) then follows with a block of oracles that constitute a prophetic announcement of the fulfillment of YHWH's signs concerning judgment against northern Israel and restoration for the

---

84. Sweeney, *Isaiah 1–39*, 112–21.
85. Sweeney, *Isaiah 1–39*, 175–88.
86. See, e.g., Lenowitz, *Jewish Messiahs*.

royal House of David.[87] Isaiah 9:7—10:4 (ET 9:8—10:4) focuses on judgment against Israel, and Isaiah 10:5—12:6 focuses on restoration for the royal House of David.

Isaiah 9:7—10:4 (ET 9:8—10:4) presents a sequence of oracles that constitute a prophetic warning to the leaders of northern Israel that their alleged rejection of YHWH will lead to judgment.[88] There are four oracles in the sequence, each of which concludes with the formula "in all this, His [YHWH's] anger has not turned back, and His hand is still stretched out." This formula presupposes the plague narratives presently found in Exodus 7-13, which recounts how Moses' outstretched hand, representing the hand of YHWH, signals the onset of the plagues against Egypt and other actions taken by YHWH on behalf of Israel, such as the parting of the Reed Sea in Exodus 14-15. The four oracles focus on: YHWH's word against Israel (9:7-11; ET 9:8-12); the people's failure to turn to YHWH (9:12-16; ET 9:8-17); the consequences for the people (Isa 9:17-20; ET 9:18-21); and a woe oracle[89] that condemns the leadership of Israel (10:1-4). The woe formula employed in Isaiah 10:1-4 provides an intertextual link with the woe sequence in Isaiah 5:8-24, which enables Isaiah 5:1-30 and Isaiah 9:7—10:4 (ET 9:8—10:4) to frame the so-called "memoir" of Isaiah in Isaiah 6:1—9:6 (ET 6:1—9:7). The four oracles presuppose the Assyrian invasions of northern Israel from the Syro-Ephraimitic War in 735-732 BCE through the Assyrian destruction of northern Israel in 724-721 BCE.

Isaiah 10:5—12:6 then presents a sequence of oracles that are ultimately concerned with the restoration of the royal House of David.[90] The synchronic form of this passage begins with a woe oracle directed against Assyria (10:5-11)[91] followed by a lengthy announcement of judgment against Assyria, accompanied by attention to the rise of a new Davidic king who will deliver Israel (10:12—12:6). The announcement of judgment proper, directed especially to the Assyrian king, appears in Isaiah 10:12-19. A series of five elaborations on this announcement, each of which is introduced with formulaic language that points to the future realization of this judgment, then follow in Isaiah 10:20—12:6. Although the temporal formulas are sometimes considered as eschatological, we have already

---

87. Sweeney, *Isaiah 1-39*, 112-21.
88. Sweeney, *Isaiah 1-39*, 188-96.
89. Sweeney, *Isaiah 1-39*, 543.
90. Sweeney, *Isaiah*, 112-21, 196-211.
91. Sweeney, *Isaiah 1-39*, 543.

indicated that analysis of the temporal forms demonstrates that they are nothing more than indications of a future time.[92] The elaborations include Isaiah 10:20-26, which anticipates future relief of the remnant of Israel from Assyrian oppression; Isaiah 10:27—11:9, which anticipates the fall of the Assyrian king coupled with the rise of a new Davidic king; Isaiah 11:10, which anticipates the recognition of the new Davidic king by the nations; Isaiah 11:11-16, which anticipates the future restoration of Israel; and Isaiah 12:1-6, which presents a concluding hymn of thanksgiving that draws heavily on the language and concerns of the Song of the Sea in Exodus 15.

Although the synchronic form of the passage is clear, it is equally clear that the present form of the text is the product of extensive diachronic composition that ranges from the time of Isaiah ben Amoz, the late eighth-century prophet, through the reign of the seventh-century King Josiah ben Amon of Judah, and finally through the late sixth-century edition of the book of Isaiah that anticipates the downfall of Babylon and the restoration of Judah under Achaemenid Persian rule. Key to the recognition of the diachronic redaction of this passage is Isaiah 13:1—14:32, which also shows clear signs of redaction.[93] Although Isaiah 13:1—14:27 is concerned with the downfall of Babylon, its portrayal of the descent of the Babylonian king to Sheol after having been left unburied on the battlefield in Isaiah 14:4b-23 indicates that the portrayal of the dead king is not of a *Babylonian* king. No Babylonian king was killed in battle and his body left unburied; rather, that particular fate is left only to King Sargon II of Assyria, who was killed in battle against the kingdom of Tabal, located in Anatolia, in 705 BCE, and the Assyrian defeat was so severe that his body was never recovered for burial. A further indication of the redaction of this passage appears in Isaiah 14:24-27, which anticipates the defeat of Assyria, not Babylon. The taunt song against the (Assyrian) king in Isaiah 14:4b-23 and the anticipation of Assyria's defeat in Isaiah 14:24-27, which employs some of the language and motifs of Isaiah 10:5-34, apparently were originally intended to follow the oracular account of the downfall of Assyria and the Assyrian king in Isaiah 10:5-34.

The use of tree imagery throughout this passage is particularly important for its interpretation.[94] The woe oracle in Isaiah 10:5-11 condemns

92. De Vries, *From Old Revelation to New*, 38-63.

93. For detailed discussion of Isaiah 13-14, see below, pp. 59-62, and Sweeney, *Isaiah 1-39*, 218-39.

94. See esp. Nielsen, *There Is Hope for a Tree*.

Assyria for its arrogance in threatening Jerusalem and other nations, and it depicts YHWH's rod, a motif drawn from the plague narratives in Exodus 5–13, as the instrument of punishment against Assyria. The imagery of an axe and a saw employed for cutting down a tree and the imagery of tree burning appear in the announcement of judgment against Assyria in Isaiah 10:12–19. The imagery of the rod of YHWH employed to punish Assyria, like the punishment inflicted by YHWH on Egypt, appears in the first elaboration in Isaiah 10:20–26. The use of the rod to beat the branches of the tree, here depicted as tree crowns, follows in Isaiah 10:27—11:9, followed by the new growth from a tree stump representing the emergence of a new Davidic king as a branch that grows from that stump. The "root" of Jesse, a metaphorical reference to the tree root of Jesse, the father of David and thus of the entire House of David, then stands as a signal to the peoples of the restoration of the House of David in Isaiah 11:10. The hand of YHWH, again citing the Exodus plague motif, then employs the restored Davidic king to defeat Israel's enemies and reunited Israel and Judah in Isaiah 11:10–16. Finally, Isaiah 12:1–6 celebrates YHWH's defeat of Assyria and restoration of the House of David by citing the Song of the Sea from Exodus 15 in which YHWH delivered Israel from Egyptian bondage.

Although Nielsen recognized the importance of the tree motif in the book of Isaiah, she overlooked an important dimension of the motif. In ancient Assyrian mythology, the Assyrian king is considered as the ideal human being, sent by the Assyrian gods to establish order, justice, righteousness, etc., among human beings on earth.[95] The imagery employed to depict the Assyrian king in this mythology is a tree, sometimes growing upside down from heaven toward earth with its roots planted in heaven and its branches growing toward the earth. The branches of the tree embody the qualities allegedly inherent in the Assyrian king as the ideal human (e.g., justice, righteousness, a sweet smell, etc.), which were to be brought to humanity by the Assyrian king and practiced by his subjects.

95. The Sumerian King List begins with the statement, "When kingship was lowered from heaven . . . ," and the motif is represented in Assyrian iconography with a depiction of the king as a tree growing upside down from heaven to earth (see Jacobsen, *Sumerian King List*, 58–59, 70–71); Jacobsen, *Treasures of Darkness*, 113–14; cf. Grayson, "Assyrian Civilization," 194–99. For discussion of the Assyrian tree of life, see Widengren, *King and the Tree of Life*; Parpola, "Assyrian Tree of Life," although Parpola's attempt to connect the Assyrian tree of life with the later Kabbalistic system of the Ten Sefirot is generally considered as unsuccessful (see Sweeney, "Ten Sefirot"); Cooper, "Assyrian Prophecies." For full discussion of the history of research on the Assyrian tree, see Giovino, *Assyrian Sacred Tree*, esp. 19–20.

But in Isaiah 10:5—12:6, the Assyrian king fails to represent these ideals. He therefore must be punished and replaced by a Davidic king, who will better embody the ideals expected of the Assyrian king. The Assyrian king is punished by the rod of YHWH, just as the Egyptian pharaoh was punished in the exodus narratives. The imagery of YHWH's punishment of the Assyrian king is especially evident in Isaiah 10:27–34 in which the branches of the tree representing the Assyrian king are to be cut off with an axe and the branches are beaten with a rod by the hand of YHWH, just as one harvests the fruit of an olive tree to retrieve its harvest. Isaiah 11:1–9 then follows with a depiction of the new, ideal Davidic king, growing as a branch and shoot from the stump of Jesse, apparently employing the imagery of the stump that remains following the punishment of Israel in Isaiah 6:12–13. The new Davidic king will then embody the qualities of justice, righteousness, wisdom, understanding, sweet smell, etc., that the Assyrian king lacks. The portrayal of the new Davidic king as a little boy and a baby playing safely in the hole of a snake in Isaiah 11:8–9 apparently presupposes King Josiah of Judah, who ascended the throne of Judah in 640 BCE at the age of eight following the assassination of his father, Amon ben Manasseh, in an attempted coup against the House of David. Although Josiah's reign ended in failure when he was killed at Megiddo by Pharaoh Necho of Egypt in 609 BCE, his interest in national restoration is manifested in his attempts to reclaim the territory of the former northern kingdom of Israel and to subjugate his neighbors as part of his efforts to restore the Davidic Empire.

The hymn of thanksgiving in Isaiah 12:1–6 would have concluded the seventh-century BCE edition of this text with its focus on the new, ideal Davidic king. The hymn cites the Song of the Sea extensively together with other motifs from Psalms (e.g., Isa 12:2b cites Exod 15:2a; Isa 12:5a cites Exod 15:1b; and Isa 12:4a draws upon Ps 105:1).[96]

Prior to the composition of Isaiah 11:1–16 in the seventh century BCE to support King Josiah's reign, the oracles concerning Assyria and the Assyrian king in Isaiah 10:5–34 would have been followed by the taunt song in Isaiah 14:4b–31 concerning the death of King Sargon II of Assyria in battle and the failure to retrieve his body in 705 BCE and the announcement of Assyria's impending defeat in Isaiah 14:24–27. It was only following the Babylonian exile and the impending fall of Babylon in the late sixth century BCE that these passage were reinterpreted in relation to the downfall and death of the Babylonian king in the present form of Isaiah 13–14 as part of the late sixth-century edition of the book of Isaiah.

---

96. Sweeney, *Isaiah 1–39*, 118.

3

Isaiah 13–27

I. Overview

ISAIAH 13–27 PRESENTS A prophetic announcement concerning the preparation of the nations for YHWH's world rule.[1] The section opens with a superscription in Isaiah 13:1 that introduces both the section at large and the unit in Isaiah 13:1—14:32, which is concerned with the prophetic "pronouncement" or "oracle" concerned with Babylon. The Hebrew word *maśśā'* has often been mistranslated as "burden" in the past because the word is derived from the verbal root *nś'*, which means "to lift up."[2] The translation, "burden," is then based on an understanding of "to lift up" as an action that calls for carrying a burden. But this understanding is mistaken. The use of the verbal root *nś'* in oracular prophecy is based on the understanding of the verb to call for lifting up one's voice to speak an oracle, pronouncement, or proverb. Examples of the use of this verbal form appear throughout the account of Balaam's prophecies concerning Israel in Numbers 22–24 (see Num 23:7; 23:18; 24:3; 24:15; 24:21).

The superscription in Isaiah 13:1 introduces both the textual unit concerned with Babylon in Isaiah 13:1—14:32 and the entire textual unit in Isaiah 13–27. This is due to the specific reference to Babylon in Isaiah 13:1

---

1. Sweeney, *Isaiah 1–39*, 39–62.
2. BDB 672.

and the formulation of the superscription at large as "The pronouncement of Babylon that Isaiah ben Amoz perceived." This formulation is similar to the superscription concerning Isaiah's perception of the visions concerning Judah and Jerusalem in Isaiah 1:1 and 2:1, both of which introduce major sub-units within the formal structure of the book of Isaiah. In the case of Isaiah 13:1, the superscription introduces a sequence of superscriptions concerning the nations:

- Isaiah 13:1, Babylon (13:1—14:32; Philistia is included with the oracle concerning Babylon in 14:28–32, with its own unique narrative superscription);
- Isaiah 15:1, Moab (15:1—16:14);
- Isaiah 17:1, Damascus (including Israel as part of the Syro-Ephraimitic coalition, 17:1—18:7);
- Isaiah 19:1, Egypt (19:1—20:6);
- Isaiah 21:1, the Wilderness of the Sea (Babylon, 21:1–10);
- Isaiah 21:11, Dumah (Edom, 21:11–12);
- Isaiah 21:13, Arabia (21:13–17);
- Isaiah 22:1, the Valley of Vision (i.e., Jerusalem, 22:1–25);
- Isaiah 23:1, Tyre (23:1–18).

Isaiah 13–23 therefore constitutes the prophetic pronouncement or oracles concerning the nations in the book of Isaiah.[3] From a diachronic standpoint, these oracles represent the nations subjugated by the Achaemenid Persian Empire, initially ruled by King Cyrus of Persia in the late sixth century BCE. Insofar as they are presented as oracles of YHWH revealed to Isaiah ben Amoz and presumably spoken by him, they represent a late sixth-century edition of the book of Isaiah, which identified the rise of the Achaemenid Persian Empire with the will of YHWH. Isaiah 40–55 indicates that King Cyrus of Persia is YHWH's chosen messiah and Temple-builder (Isa 44:28; 45:1) and so it calls upon Jews exiled in Babylonia to return to Jerusalem to restore the city as the site for YHWH's worldwide sovereignty over creation and the nations.

Although Isaiah 24–27 is oftentimes understood to be "the Apocalypse of Isaiah," closer analysis of this textual block indicates that it is not

---

3. Sweeney, *Isaiah 1–39*, 212–17.

apocalyptic or eschatological at all.[4] Instead, it is an example of the use of mythological language in a prophecy of salvation serving to depict the restoration of Jerusalem/Zion as the holy center of creation and the capital of a restored Israel and Judah. Ancient Judean thought understood YHWH's Temple in Jerusalem to be the holy center of creation, which is how most ancient Near Eastern temples were understood to function in their respective cultures.[5] Consequently, the depiction of a ruined creation portrays the effects of the Jerusalem Temple profaned, either by physical destruction or by the introduction of unholy practices in the Temple. With the Temple restored and celebrated by holy offerings that are eaten in a festival meal by the priests and people of Judah (and Israel) in the Temple, creation is understood to be restored. Insofar as Isaiah 24–27 is appended to the oracles concerning the nations in Isaiah 13–23, it portrays the festival celebration in the restored Temple as YHWH's world rule over the nations and creation at large is reestablished with the re-sanctification of the Jerusalem Temple. As such, Isaiah 24–27 is part of the late sixth-century edition of the book of Isaiah, and a recent study by Hays argues that it originated with celebration of the downfall of Assyrian rule over Judah and Jerusalem in the late seventh century BCE.[6]

II. Isaiah 13:1—14:32

Isaiah 13:1—14:32 presents the prophetic pronouncement (oracle) concerning Babylon with an appendix concerned with a prophetic pronouncement concerning Philistia.[7] The passage comprises three major constituent units: the superscription in Isaiah 13:1; the prophetic pronouncement concerning Babylon in Isaiah 13:2—14:27; and the appendix concerning Philistia in Isaiah 14:28–32.

Superscriptions by their very nature stand apart structurally from the material that they introduce.[8] Consequently, the superscription in Isaiah 13:1 is the first major sub-unit of Isaiah 13:1—14:32.

Isaiah 13:2—14:27 constitutes the prophetic pronouncement concerning Babylon proper, insofar as it is concerned throughout with presenting

4. Sweeney, *Isaiah 1–39*, 311–25.
5. Levenson, "Temple and the World."
6. Hays, *Origins of Isaiah 24–27*.
7. Sweeney, *Isaiah 1–39*, 218–39.
8. Tucker, "Prophetic Superscriptions."

YHWH's oracle concerning Babylon through the agency of the prophet, Isaiah ben Amoz. The oracle begins with a summons to war in Isaiah 13:2–5 in which the prophet recounts YHWH's summons of warriors to attack Babylon. It continues with a lengthy oracular sequence in Isaiah 13:6—14:23 that announces the Day of YHWH against Babylon. Some scholars have attempted to argue that the Day of YHWH is an eschatological event, but the portrayal of the Day of the L-rd (YHWH) as an eschatological event is derived from Acts 2:16–20, which cites Joel 3:1–5 (ET Joel 2:28–32) to portray the Day of the L-rd as an eschatological event that portends the second coming of Jesus. Although the text of Joel portrays the Day of the L-rd as a day when the sun turns dark and the moon turns to blood, these are only the natural effects of the sirocco winds, known in the Middle East as the *Sharav* in Hebrew and the *Ḥamsin* in Arabic and as the Santa Ana winds in the American Southwest.[9] The winds are a natural phenomenon at the turn of the seasons, dry to rainy in the fall and rainy to dry in the summer, when high pressure systems settle over eastern deserts, i.e., the Arabian Desert over Jordan in the Middle East and the Mojave Desert in the American Southwest. The high pressure systems force air to reverse its normal course of movement from west to east to east to west, which results in hot, dry winds that blow great quantities of dust, thereby blocking out the sun and making the moon appear blood red. In the Hebrew Bible, they are the east wind, featured in the Exodus Reed Sea narratives of Exodus 14–15 and other texts in which they demonstrate YHWH's power over creation to defend Israel from enemies. The Day of YHWH is nothing more than a mythological portrayal of YHWH's efforts to employ the sirocco winds of creation to protect Israel and Judah from enemies, such as Egypt. In addition to the imagery of creation, the oracle employs the imagery of childbirth to depict the turmoil caused by YHWH against the enemies of Israel and Judah (Isa 13:8). There is reference to an attack against Babylon by the Medes (Isa 13:17–18), a nation located north of the Tigris River and a former ally of Babylon, who joined King Cyrus the Great of the Persian Empire in his campaign against Babylon in 545–535 BCE.[10] The impending destruction of Babylon is compared to the destruction of Sodom and Gomorrah (Isa 13:19; cf. Gen 18–19).

A distinctive feature of the oracle concerning Babylon is the portrayal of the Babylonian king descending to Sheol, the underworld where all the

9. Fitzgerald, *L-rd of the East Wind*.
10. Wiesehöfer, "Meses, Media."

dead go (Isa 14:3–23).[11] This portrayal appears in the form of a taunt song, which portrays the Babylonian king, killed in battle and his body left unburied on the battle field. No Babylonian king of the time suffered such a fate. The taunt song was apparently composed to mark the death of King Sargon II of Assyria in battle against the kingdom of Tabal, located in what is now eastern Turkey, in 705 BCE. The Assyrian army was badly mauled, Sargon II was killed, and his body remained unburied and unclaimed on the battle field. This suggests that the taunt song in Isaiah 14:3–23 was written about Sargon II originally,[12] and presumably was intended to follow upon the oracle against the Assyrian king in Isaiah 10:5–34. The statements made about Assyria in Isaiah 14:24–27 use language similar to that of Isaiah 10:5–34, which indicates a relationship with the earlier oracle against the Assyrian king. The taunt song in Isaiah 14:3–23 was edited and applied to the expected fate of the Babylonian king during the late sixth century BCE when Cyrus of Persia threatened Babylon. But by 539 BCE, Cyrus struck a deal with Babylon for it to accept him as king, and he and his army entered Babylon peacefully when the Babylonian priesthood named him as their next monarch, chosen by Marduk, the city god of Babylon.

The third major sub-unit of the prophetic pronouncement concerning Babylon is the appended oracle concerning Philistia in Isaiah 14:28–32.[13] Some interpreters might speculate that the Philistine oracle in Isaiah 14:28–32 was located after Isaiah 14:4b–27 in an earlier edition of Isaiah's oracles, but there is no clear evidence that this was the case. The reason for the location of Isaiah 14:28–32 at the end of the originally anti-Assyrian oracle in Isaiah 14:4b–27 is to signal the Assyrian strategy of first advancing against Philistia to prevent the Egyptians from intervening in Israel and Judah, thereby allowing the Assyrian army to subdue Israel and Judah without Egyptian interference. By initially moving against Philistia, the Assyrians blocked Egypt from moving its army northward to support Israel and Judah against Assyrian attack. Having blocked the Egyptians, the Assyrians were free to do whatever they liked to Israel and Judah. This was the strategy of Sargon II in 720 BCE and Sennacherib in 701 BCE. The Babylonians did not employ this strategy. When they attacked Judah in 598, 587, and (presumably) 582 BCE, they advanced down the Jordan

---

11. Sweeney, *Isaiah 1–39*, 218–39; Gosse, *Isaïe 13,1–14,23*; Erlandsson, *Burden of Babylon*.

12. See esp. Sweeney, *Isaiah 1–39*, 231–35; Erlandsson, *Burden of Babylon*, 109–66.

13. See esp. Sweeney, *Isaiah 1–39*, 233–34.

River Valley and approached Jerusalem from the east in order to subdue the Trans-Jordan and cut it off from Judah.

III. Isaiah 15:1—16:14

Isaiah 15:1—16:14 presents the prophetic announcement concerning Moab, including the superscription to the passage in 15:1a; the prophetic pronouncement proper in 15:1b—16:12;[14] and the summary appraisal in 15:13-14. The prophetic pronouncement proper appears in Isaiah 15:1b—16:12, and it includes three major sub-units. The first is the prophetic first-person lament over the fate of Moab in Isaiah 15:1b-9.[15] The lament appears in the classic 3/2 meter of mourning, Qinah ("lament"), which presupposes a halting funeral march of three steps followed by two steps as the burial party carries the body of the dead to the tomb. The lament mourns especially for the Moabite regions and cities of the north, including Ar-Moab, Kir-Moab, Dibon, Nebo, Medeba, Heshbon, and Elealah in Isaiah 15:1b-4 as well as lamentation for Moabite refugees who are fleeing to the cities of the south, including Zoar, Eglath-Shelishiyah, the ascent of Luhith, the road to Horonaim, the waters of Nimrim, and the Wadi of Willows in 15:5-7.[16] Isaiah 15:8-9 names Eglaim in the south and Beer-Elim in the north. The division into north and south presupposes the regions to the north and south of the Arnon River, insofar as the territory north of the Arnon had once been the lands inhabited by the Israelite tribes of Reuben, Gad and half-Manasseh, whereas the territory south of the Arnon was Moab proper. Such a portrayal indicates an invasion of the Trans-Jordan from the north.

Interpreters have argued for various scenarios to explain the invasion of Moab. The most persuasive is the assault launched against Aram, the Trans-Jordan, and Israel by the Assyrian king, Tiglath-Pileser III, during the Syro-Ephraimitic War of 735-732 BCE. Tiglath-Pileser III attacked at the behest of King Ahaz ben Jotham of Judah to deliver him from the assault of the Syro-Ephraimitic coalition of Aram and Israel (see 2 Kgs 16). Tiglath Pileser III was only too happy to comply because it gave him the opportunity to take control of Aram and Israel and to impose even greater

---

14. Sweeney, *Isaiah 1-39*, 252; see also Jones, *Howling Over Moab*.
15. Sweeney, *Isaiah 1-39*, 523; Gerstenberger, *Psalms, Part 1*, 10-11.
16. For discussion of sites in Moab, see Miller, "Moab and the Moabites"; Miller, *Archaeological Survey*.

tribute on Judah for saving Ahaz's life. He destroyed Damascus in 732 BCE and stripped northern Israel of its peripheral territories in the Trans-Jordan, the Galil, and the coastal plain, leaving Israel with only its territory in the Israelite hill country, now known as the northern portion of the West Bank.[17] The Moabite Stone addresses the defeat of Israel in the northern Trans-Jordan, which enabled King Mesha of Moab to take control of Israel's territories located east of the Jordan River and north of the River Arnon.[18]

The second major component of Isaiah 15–16 is Isaiah 16:1–5, which presents the prophet's proposal to refugees from the Trans-Jordan to take shelter with Judah and Jerusalem, here named metaphorically as "Daughter Zion" (Hebrew, *bat-ṣiyôn*). Such a name presumes the typical practice in the ancient world of identifying cities with a matron goddess; in the case of Judah, Bat-Zion was considered as the bride of YHWH, who would then presumably enjoy YHWH's protection and support.[19] The offer of refuge to inhabitants of northern Moab would then presume their identities as members of the tribes of Gad and Reuben and possibly the half-tribe of Manasseh. Such an offer would indicate Judah's interest in reestablishing the authority of the House of David over some of the northern Israelite tribes.

The third major component of Isaiah 15–16 appears in Isaiah 16:6–12, which constitutes the prophet's renewed first-person lament over Moab. The poem again employs the classic 3/2 meter of the Qinah (Hebrew for "the lament"). Kir-haresheth, Heshbon, Sibmah, Baalei-goiim, and Jazer were apparently known for their vineyards, which would have produced the raisin cakes for which the starving refugees long.

Finally, Isaiah 16:13–14 follows the prophetic pronouncement with a summary-appraisal form, which notes that YHWH's oracle concerning Moab had been spoken long ago, presumably by Isaiah ben Amoz during the Syro-Ephraimitic War in 735–732 BCE. Such a statement presupposes a later time in which Moab will suffer punishment and be left as only a remnant of its former self. Such a later time would be the late seventh-century reign of King Josiah ben Amon of Judah (640–609 BCE), who envisioned the reestablishment of Davidic rule over Moab and the other nations of the Trans-Jordan, as portrayed in Zephaniah 2:8–11, who prophesied during

---

17. Pitard, *Ancient Damascus*, esp. 145–89.
18. Pritchard, *ANET*, 320–21; Dearman, *Studies in the Mesha Inscription*.
19. See esp. Baumann, *Love and Violence*, esp. 175–202.

Josiah's reign,[20] and Isaiah 11:14, which is part of a Josian-period oracle in Isaiah 11:1–16. Jeremiah 48:29–38 reproduces much of Isaiah 16:6–12 and elements of Isaiah 15:1b–9, which further supports the thesis that figures such as Jeremiah were reflecting on the earlier Isaian text in the late seventh or early sixth century BCE.[21]

IV. Isaiah 17:1—18:7

Isaiah 17:1—18:7 presents the pronouncement concerning Damascus.[22] This passage is somewhat puzzling because it does not discuss Damascus exclusively throughout. Instead, it takes up Damascus in Isaiah 17:1–3, and it includes Ephraim and Israel in its discussion of the announcement of punishment against Damascus. Such a combination suggests that the oracle is fundamentally concerned with the Syro-Ephraimitic coalition in which King Rezin of Damascus and King Pekah ben Remaliah of Israel allied with each other in an attempt to revolt against the Assyrian Empire in 735–732 BCE. As noted in the discussion of Isaiah 7:1—8:15 above, the Syro-Ephraimitic coalition failed in its attempt to force Judah into its alliance, and the coalition was ultimately destroyed when King Ahaz ben Jotham of Judah appealed to his Assyrian overlord, King Tiglath Pileser III of Assyria, to come to deliver him from the Syro-Ephraimitic attack (see 2 Kgs 16).

But the concern with Damascus at the outset and the potential focus on the Syro-Ephraimitic coalition does not exhaust the concerns of this text. A new superscription concerned with a pronouncement concerning Egypt appears only in Isaiah 19:1, thereby leaving Isaiah 17:4—18:7 open to interpretation in relation to the initial concern with the punishment of Damascus and Israel in Isaiah 17:1–3. At this point, readers must recognize that Isaiah 17:4—18:7 takes up a variety of concerns that must be fully understood in order to interpret the overall concerns of the passage.

First, readers must note that Isaiah 17:4–6 follows upon Isaiah 17:1–3 with an oracle, introduced by the temporal formula *wĕhāyâ bayyôm hahû'* ("and it shall come to pass in that day"), which focuses further on the punishment of Jacob, i.e., the northern kingdom of Israel. As De Vries has shown, the temporal formula "and it shall come to pass in that day" is nothing more than an indication of a future time; it is not an eschatological

20. Sweeney, *Zephaniah*, 133–44.
21. See also Wildberger, *Isaiah 13–27*, 122–26.
22. Sweeney, *Isaiah 1–39*, 252–62.

formula as so many interpreters have posited.[23] Furthermore, it is joined to the preceding oracle in Isaiah 17:1–3 by the conjunction *wĕ-* ("and"), which means that Isaiah 17:1–3 and 17:4–6 are joined together to produce a longer oracle concerned with Israel/Ephraim/Jacob due to its alliance with Damascus as part of the Syro-Ephraimitic coalition. Overall, the combined oracle focuses first on Damascus and then on Israel, and it employs the imagery of ruined cities that have been deserted to become places inhabited by grazing flocks (Isa 17:1–3) followed by the imagery of harvested fields and olive trees to portray how Jacob has become diminished as a result of its punishment in terms similar to those of Assyria in Isaiah 10:5–34.

Secondly, a sequence of further temporal formulas appears initially in Isaiah 17:7 and 17:9, albeit without the conjunction *wĕ-* ("and"), i.e., *bayyôm hahû'* ("in that day"). Like the formula in Isaiah 17:4, they are nothing more than references to a future time, but the absence of the conjunction in each case indicates that they represent a shift in focus from that of Isaiah 17:1–6. Rather than focusing specifically on the punishment of Damascus and Israel, the first passage in Isaiah 17:7–8 focuses on the need for human beings in general to focus on their Maker, viz., YHWH, the Holy One of Israel, rather than upon altars, sacred posts, and incense burners made by their own hands. The second passage in Isaiah 17:9 then focuses on the abandoned cities of Horesh and the Amir, apparently references to the Hivvites and the Amorites who inhabited the land of Canaan prior to the arrival of the Israelites,[24] in an effort to argue that Israel is suffering punishment like that of the earlier Canaanite peoples whom YHWH expelled from the land due to their alleged wrongdoing. The following material in Isaiah 17:10–11 then observes that the people of Israel have neglected YHWH, by relying instead on an alliance with foreigners in Damascus, and that the land is responding by failing to produce adequate harvests so that the people might live.

Two woe oracles then follow in Isaiah 17:12–14 and 18:1–7.[25] Isaiah 17:12–14 warns of the danger of hostile nations, which will attack Israel just as the sea attacks the shore line of the Mediterranean coast, but it notes that YHWH alone, the G-d of creation and of Israel, protects the dry land

23. De Vries, *From Old Revelation to New*, 38–63.

24. See the Septuagint translation of this verse; but cf. Wildberger, *Isaiah 13–27*, 160; Blenkinsopp, *Isaiah 1–39*, 302. The Hebrew Masoretic text reads *haḥōrēš wĕhāāmîr*, "the wooded height and the (wooded) mountain peaks."

25. Sweeney, *Isaiah 1–39*, 543.

against the sea to ensure stability in creation, much like YHWH protects the people of Israel to ensure stability in the world of human affairs.

Isaiah 18:1–7 then follows with a lengthy woe oracle that warns of the dangers of messengers sent by sea, presumably by Israel, to Cush (Ethiopia) to seek assistance against a threat of foreign invasion, apparently by Assyria. Indeed, Israel suffered disaster as a result of the Assyrian invasion of Tiglath Pileser III in 732 BCE when the Assyrians destroyed Damascus and stripped Israel of its border territories in the Trans-Jordan (modern-day Jordan) to the east, the Galilee region to the north of the Jezreel Valley, and the Way of the Sea located along the coastal plain adjacent to the Mediterranean Sea to the west (see Isa 8:23). This loss of territory left Israel with only the hill country of Ephraim and Manasseh, the northern portion of the modern West Bank.

But northern Israel did not see itself as defeated by this loss of territory. Instead, the nation was outraged and vowed to restore its losses by revolting against Assyria a second time in 724 BCE under the rule of King Hoshea ben Elah. As part of his efforts to prepare for revolt, 2 Kings 17:4 states that Hoshea sent messengers to Pharaoh So to seek Egyptian support against Assyria (2 Kgs 17:1–6). Pharaoh So has been identified as a reference to the pharaoh at Sais, the Nile Delta capital of the 24th Egyptian dynasty, which was later controlled and then succeeded by the 25th Ethiopian dynasty. But the time at which the 25th Ethiopian dynasty succeeded the 24th dynasty is not entirely clear as the 25th dynasty appears to have exerted considerable influence on the 24th dynasty even before the 24th dynasty came to an end. The pharaoh in question may have been Tefnakhti (726–716 BCE) or his successor, Bakenrenef, both of the 24th dynasty, or Piye (Piankhi, 744–714 BCE), an early pharaoh of the 25th dynasty.[26] When King Shalmaneser V learned of Hoshea's actions, he arrested Hoshea and invaded the northern kingdom of Israel. Following a three-year siege, Shalmaneser captured Samaria, the capital city of the northern kingdom of Israel, and exiled many Israelites to Assyria, Medea, and elsewhere in the Assyrian Empire, beginning in 721 BCE. Apparently Shalmaneser V died at some point during this campaign, apparently of natural causes, and his son, Sargon II, became king of Assyria and took command of the invasion of Israel.

Isaiah 18:1–7 condemns Israel's efforts to ally itself with Ethiopia and announces that YHWH will remain in YHWH's place and ultimately trim

---

26. Sweeney, *1–2 Kings*, 393, for bibliography. See esp. Goedicke, "End of 'So, King of Egypt'"; Cogan and Tadmor, *2 Kings*, 196.

land with pruning hooks, apparently a metaphor to depict the punishment of the land as a trimming of branches as one might trim a vineyard. And in the end, Isaiah 18:7–8 announces that it will be YHWH, not Ethiopia, who will ultimately deliver Israel from its enemies. The deliverance will come out from YHWH's home in Jerusalem, i.e., the Temple of YHWH at Mt. Zion.

V. Isaiah 19:1—20:6

Isaiah 19:1—20:6 presents the prophetic pronouncement concerning Egypt.[27] Following the superscription in Isaiah 19:1a, the prophetic pronouncement proper appears in Isaiah 19:1b—20:6. It includes two major components. The first component appears in Isaiah 19:1b–25, which presents a prophetic announcement concerning Egypt. This announcement comprises three major parts. The first is a theophanic announcement in Isaiah 19:1b–10 concerning YHWH's punishment of Egypt. The theophanic element represents an appearance of YHWH in human affairs. The passage presents the metaphorical portrayal of YHWH riding on a cloud to symbolize YHWH riding through the heavens on a throne chariot, much like Assyrian iconography portrayed the chief Assyrian god, Assur, riding through the heavens on his own winged chariot with his bow drawn to defeat enemies.[28] The second is a taunt against the pharaoh and his officials concerning their foolishness and incompetence before YHWH, who has confused the Egyptian leadership so that the country will go astray. And the third element appears in Isaiah 19:16–25, which presents an announcement of future consequences and blessings that YHWH will direct on the Egyptians. The second major component of the passage appears in Isaiah 20:1–6, which presents an account of Isaiah's symbolic action by walking naked in the streets of Jerusalem to symbolize the Assyrian attack against the Philistine city of Ashdod in 720 BCE, an attack that resulted

---

27. Sweeney, *Isaiah 1-39*, 263–76.

28. See Pritchard, *ANEP*, 536. Note also Psalms 68, esp. verse 5; 104, esp. verse 3; 2 Samuel 22, esp. verses 10–11 (see also Psalm 18, esp. verses 10–11); Ezekiel 1–3; and Habakkuk 3, esp. 3, 8–9, all of which portray YHWH riding through the heavens on the clouds, representing the divine chariot. Such imagery is typical in Assyria with its imagery of Assur flying in his winged chariot; Ugarit, where Baal, the Canaanite/Ugaritic storm god, is called "rider of the clouds" to bring rain to the land and order to creation; and Egypt, where solar imagery informs the chariot imagery of Amun-Re, the Egyptian sun god, traveling through the heavens to bring light and life to the earth.

in Ashdodite prisoners led away naked by the Assyrians (cf. Isa 7:20). Although the Egyptians had promised to defend Ashdod, their efforts proved to be ineffective. The Egyptians later promised to support Ashdod in its revolt against Assyria in 713–11 BCE, but once again, the Egyptians were unable to deliver Ashdod from the Assyrian army led by Sargon II.[29]

Interpreters have correctly argued that Isaiah 19:1—20:6 is a composite text that includes materials written in several historical settings. Wildberger argues that Isaiah 19:1b–15 is a composite text because verses 1b–4 and 11–14 portray political chaos in Egypt, whereas verses 5–10 are concerned with other matters.[30] Specifically, verses 5–10 portray the natural disaster of the Nile River dried up and therefore unable to support the agricultural harvest on which life in Egypt depends. It is clear, however, that the Egyptians—and other ancient Near Eastern cultures—typically correlated political chaos with the disruption of the natural world of creation. Examples of such correlation appear in so-called prophetic texts, such as The Admonitions of Ipu-Wer and The Prophecy of Nefer-Rohu, both of which correlate portrayals of chaos in the social order and in the natural order of creation to charge past pharaohs with incompetence in their rule.[31] Such chaos is then employed to justify the rise to power of a new pharaoh who will bring order into the world of human events and creation to end the chaos caused by his predecessors. Wildberger's concerns were also triggered by uncertainties concerning the ruling the dynasties in Egypt, but as observed in the discussion of Isaiah 17:1—18:7 above, it is clear that the 25th Ethiopian dynasty was able to intimidate and influence the two pharaohs of the 24th Saite dynasty before the Ethiopians took full control of the country. Isaiah 19:1–15 consequently should be viewed as a unified text.

Isaiah 19:16–25 is especially open to questions concerning the composition of its various elements. In many cases, interpreters view this text as a collection of late, eschatological statements concerning the future of Egypt, due especially to the repeated formula *bayyôm hahû'* ("in that day"), which introduces its various sub-units in Isaiah 19:16, 18, 19, 23, and 24. But as observed earlier, De Vries has demonstrated that this formula is nothing more than a common reference to the future that does not entail

---

29. See the Annals of Sargon II concerning his relations with Ashdod in Pritchard, *ANET*, 286–87. For portrayals of prisoners led away by the Assyrians, see Pritchard, *ANEP*, 366–67 (Tiglath Pileser III); 371; and 373 (Sennacherib).

30. Wildberger, *Isaiah 13–27*, 235–39; but see Childs, *Isaiah*, 143.

31. Pritchard, *ANET*, 441–44, 444–46.

any eschatological meaning.³² Furthermore, some scholars have argued that the future blessing for Israel, Egypt, and Assyria indicate later composition.³³ But such a view must be rejected as the text entails nothing more than a view that the conquest of Egypt by the Assyrian monarch Esarhaddon in 671 BCE and the installation of the 26th Saite dynasty would entail a period of peaceful cooperation. But subsequent events proved such a view to be unwarranted, insofar as the 26th Saite dynasty proved to be loyal allies of Assyria and helped Assyrian to retain control over Judah, even during the reign of King Josiah of Judah (640–609 BCE), who attempted to assert Judean independence and to reunify the territory of the former northern kingdom of Israel with that of Judah under the rule of the House of David.³⁴ Indeed, Pharaoh Necho II of Egypt killed King Josiah at Megiddo when Josiah attempted to stop the Egyptian advance to support the Assyrians at Haran in 609 BCE. The Babylonian Empire was able to defeat the Assyrian army and put an end to the Assyrian Empire, thereby leaving Judah under Egyptian control. Although there may be grounds to view a distinction between the composition of verses 16–17 and verses 18, 19–25 based on the shift between the portrayal of anxiety in verses 16–17 and blessing in verses 18, 19–25, the whole must be viewed as the product of the late seventh-century edition of Isaiah when the prospects for the success of Josiah's ambitions were still anticipated.

Finally, Isaiah 20:1–6 emphasizes the failure of Egypt to liberate Ashdod or anyone else from Assyrian control. Once again, this brief narrative appears to represent the views of the seventh-century edition of the book of Isaiah, which anticipated the success of Josiah's reign and his program of religious reform and national restoration.

VI. Isaiah 21:1–10

Isaiah 21:1–10 in its present form constitutes a prophetic pronouncement concerning the Wilderness of the Sea.³⁵ The passage comprises two major portions. Following the superscription in Isaiah 21:1a, the first appears in Isaiah 21:1b–4 as a report of a prophetic audition in which the prophet, presumably Isaiah, hears about an attack that will threaten the Wilderness

32. De Vries, *From Old Revelation to New*, 38–63.
33. See Kaiser, *Isaiah 13–39*, 104–12; cf. Blenkinsopp, *Isaiah 1–39*, 316–20.
34. See Sweeney, *King Josiah of Judah*.
35. Sweeney, *Isaiah 1–39*, 284.

of the Sea. The second appears in Isaiah 21:5–10, which confirms the audition and issues commands to go to battle stations in order to defend the land against the approaching attack.

The Wilderness of the Sea is understood to be a reference to the southeastern regions of Babylonia where the Tigris and Euphrates flow together and then empty into the Persian Gulf. Insofar as Isaiah 21:2 refers to the advance of Elam and Medea against Babylon and Isaiah 21:9 refers to the fall of Babylon, it would appear that this oracle is the product of the late fifth- and early fourth-century BCE edition of the final form of the book of Isaiah, which some scholars date to the early Persian period following the end of the Babylonian exile in 539 BCE.[36] But Babylon never fell to Elamite and Medean arms—or even to Persian military might; rather, Babylon submitted peacefully to Cyrus the Great, king of Achaemenid Persia, in 539, and accepted him as king of Babylon, chosen by Marduk, the city god of Babylon.

As a result of these and other considerations, Macintosh postulates that Isaiah 21:1–10, together with 21:11–12 and 21:13–17, constitutes a form of palimpsest, an older manuscript that has been updated and reworked by later scribes.[37] The oracle concerning "the Wilderness of the Sea" refers, as mentioned above, to the southern regions of Babylonia where the Tigris and Euphrates Rivers flowed together and continued on into the Persian Gulf. This is the region where King Hezekiah's ally in revolt against Sennacherib, Prince Merodach-Baladan, lived and established his power base. The area was known in Akkadian as *mat tamti*, "Land of the Sea," due to its proximity to the Persian Gulf. Following his siege of Jerusalem, Sennacherib left Hezekiah on the throne in Jerusalem and marched his army back to Babylonia to pursue Merodach-Baladan and put down the Babylonian revolt in the region of *mat tamti*. Even as late as 689 BCE, Sennacherib had not captured or killed Merodach-Baladan, and there is no evidence to suggest that he ever did.[38] Indeed, scholars presume that Merodach-Baladan must have died, and they posit that Sennacherib must have killed him despite the absence of any evidence that he did so. Macintosh therefore proposes that Isaiah 21 must have been written in the late eighth or early seventh century BCE, and that it was later updated for the fifth/fourth-century BCE edition of the book of Isaiah. He understands the commands to "go up, O Elam! Fortify,

---

36. E.g., Gosse, *Isaïe 13,1—14,23*, esp. 43–67.
37. Macintosh, *Isaiah XXI*.
38. Brinkman, "Merodach Baladan II."

O Medea!" in Isaiah 21:2 to function as commands to Elam and Media, presumed allies of Babylonia against Assyria, to prepare defenses for the coming attack. Indeed, Elam and Medea were later key allies of Babylonia when it revolted successfully against Assyria in 628–629 BCE.

VII. Isaiah 21:11–12

The brief passage in Isaiah 21:11–12 constitutes a prophetic pronouncement against Dumah.[39] Following the superscription in Isaiah 21:11a, the pronouncement in 21:11b–12 comprises two basic components. Isaiah 21:11b recounts the report of a watchman, who is asked about the safety of Dumah during the night. Isaiah 21:12 presents the response of the watchman that there is no news to report. Presumably, Dumah is safe.

Like the preceding pronouncement concerning the Wilderness of the Sea, Macintosh views the pronouncement concerning Dumah as part of a palimpsest that was first written in the late eighth or early seventh century BCE and later reinterpreted in the late fifth to early fourth century BCE.[40] In this case, the reference is to Seir, a term for the region south and east of the Dead Sea where the ancient kingdom of Edom stands. Ephal has identified Dumah as a desert oasis known in Akkadian as *Dumat al-Jandal*, located in the Wadi Sirhan along the main trade route through the north Arabian Desert that lies between Babylonia and Syria.[41] Although Sennacherib attacked Judah in 701 BCE by crossing west through the Jezreel Valley and advancing south along the coastal plain to block any relief forces coming from Egypt, he also sent emissaries east through the Negev Desert to demand tribute from the Arab tribes roaming about in the Arabian Desert and south along the western Arabian trade routes.

Although Isaiah 21:11–12 would have been written in the late eighth or early seventh century BCE, it would have been adapted to the late fifth- or early fourth-century edition of the book of Isaiah, insofar as the Achaemenid Persian Empire would have an interest in securing the loyalty of the Arabian Desert tribes and collecting tribute from them.

---

39. Sweeney, *Isaiah 1–39*, 284–86.
40. Macintosh, *Isaiah XXI*.
41. Ephal, *Ancient Arabs*, 118–25.

VIII. Isaiah 21:13–17

Isaiah 21:13–17 presents the prophetic pronouncement concerning Arabia.[42] Following the superscription in Isaiah 21:13a, the prophetic pronouncement in 21:13b–17 comprises two major portions. Isaiah 21:13b–15 recounts reports that fugitives in the Arabian Desert are receiving water and food from two Arab tribes known as the Dadanites and the Temanites. The passage reports that the fugitives are escaping armed forces. Presumably, these forces are soldiers from Sennacherib's army who are attacking fugitives who have escaped from either Israel or Judah in 705–701 BCE or from Babylonian in 691–689 BCE. Given Sennacherib's advance against Judah from the coastal plain by Lachish, the latter seems likely, although the appearance of the Rab Shakeh before Jerusalem in Isaiah 36–37 indicates that Sennacherib was fully capable of sending envoys and detachments throughout the land. The second portion in 21:16–17 reports that in another year, Kedar's warriors will likely disappear. Kedar is another Arabian tribe, and the statement indicates efforts to eliminate them on the part of the Assyrian invaders. Again, Isaiah 21:13–17 is part of Macintosh's presumed palimpsest. Although an attack against the Arabian Desert took place in 705–701 BCE, it seems more likely that the moves against the Arabian Desert spoken of here were made during Sennacherib's campaign against Babylonia in 691–89 BCE. Again, Achaemenid Persia would have similar interests in suppressing Arabian Desert tribes in late fifth and early fourth centuries BCE.

IX. Isaiah 22:1–25

Isaiah 22:1–25 presents the pronouncement concerning the Valley of Vision, which refers to the city of Jerusalem.[43] The use of the term Valley of Vision (Hebrew, *gê' ḥizzāyôn*) is a deliberate play on words and imagery to highlight the prophet's visionary understanding of what has happened to Jerusalem. It plays with the concept of the Wadi Kidron, a stream bed that fills with water during times of rain and remains dry during the dry summer season. The Wadi Kidron forms the eastern boundary of the ancient city of Jerusalem, and the main gate to the city, including access to its water source in the Gihon Stream, where the Assyrian Rab Shakeh, "the Chief

---

42. Sweeney, *Isaiah 1–39*, 286–87.
43. Sweeney, *Isaiah 1–39*, 288–302.

Cup Bearer," will stand in Isaiah 36–37 when demanding the unconditional surrender of Jerusalem. Because the name Kidron (Hebrew, *qidrôn*) means "darkness," insofar as the walls of the city of Jerusalem from the west and the shadow of the Mount of Olives from the east would shade the Wadi Kidron, it would serve as the basis of the wordplay. Valley of Vision entails a valley, in this case formed by a wadi, that can be seen, whereas the name Wadi Kidron entails a valley (wadi) that is obscured and difficult to see. The play on words accentuates the revelatory character of the prophet's vision in Isaiah 22.

Following the superscription in Isaiah 22:1a, the prophetic pronouncement in 22:1b–25 comprises two major portions. The first major portion appears in 22:1b–14, which presents a prophetic disputation speech concerning the meaning of the Assyrian siege of Jerusalem in 701 BCE. A disputation speech is a speech that begins by quoting a premise or an idea that the speaker or writer of the text wishes to challenge, followed by argumentation for an alternative premise or idea.[44] The prophet's counter thesis appears in Isaiah 22:1b–14, in which the prophet argues that the lifting of the Assyrian siege of Jerusalem is not a time for rejoicing as the people would contend. Instead, it is a time for weeping. The prophet's argument begins by observing how the people are rejoicing at the lifting of the siege by climbing to the rooftops of their houses to celebrate the departure of the Assyrian army, presumably with a lot of joyous noise, dancing, singing, drinking, etc. But the prophet asks about all the people who were killed in the Assyrian invasion of Judah, all of the officers who fled when the battle turned against them, and all the prisoners who were taken back to Assyria by the Assyrian army. These factors are signaled in Sennacherib's account of his 701 BCE invasion of Judah in which he claims victory, the besieging of forty-six Judean walled cities, and the exile of some 200,150 Judean inhabitants.[45] The prophet concludes this part of his challenges by stating that he will weep for all that has been lost rather than celebrate.

The second part of the disputation appears in Isaiah 22:5–14 with the prophet's argument that the Assyrian siege of Jerusalem was an expression

---

44. Sweeney, *Isaiah 1–39*, 519; Graffy, *Prophet Confronts His People*. Contra Childs, *Isaiah*, 159–60, who argues that Isaiah 22 cannot be considered a real disputation, among other considerations. But he misses the methodological issue that, in contemporary form-critical research, scholars have recognized that genres do not constitute texts; rather, they function within uniquely formulated texts. Sweeney, "Form Criticism"; Knierim, "Form Criticism Reconsidered."

45. Pritchard, *ANET*, 287–88.

of the Day of YHWH against the city of Jerusalem and the land of Judah. The Day of YHWH is normally understood as a day of judgment against Israel's enemies, but the prophets were capable of using the motif of the Day of YHWH to express a day of judgment against Israel or Judah too.[46] Amos employed the motif as a Day of judgment against Israel in Amos 5:18-20, and Isaiah has already employed the motif against Jacob (Israel) in Isaiah 2:6-21. A later author employed the motif against Babylon in Isaiah 13:1—14:23, and Zephaniah employed it again as a potential punishment for Judah if the people did not adopt King Josiah's reforms to repent and return to YHWH in Zephaniah 1:14-18. In the case of Isaiah 22:5-14, the prophet envisions an army that includes nations such as Kir and Elam to attack Judah. Although some might object that Elam was an ally of Babylon as noted in discussion of Isaiah 21:1-10, Elam was a vassal of Assyria in the late eighth century BCE, and it was therefore obligated by its treaty with Assyria to provide troops to the Assyrian king (Sennacherib), the suzerain monarch, when required. Although the Assyrians never stormed the city of Jerusalem, the Rab Shakeh would likely have been accompanied by a sizable force of soldiers when he demanded the unconditional surrender of the city in Isaiah 36-37. The presence of soldiers would have underscored the threat to Jerusalem, particularly to the Judean soldiers on the walls of the city who would likely die when the Assyrian assault commenced. Isaiah notes the preparations undertaken by Hezekiah: the strengthening of the walls of the city, which were evident through the building of the broad wall to enclose the western Mt. Zion that had previously stood outside of Jerusalem's fortification; the patching of any breaches or weak points in the wall; the building of a new water system for the city that would ensure its supply of drinking water; and the eating of meat and drinking of wine during the preparations because the people believed that "tomorrow we will die," as expressed in Isaiah 22:13.[47] But Isaiah recalls the weeping and mourning of the people, and how they shaved their heads in mourning and wore sackcloth as expressed in Isaiah 22:12, but now they rejoice. In Isaiah 22:14, the prophet states that YHWH will remember how they forgot their G-d, who stood ready to protect them as expressed in the eternal covenant

---

46. See my discussion of the Day of YHWH in Sweeney, *Zephaniah*, 52–54; see also Kim, "Day of the L-rd," 299–301.

47. For overview discussion of the fortifications and water system of Jerusalem in the late eighth century BCE, see B. Mazar and Shiloh, "Jerusalem"; E. Mazar et al., "Jerusalem."

of the Davidic/Zion tradition of divine protection for the House of David and the city of Jerusalem (2 Sam 7).

The second major portion of the prophetic pronouncement appears in Isaiah 22:15–25, which focuses especially on the judgment of Shebna, a royal official who was in charge of the royal household or palace. The office of the one "who was over the house [palace]" refers to a highly ranked administrator in the royal House of David, who had charge of the royal palace and general royal affairs.[48] The prophet accuses Shebna of having carved out a burial tomb on a high rock to memorialize himself when he dies. The office is well known in biblical literature, and so is Shebna. He is one of the officials who stood on the wall of the city to receive the Assyrian Rab Shakeh's demand for unconditional surrender in Isaiah 36–37 (cf. 2 Kgs 18–19), and Hezekiah sent him as part of the delegation to consult with the prophet in the same narrative. But in Isaiah 37:2 he is not identified as being in charge of the house; rather, he is identified as "the scribe," and Eliakim ben Hilkiah was identified as the official in charge of the royal house. The office of one "over the house" is known from tombs, as several tombstones inscribed with the title "royal steward" (i.e., "over the house") were discovered in the ancient Judean burial chambers on the Mount of Olives across from the Wadi Kidron. (One tomb preserves part of a name, -yahu, which might be a longer form of the name, Shebna, i.e., Shebnayahu, but it is not certain that this was the name intended.)

Speaking on behalf of YHWH, Isaiah declares that YHWH will cast Shebna down from the heights by seeing to it that he will die in exile in a broad land, a likely reference to Mesopotamia where Assyria is located, instead of the hill country of Jerusalem and Judah. The prophet also declares that Shebna will be replaced in his position as overseer of the royal house by Eliakim ben Hilkiah, presumably the same man who is named in Isaiah 36–37 as holding the position of overseer of the royal house. Eliakim and his father's household will then receive the honors that Shebna had envisioned for himself as his "peg," a metaphorical way of saying that the means of support that Shebna enjoys will collapse.

We will never know what happened to Shebna, but the reference to Eliakim as the overseer of the royal house in Isaiah 37:2, Sennacherib's own references to having exiled thousands of Judeans, and the absence of a clear reference to Shebna's name on the above-noted tombstones dedicated to an overseer of the royal house suggest that the present oracle in Isaiah 22 could

---

48. Fox, *In the Service of the King*, 81–96.

have been actually realized. Shebna may well have been the royal messenger sent by Hezekiah with Sennacherib to Assyria as "his [Hezekiah's] royal messenger . . . to deliver the tribute and do obeisance as a slave."[49] Such a hypothesis entails that Hezekiah chose Shebna to lead the Judean delegation to deliver tribute to Sennacherib in Nineveh, and that Shebna never returned to Jerusalem and Judah to be buried in the magnificent tomb that he had prepared for himself. But, of course, we will never know the identity of this man to whom Sennacherib refers in his own account of the outcome of the siege.

X. Isaiah 23:1-18

Isaiah 23:1-18 presents the pronouncement concerning Tyre.[50] Following the superscription in Isaiah 23:1a, 23:1b-18 comprises two major components. The first is the pronouncement concerning Tyre proper in 23:1b-14, which is demarcated by an inclusion, "Wail, O ships of Tarshish . . . ," in verses 1b and 14 and formulated as a call for communal complaint directed to Phoenicia. The second major component is a prophetic announcement of future events concerning the seventy-year punishment of Tyre and its following restoration.

The passage is ascribed to Isaiah ben Amoz, and Tyre was indeed under threat during his lifetime in the late eighth century BCE. The city was first established in the third millennium BCE, and it was built on a rocky island off the Phoenician coast in the Mediterranean, facing a shore-based city.[51] It was known for its powerful navy, which enabled the city to defend itself and engage in sea-based trade throughout the eastern Mediterranean, especially between north Africa (Egypt and beyond) and southern Europe (Iberian Peninsula; Rome; Greece; Asia Minor). During the late eighth century BCE, Tyre was allied with King Hezekiah of Judah in his attempt to revolt against the Assyrian Empire.[52] When Sennacherib's forces attempted to besiege Tyre, they were unable to conquer it for lack of naval forces and expertise, but they were able to negotiate submission to the Assyrian Empire. The reference to the seventy-year punishment and restoration of Tyre may presuppose a later date in the seventh century BCE. During this period,

---

49. Pritchard, *ANET*, 288.
50. Sweeney, *Isaiah 1-39*, 302-11.
51. For discussion of the history of Tyre, see Katzenstein, *History of Tyre*.
52. See Katzenstein, *History of Tyre*, 220-58, esp. 246-58.

King Esarhaddon, the son of Sennacherib, is known to have referred to the seventy-year desolation of Sumer and Akkad in his inscriptions.[53] Seventy years refers to the lifetime of a king, and it corresponds roughly to the period when Tyre's influence was restricted due to Assyria's domination over its coastal territories. But with the decline of the Assyrian Empire in the late seventh century, Tyre began to restore its power once again. Such a scenario suggests that Isaiah's oracle was intended to address the decline of Tyre, but Tyre was not destroyed in the late eighth century. Consequently, the notice of Tyre's restoration after seventy years may indicate the editing of Isaiah's Tyrian oracle in the late seventh-century edition of Isaiah's oracle written during the reign of King Josiah of Judah (640–609 BCE), who presided over an attempted restoration of Judah during the period of Assyria's decline.

A similar scenario for Tyre appears during the campaigns of King Nebuchadnezzar of Babylon, who defeated the Assyrian army at Haran in 609 BCE and brought the Assyrian Empire to an end.[54] Nebuchadnezzar subjugated Babylon's former ally, Judah, in 605 BCE, and treated Judah as an enemy. Babylon's treatment of Judah provoked a series of revolts. The first was by King Jehoiakim ben Josiah of Judah in 598 BCE, which resulted in Jehoiakim's death and the exile of his son, Jehoiachin, and many other Judeans to Babylonia. The second revolt was in 588 BCE, which resulted in the destruction of Jerusalem and the Temple of Solomon in 586 BCE. Nebuchadnezzar laid siege to Tyre in 585 BCE, apparently because Tyre had aligned itself with Jerusalem. Unfortunately, the records of this siege are incomplete. Judah's third revolt against Babylon took place in 582 BCE, beginning with the assassination of Gedaliah ben Ahikam ben Shaphan, a Judean noble who had been appointed by the Babylonians to administer Judah on their behalf. It appears that Nebuchadnezzar never conquered Tyre, but he did force its submission by 572 BCE, much as Sennacherib had done over a century earlier.

It is also noteworthy that Tyre founded a north African colony known as Carthage in the late ninth century BCE at a time when Tyre had been a close ally of the House of Omri, which ruled northern Israel during this period.[55] Indeed, King Ahab ben Omri of Israel married a Phoenician princess, Jezebel bat Ittobaal of Tyre, to seal the alliance. Carthage is the

---

53. Luckenbill, *Ancient Records of Assyria and Babylonia*, e.g., 2:650, p. 245; see also Katzenstein, *History of Tyre*, 259–94.

54. See esp. Katzenstein, *History of Tyre*, 295–347.

55. Vainstub, "Carthage."

Latinized form of the Phoenician name for the city, *qrt ḥdšt*, probably pronounced *Qarat Ḥadašat*, which means "new city." Carthage, located in what is now northern Tunisia, became a powerful trading city. Its most famous ruler and military commanded was Hannibal, 247–183 or 181 BCE, who invaded southern Europe and threatened Rome. The Romans eventually defeated Hannibal and drove him back to Carthage. The Romans later besieged Carthage and destroyed it in 146 BCE.

Carthage is important for treatment of Isaiah 23:1–18 because the Greek Septuagint version of the oracle rewrites it as an oracle that anticipates the destruction and eventual restoration of Carthage, the colony of Tyre.[56] In the Hellenistic period, the purpose of prophecy shifted from oracles intended to analyze the actions of the gods in the world of humanity to oracles that were intended to predict the future.[57] Insofar as Tyre had not been destroyed in Isaiah's lifetime or even in the centuries that followed through the formation of the book of Isaiah in late fifth or early fourth century BCE, there was no fulfillment of Isaiah's oracle. But Hellenistic readers of Isaiah were familiar with the siege of Tyre by Alexander the Great, king of Macedon, who conquered the ancient Near East during his last years, 333–323 BCE. Alexander did conquer Tyre by dismantling the coastal city of Tyre and its defensive walls, and by utilizing Phoenician prisoners to use the stones of the city to build a causeway that formed a peninsula to connect the rocky island of Tyre to the Phoenician coast. The artificial peninsula then enabled Alexander to bring up his siege engines against Tyre and conquer the city. By the time of the Greek translation of Isaiah, apparently in the first century BCE, Tyre's colony in Carthage had also been destroyed and provided ample confirmation that Isaiah's "prediction" concerning Tyre had been fulfilled.

XI. Isaiah 24–27: Overview

Isaiah 24:1—27:13 presents a prophetic announcement of YHWH's new world order, which is composed as a prophetic announcement of salvation or restoration for Zion and Israel.[58] The passage is demarcated at the outset by the particle *hinnēh* ("behold!") and its focus on the entire earth or land,

---

56. See esp. Kooij, *Oracle of Tyre*; see also Kooij, *Alten Textzeugen des Jesajabuches*, 22–73.

57. Cook, *"Cessation of Prophecy."*

58. Sweeney, *Isaiah 1–39*, 311–25.

which has descended into chaos. It concludes with scenarios of restoration in Isaiah 27:12–13, which portray the return of Jewish exiles from Assyria and Egypt. A woe oracle beginning in Isaiah 28:1 marks the beginning of a new structural unit concerned with "the drunks of the tribe of Ephraim."

Isaiah 24–27 was often characterized in past scholarship as an apocalyptic or an eschatological text concerned with the end time, but more recent scholarship has recognized that it is nothing more than a mythological portrayal of punishment and restoration that will be realized at some time in the future. As we have previously noted, De Vries's reevaluation of the temporal formulas (e.g., "in that day," etc.) has been especially instrumental in reevaluating these chapters as has the recognition of the function of mythological language in the ancient world.[59]

Isaiah 24–27 comprises two major components. The first is a prophetic announcement of the punishment of the earth, which depicts chaos in the world of creation (Isa 24:1–23). The second is a prophetic announcement of blessing for the entire earth (Isa 25:1—27:13), which includes discussion of the implications for the restoration of Zion and Israel as the holy center for YHWH's plans to establish a new world order based in Zion and Israel in which YHWH will be recognized as the sovereign deity of the world at large.

Isaiah 25–27 also comprises two major components. The first is an announcement of YHWH's plans to bless the entire earth at Zion (Isa 25:1–12). The second is an announcement of the results of YHWH's blessing, viz., the return of Israel's exiles from Assyria and Egypt (Isa 26:1—27:13). This second section includes three elements. Isaiah 26:1–21 presents Judah's petition to YHWH for deliverance from the chaos previously described. Isaiah 27:1 presents a notice of YHWH's defeat of Leviathan, the sevenheaded dragon, presumably understood to be a sea monster or crocodile, who brings chaos into the world of rivers and seas. Finally, Isaiah 27:2–13 presents an exhortation to Israel to accept YHWH's offer of restoration, return, and reconciliation.

Although many scholars have presumed that Isaiah 24–27 must be a very late text, dating to the Persian or Greco-Roman period, due its presumed apocalyptic or eschatological character,[60] more recent scholarship points to the late monarchic period, particularly the reign of King Josiah

---

59. De Vries, *From Old Revelation to New*.
60. For recent studies, see Polaski, *Authorizing an End*; Hibbard, *Isaiah 24–27*.

ben Amon of Judah, who presided during the period of Assyria's decline with its potential for the reestablishment of an independent Judean state.⁶¹

Isaiah 24–27 now appears to have been formulated during the late seventh century BCE, but its position following the oracles concerning the nations in Isaiah 13–23, which appears to be the product of the late fifth- or early fourth-century edition of the book of Isaiah, indicates that Isaiah 24–27 is intended to portray the celebration on Mt. Zion once the nations of the earth have suffered their own punishment from YHWH in keeping with Isaiah 2:6–21. Even though the redactional reformulation of Isaiah 13:1—14:27 casts it as an oracle about Babylon, it would appear that the oracle was originally concerned with Assyria and that Isaiah 24–27 was a celebration at the downfall of Assyria, Judah's earlier oppressor. Although Isaiah 13:1—14:27 was reformulated into an oracle concerned with the punishment of Babylon for the fifth/fourth-century edition of Isaiah, Isaiah 24–27 appears to have retained its position most likely because of its enigmatic references to "the city of chaos," which would have been read as references to Babylon despite the final reference to Assyria and Egypt in Isaiah 27:12–13.

A. Isaiah 24:1–23

Isaiah 24:1–23 presents a prophetic announcement of YHWH's punishment of the earth.⁶² Although most interpreters consider this passage to be directed against the entire earth, the Hebrew term employed here is *hāʾāreṣ* ("the land"), which refers specifically to the land of Israel. Many interpreters also understand the passage to be proto-apocalyptic and eschatological. It may be considered to function as an apocalyptic text, insofar as it is revelatory, but it is not eschatological, insofar as it does not portray the end of the world. The problem lies in the common definition of apocalyptic, formulated by John J. Collins: "a genre of revelatory literature with a narrative framework, in which a revelation is mediated by an otherworldly being to a human recipient, disclosing a transcendent Reality which is both temporal, insofar as it envisions eschatological salvation, and spatial insofar it involves another supernatural world."⁶³

---

61. Hays, *Origins of Isaiah 24–27*; cf. Sweeney, *King Josiah of Judah*.

62. Sweeney, *Isaiah 1–39*, 325–33.

63. Collins, "Introduction: The Genre Apocalypse," 4–5; for discussion, see Sweeney, *Jewish Mysticism*, 167–69.

Isaiah 13–27

Collins's definition is applicable to Isaiah 24–27 insofar as those chapters do portray a revelation of the divine will to a human agent, presumed to be Isaiah (although the text postdates Isaiah). However, it does not apply insofar as it characterizes the genre as eschatological, a concept developed in early Christianity to portray the anticipated second coming of Christ and the judgment or redemption of the entire world. Isaiah 24–27 is not eschatological in anything like that sense. So is it apocalyptic? Not on Collins's maximalist definition, but on a more minimalist definition, one that sees eschatology as a non-essential ingredient in apocalyptic, it is proto-apocalyptic.

Isaiah 24:1–23 is instead a mythologically informed composition that portrays an impaired land in striking and impactful ways. Such an understanding presupposes that the Jerusalem Temple is the holy center of creation,[64] and that any impurity associated with the Temple—such as its desecration by human ritual or ethical wrongdoing—will impair the land, rendering it unholy and therefore unable to sustain life. Such impairment entails chaos in creation, e.g., floods, earthquakes, drought, and other natural forms of disruption, or the invasion of enemies, who will kill or exile the inhabitants of the land. Both forms of impairment are evident in Isaiah 24–27.

Isaiah 24:1–23 comprises three major components, the first of which is 24:1–2, which presents an introductory announcement of YHWH's punishment of the earth or land.

The second component is a prophetic announcement of the basis for the punishment of the land (Isa 24:3–13). The land is here portrayed as withered and desolate and unable to support its inhabitants, rich or poor, high-standing or low-standing, no matter who they might be. A key element of this disruption of the charge in verse 5 is that the land's inhabitants have transgressed YHWH's instructions (Hebrew, *tôrōt*), ignored statutes (Hebrew, *ḥōq*), and violated the covenant of the world (Hebrew, *běrît ʿôlām*). The Hebrew term *běrît ʿôlām* is often correctly understood to refer to "eternal covenant," but the basic meaning of the term *ʿôlām* is "world," that is, "the world of creation." Such an understanding is consistent with the ancient view that the Jerusalem Temple is the holy center of creation and that the integrity of the Temple ensures the integrity of the world of creation. The concept of temple as holy center of the world is shared by

---

64. Levenson, "Temple and the World"; see also Levenson, *Sinai and Zion*; Levenson, *Creation and the Persistence of Evil*.

most ancient Near Eastern cultures of the time, particularly Aramean, Assyrian, and Babylonian.

A second key concept here is the destruction of "the city of chaos," Hebrew, *qiryat-tōhû*, in Isaiah 24:10. This reference has been understood to refer to Jerusalem itself; to Nineveh, the capital of the Assyrian Empire; to Babylon, the capital of the Babylonian Empire; and to others. As we will see below, the term appears to refer to the site of Ramat Raḥel, located south of Jerusalem, where the Assyrians built an administrative center for controlling Jerusalem and Judah during the late eighth through seventh centuries BCE.[65]

The third component appears in Isaiah 24:14–23, which presents a prophetic announcement that explains YHWH's word, formulated as a disputation speech, which is designed to challenge a common premise held by others in favor of a different understanding favored by the presumed speaker of the text. Whereas Isaiah 24:16–20 indicates that the people of the time accept the premise that an enemy has brought punishment upon the land, Isaiah 24:21–23 argues instead that YHWH will punish the hosts of heaven and the kings of the earth, apparently a veiled reference to the Assyrian Empire, which subjugated Judah in the late eighth through the late seventh centuries BCE. In later times, these verses would have been understood to refer to the Babylonian Empire, the Seleucid Empire, the Roman Empire, and later enemies who subjugated and oppressed Judah and the Jewish people. Once these figures are punished, YHWH will be revealed as the true king of the world of creation and human events on Mt. Zion, the location of YHWH's holy Temple.

In order to make its points, Isaiah 24:1–23 cites earlier prophetic texts.[66] Isaiah 24:13 quotes Isaiah 17:17:6a, "And there shall remain of him [Jacob] gleanings, like the beatings of olives," which referred to Isaiah's earlier condemnation of Israel in the Syro-Ephraimitic War. In the present context, it refers to the punishment of the city of chaos, and the passage echoes the condemnation of the Assyrian king in Isaiah 10:5–34, who is beaten with YHWH's rod, just as one might beat an olive tree at harvest time. Isaiah 24:17–18a, "terror, and pit, and trap, are upon you, O inhabitant of the land. And the one who flees at the sound of terror will fall into the pit, and the one who ascends from the midst of the pit, will be captured

---

65. See Hays, *Origins of Isaiah 24–27*, esp. 95–126.

66. In addition to my commentary on this passage, see Sweeney, "Textual Citations in Isaiah 24–27."

in the trap," quotes the oracle against Moab in Jeremiah 48:43-48a to make the point that Judah's oppressors will not escape YHWH's punishment.

B. Isaiah 25:1—27:13

Isaiah 25:1—27:13 presents the prophetic announcement of the blessing of the earth/land and its results for Zion/Israel.

The first major component of this segment is Isaiah 25:1-12, which announces YHWH's blessing of the earth/land at Zion.[67] The passage comprises two major sections, viz., 25:1-5, a communal song of thanksgiving for YHWH's defeat of an oppressing city, and 25:6-12, an announcement of the blessing of the peoples and Israel at Mt. Zion in verses 6-8 followed by an announcement of Israel's response to the demise of Moab in verses 9-12.

The communal song of thanksgiving in Isaiah 25:1-5 celebrates the downfall of a city that has oppressed Jerusalem and Judah. Past interpretation has focused on the same cities noted above (i.e., Damascus [Aram], Nineveh [Assyria], and especially Babylon [Babylonia]) in the discussion of the city of chaos in Isaiah 24:10. More recent work by Hays points to the Assyrian administrative center at Ramat Raḥel noted above as the city in question. In Isaiah 25:4-5, the song alludes to 4:4-5, which reads, "for you [YHWH] are a refuge to the poor, a refuge for the needy in his distress, a shelter from hail, a shade from the heat. For the wind of tyrants is like rain against a wall, like heat in the desert. The noise of aliens you shall subdue, like heat in the shadow of a cloud. The song of tyrants, he [YHWH] silences." The purpose of this allusion is to celebrate the projected downfall of Moab, as indicated in Zephaniah 2:5-11, which would have signaled one of the goals of King Josiah's program for religious reform of Judah and political independence from the Assyrian Empire.[68] Insofar as Tiglath Pileser had stripped away the Trans-Jordan from northern Israelite control during the Syro-Ephraimitic War, the Moabite Stone indicates Moab's moves to take control of the Trans-Jordan north of the Wadi Arnon, which had marked the southern border of Trans-Jordanian lands assigned to the Israelite tribes of Reuben, Gad, and half of Manasseh. One of Josiah's goals was to reestablish Davidic sovereignty over these territories, although this goal was never realized due to Josiah's untimely death at Megiddo in 609 BCE at the hands of Pharaoh Necho of Egypt.

---

67. Sweeney, *Isaiah 1–39*, 333–37.
68. Sweeney, *Zephaniah*, 133–44; see also Sweeney, *King Josiah of Judah*, 185–97.

The second component of Isaiah 25:1–12 appears in 25:6–12, which presents the prophetic announcement of blessing for the nations and Israel in verses 6–8 and Israel's response to the blessing and the demise of Moab in 25:9–12. Isaiah 25:6–8 announces a rich banquet on Zion that will celebrate the demise of sorrow and death among the nations and the shame of Israel for having lost control of the nations in the Trans-Jordan. Isaiah 25:9–12 celebrates YHWH's role in making the downfall of Moab and the restoration of the Trans-Jordan to Judah possible. Isaiah 25:11b–12 reads, "And he [YHWH] shall bring down his [Moab's] pride with the skill of his hands. And the high fortifications of your walls he shall lay low, he shall bring down, he shall cast down to the earth in dust." This statement alludes to the depiction of the Day of YHWH in Isaiah 2:9–17 to celebrate once again the anticipated downfall of Moab at the hands of YHWH.[69]

The second major component of Isaiah 25:1—27:13 is 26:1—27:13, which announces the results of YHWH's blessing of the earth/land at Zion, that is, the return of Israel to Zion.[70] This component includes three major segments, each of which is introduced by the temporal formula *bayyôm hahû'* ("in that day"). As previously mentioned, this is nothing more than a simple reference to a future time.[71] Given the context of the late seventh-century reign of King Josiah of Judah (640–609 BCE), that future time would be the time when the goals of Josiah's reforms (viz., religious reform and national restoration) had been realized.[72] The first component is Isaiah 26:1–21, which presents Judah's petition to YHWH for deliverance. The second appears in 27:1, which presents YHWH's defeat of Leviathan, a mythological water monster, here identified with the Nile River Delta. The third appears in 27:2–13, the prophet's exhortation to Israel to accept YHWH's offer of reconciliation in order that the people will return to Zion.

In keeping with the full form of Isaiah 24–27, these texts date to the late seventh-century BCE reign of King Josiah of Judah, who sponsored religious reform in the Jerusalem Temple and national restoration for Israel and Judah led by the royal House of David during the period of the decline of the Assyrian Empire.

---

69. In addition to Sweeney, "Textual Citations," see Vermeylen, *Du prophète Isaïe à l'apocalyptique*, 1:365–66.

70. Sweeney, *Isaiah 1–39*, 311–25.

71. De Vries, *From Old Revelation to New*, 38–63.

72. Sweeney, *King Josiah of Judah*.

Isaiah 26:1–21 is Judah's petition to YHWH for deliverance, here formulated as a prophetic announcement of Judah's communal complaint.[73] The passage comprises two major components. The first appears in Isaiah 26:1a, which is formulated as an announcement of the complaint song introduced by the temporal formula "in that day," a reference to an unspecified future time. The communal complaint psalm is a typical liturgical genre in which the Israelite or Judean community petitions YHWH to resolve some problem facing the people, e.g., enemy invasion, failed harvest, disease, etc.[74] The communal complaint song proper follows in Isaiah 26:1b–21, which is an exhortation to the people to show confidence in YHWH. The passage includes four major parts. The first part is a song of praise for YHWH's victory (Isa 26:1b–6), which celebrate YHWH's defeat of an unnamed opponent. A likely candidate would be the Assyrian Empire. Babylonia, led initially by Nebopolassar, revolted against Assyria in 628 BCE, and the Babylonians, aided by their Medean allies, had destroyed Assur, the holy city of the Assyrian Empire dedicated to the god Assur, in 614 BCE, and Nineveh, the political capital of the Assyrian Empire, in 612 BCE. Insofar as the Assyrian army was defeated in Haran by the Babylonians in 609 BCE, marking the end of the Assyrian Empire, this period provides a likely background to the composition of this particular communal complaint.

The second part of Isaiah 26:1b–21 appears in 26:7–10, an affirmation of YHWH's righteousness, reinforced by a contrasting portrayal of the wicked and the righteous. The passage speaks only in general terms, but the point of this segment is clear, i.e., YHWH is righteous and those opposed to YHWH are not. The unspoken assumption is that the Assyrian Empire, with its treatment of Israel and Judah from the late eighth century BCE to the presumed present time of the late seventh century BCE, represents the wicked.

The third part of Isaiah 26:1b–21 appears in 26:11–19, which constitutes the petition of the people to YHWH to ask that YHWH take action against the wicked. The identity of the wicked remains anonymous as the petition takes its course for YHWH to display righteousness in defeating the wicked oppressor who has left the people in dire straits. The segment concludes with metaphorical portrayals of the people, comparing them first to a pregnant woman attempting to give birth to her child, but she is

---

73. Sweeney, *Isaiah 1–39*, 327–44.
74. Gerstenberger, *Psalms, Part 1*, 11–14.

unable to do so without YHWH's active involvement on their behalf. The metaphor then shifts to the dead who may now come to life with the assistance of YHWH, who brings life to the people.

The fourth part of Isaiah 26:1b–21 appears in 26:20–21, which is formulated as an exhortation to the people to anticipate YHWH's justice. This segment calls upon the people to go home and wait for YHWH to act on their behalf, fully confident that YHWH will do so.

Isaiah 26:1b–21 relates intertextually to other texts to make its points.[75] Isaiah 26:5, "for he [YHWH] lays low those who dwell on high, the lofty city. He brings it down, he brings it down to earth. He cast it down to the dust." The reference appears to presuppose the earlier mentioned "city of chaos," presumably the Assyrian administrative center at Ramat Raḥel, and the language of the passage appears to presuppose Isaiah's "Day of YHWH" passage in Isaiah 2:6–21, in which the prophet depicts YHWH's actions to bring down those who are high and arrogant. A second text appears in Isaiah 26:17–18, "like a pregnant woman about to give birth, she cries in pain, she cries out in her labor, thus we were because of you, O YHWH. We were pregnant, we writhed in pain, as we brought forth wind. We did not make salvation on earth and the inhabitants of the world did not fall [i.e., were not born]." The imagery of childbirth appears frequently in the book of Isaiah to signal the beginning of a new era (see Isa 7:14; 8:3; 9:5; 13:8; 21:3; 23:4–5; 33:11; 42:11; 45:10; 49:21; 51:2, 18; 54:1; 55:10; 59:3–4; 66:7–9). Two passages, Isaiah 13:8 and 66:7–9, stand out because of their close lexical association. But both appear to be later than Isaiah 26:17–18, which suggests that Isaiah 26:17–18 influenced their language.

The second component of Isaiah 26:1—27:13 is the brief text in Isaiah 27:1, again introduced by the formula "in that day," which portrays YHWH's defeat of Leviathan.[76] Leviathan is a seven-headed water monster, likely understood as a form of crocodile in relation to its identification with the Nile River in Egypt (see Isa 27:12), although he is certainly not limited to the Nile, insofar as he is identified with the Euphrates River in Isaiah 27:12. Leviathan also appears in Psalms 74:14 and 104:26; Job 3:8 and 40:25 (ET 41:1); and 1 Enoch 60:7–8, generally as a sea monster representing chaos, who is defeated by YHWH. Leviathan appears in Ugaritic literature, where he is known as Lotan, an Ugaritic vocalization of the name for a sea monster killed by the gods Baal and Anat (KTU 1.5:I.1–2), and in Mesopotamia,

---

75. Cf. Sweeney, "Textual Citations in Isaiah 24–27," 73–75.
76. Sweeney, *Isaiah 1–39*, 344–45.

where he is identified as a fire-breathing dragon who threatens the world of creation with chaos only to be defeated by heroes, such as Gilgamesh and Enkidu among others.[77] Leviathan represents a typical chaos monster that must be defeated by a deity or a human hero to preserve creation or to bring creation into being. In the present case, Leviathan's identification with the Nile and the Euphrates Rivers in Isaiah 27:12 appears to presuppose the oppressors of Judah and Israel, i.e., the Assyrian Empire, located beyond the banks of the Euphrates River in Mesopotamia, and Egypt, a vassal and later a close ally of Assyria during the seventh century BCE, located along the Nile River in northeast Africa.

The third and final component of Isaiah 26:1—27:13, again introduced with the formula "in that day," appears in 27:2-13. It is a prophetic exhortation to Israel to accept YHWH's offer of reconciliation.[78] Isaiah 27:2-13 comprises two major components. The first is 27:2-6, a new vineyard allegory, which complements the earlier vineyard allegory in 5:1-7. Whereas Isaiah 5:1-7 announced YHWH anger at the vineyard, which represented Israel and Judah, Isaiah 27:2-6 offers reconciliation to the people now that the punishment is about to come to an end.[79] The second component appears in 27:7-13, which presents the exhortation to Israel proper by employing the disputation genre to apply the new vineyard allegory offering reconciliation to Israel.[80] The passage begins by questioning whether Israel had suffered as much as its oppressor, and claiming that punishment was necessary to purge the people of their sins. But at the end of the passage in Isaiah 27:12-13, the text draws upon 11:10-16 to reiterate the earlier claims that YHWH had defeated Leviathan (Isa 11:15; 27:1) and that YHWH had beaten the oppressors as one beats an olive tree at harvest to redeem the people of Israel and Judah from Assyria and Egypt to restore them to Zion, YHWH's holy mountain in Jerusalem.

---

77. Korpel, "Leviathan"; see esp. Day, *G-d's Conflict with the Dragon*.
78. Sweeney, *Isaiah 1-39*, 345-53.
79. Sweeney, "Textual Citations in Isaiah 24-27," 75; Sweeney, "New Gleanings."
80. Sweeney, "Textual Citations in Isaiah 24-27," 75-76.

4

Isaiah 28–33

I. Overview

ISAIAH 28–33 IS PROPHETIC instruction concerning YHWH's plans and purposes for Jerusalem, which culminates in the announcement of a royal savior.[1] The formal literary structure of this textual block includes five major components: (1) Isaiah 28:1–29 constitutes prophetic instruction concerning YHWH's purpose in bringing Assyrian hegemony upon Israel and Judah; (2) Isaiah 29:1–24 offers prophetic instruction concerning YHWH's purpose in brining about assault against Ariel/Zion; (3) Isaiah 30:1–33 presents prophetic instruction concerning YHWH's delay in delivering the people from Assyria; (4) Isaiah 31:1–9 is parenesis concerning reliance on Egyptian aid against Assyria; and (5) Isaiah 32:1—33:24 lays out prophetic instruction concerning the announcement of a royal savior who will deliver Israel/Judah/Jerusalem from its oppressors. This last component is further sub-divided into two major sub-units: (a) Isaiah 32:1–20 is prophetic instruction concerning the upcoming announcement of a royal savior/deliverer, and (b) Isaiah 33:1–24 is a prophetic announcement concerning the royal savior/deliverer proper.

Altogether, Isaiah 28–33 functions as a fitting conclusion to the first part of the final form of the book of Isaiah in chapters 1–33 by pointing to

---

1. Sweeney, *Isaiah 1–39*, 353–58.

the emergence of a royal savior/deliverer who will be made known in the second part of the book, Isaiah 34–66. Although the first half of the book of Isaiah gives considerable attention to the emergence of a righteous Davidic monarch, no such monarch appears in the second part of the book following the introductory material in Isaiah 34–39. Ultimately, Isaiah 34–66 will identify King Cyrus of Persia as YHWH's messiah and Temple-builder in 44:28 and 45:1. The eternal covenant with the royal House of David will be applied to the people of Israel at large in Isaiah 55, insofar as no Davidic monarch is evident in Isaiah 40–66 or in the Persian period. There is an attempt to establish Zerubbabel ben Shealtiel, the grandson of King Jehoiachin ben Jehoiakim, as the next Davidic monarch during the period when the Jerusalem Temple was rebuilt (520–515 BCE; see Hag 2:20–24; Zech 6:1–15), but this effort is ultimately unsuccessful, and no certain information is available concerning the ultimate fate of Zerubbabel.

In its present form, Isaiah 28–33 is a redactional block that dates to the late fifth- or early fourth-century edition of the book of Isaiah. It is held together by the introductory "woe" (Hebrew, *hôy*) oracle forms, which introduce each of the major constituent chapters in Isaiah 28; 29; 30; 31; and 33. Isaiah 32 begins with an introductory "behold" (Hebrew, *hēn*) to indicate its role as the introduction to the concluding component in the sequence of oracles that build their respective instructions into the current textual block. This conclusion is evident especially from the sequence of arguments offered in the building blocks of this text as well as the role of Isaiah 33. Beuken identifies Isaiah 33 as a "mirror text" (German, "*Spiegeltext*") insofar as it cites or alludes to numerous Isaian texts throughout the first part of the book of Isaiah, especially Isaiah 1, which serves as an introduction to the final fifth/fourth-century BCE edition of the book.[2] Isaiah 33 also points forward to Isaiah 65–66, which looks to the fulfillment of the purging of Jerusalem announced in Isaiah 1.

Although the present form of Isaiah 28–33 dates to the late fifth- or early fourth-century edition of the final form of the book of Isaiah, it is evident that an earlier form of this textual block in Isaiah 28–32 underlies the present form. This block of texts was intended to point to the emergence of a royal savior or deliverer who would deliver Israel, Judah, and Jerusalem from oppression. The concerns with the Assyrian Empire and Egypt evident in these texts would have been read in relation to the late seventh-century reign of King Josiah ben Amon of Judah (640–609 BCE), who pursued a

---

2. Beuken, "Jesaja 33 als Spiegeltext"; Beuken, *Isaiah 28–39*, 239–77.

program of religious reform and national restoration for the House of David and its rule from Jerusalem over Judah and the former territory of the northern kingdom of Israel.[3] But with Josiah's untimely death at the hands of Pharaoh Necho of Egypt in 609 BCE, Josiah's ambitions came to naught, and the kingdom of Judah (and Israel) was subjugated to the Babylonian Empire in 605 BCE. Jerusalem itself, including the Temple of Solomon, was destroyed during the second Babylonian invasion of Judah in 588–586 BCE. Even so, the major components of Isaiah 28–32 (i.e., Isa 28; 29; 30; 31; and 32) appear to have been written by Isaiah ben Amoz in the late eighth century BCE, and they were later reread in relation to Josiah's program of religious reform and national restoration in the late seventh century BCE.

II. Isaiah 28:1–29

Isaiah 28:1–29 is a prophetic instruction regarding YHWH's purpose in bringing Assyrian hegemony over the northern kingdom of Israel.[4] The passage begins with a "woe" (Hebrew, *hôy*) oracle in 28:1–4 directed to the so-called "proud crowns of the drunkards of Ephraim," insofar as Ephraim is the major power tribe of the northern kingdom of Israel.[5] The portrayal of the Ephraimites as drunkards is metaphorical and intended to assert that the leadership of the tribe of Ephraim had employed incredibly poor judgment in revolting against the Assyrian Empire, thereby bringing about the demise of the northern kingdom of Israel in 724–721 BCE. The reference to "proud crowns" apparently refers to the headgear, perhaps turbans held in place by crowns decorated with engraved flowers to indicate the king and royal officials of the northern Israelite monarchy who led the northern kingdom into its revolt against Assyria, ultimately ensuring its destruction. The reference to "wilting flowers" on the heads of these men indicates their failures as national leaders, and the references to their rich food and wine indicates that they paid more attention to their own appetites than they did to the affairs of state. Their demise is signaled in the opening woe oracle by metaphors of hail, pestilence, torrential rain, trampling, and the fig harvest to suggest, again metaphorically, that northern Israel was "harvested" by its Assyrian invaders who brought the kingdom to its end.

3. Sweeney, *King Josiah of Judah*.
4. Sweeney, *Isaiah 1–39*, 359–73.
5. Sweeney, *Isaiah 1–39*, 543.

The second major sub-unit of the chapter appears in Isaiah 28:5–29, which is introduced in verse 5 by a temporal formula, "in that day" (Hebrew, *bayyôm hahû'*), which points to the future, to indicate that ultimately YHWH will become a crown of beauty on the heads of the leadership of the remnant of Israel (i.e., the kingdom of Judah) when YHWH will resume protection of the people of Israel (Isa 28:5–6).

Altogether, Isaiah 28:5–22 constitutes the first major sub-unit of Isaiah 28:5–29, which is concerned with announcing the removal of Israel's past, failed leadership. The first major part of this sub-unit appears in the above-noted 28:5–6, which announces that YHWH will assume leadership of the remnant of the people (i.e., Judah), presumably to bring about the restoration of the whole of Israel.

The second part of Isaiah 28:5–22 appears in 28:7–13, which returns to the condemnation of Ephraimite leadership and the metaphor of its drunkenness to assert its incompetence. The background to this portrayal appears in the form of an ancient festival observance known in Hebrew as the *marzēaḥ*, often understood as a "cultic celebration," and sometimes as a funerary celebration.[6] The celebration is well-known in West Semitic texts, particularly those from Ugarit, e.g., KTU 1.114, El's Banquet, which portrays El as so drunk that he must be carried back to his house where he falls down into his own vomit and excrement.[7] References also appear in the Bible in Jeremiah 16:5 and Amos 6:7. Although the *marzēaḥ* is often portrayed as a funerary celebration in keeping with Jeremiah 16:5, it must be understood in a much broader context. The *marzēaḥ* appears to be a celebration connected with the conclusion of the fall fruit harvest, known as Sukkot, "Booths, Tabernacles," in ancient Israel and Judah and in post-biblical Judaism. Sukkot is the time when the fruit harvest—including grapes, figs, olives, etc.—is brought in before the fall rainy season begins. It would therefore be a time to process the fruit into juices that would be stored in clay vessels where it could ferment into wine and other alcoholic beverages. This would necessitate the drinking of any leftover alcohol from the previous year, which would explain the drunken celebration that accompanies the festival. In the case of cultures such as Ugarit and other ancient Canaanite cultures, the fall Sukkot celebration would mark the return of the storm god, Baal, from the underworld where he had been left for dead during the dry summer season. Baal's return would signal the onset of the fall

---

6. See *HALOT* 634; Schmidt, "Marzeah."
7. See Wyatt, *Religious Texts from Ugarit*, 404–13.

rains and give cause for celebration due to the expectation of a rich harvest for the coming year. Such an understanding of the Canaanite roots for the festival would explain the funerary dimensions once Baal was metaphorically brought back to life. Isaiah, who appears to be an expert in the care of fruit trees and vines and frequently makes reference to drunkenness of Israel's leaders (see Isa 5:22–24), would be very familiar with the *marzēaḥ*, and he would presumably cite the theme of drunkenness from this festival to characterize leadership that he would have considered incompetent in ancient Israel and Judah. Drunkenness would also explain the stammering speech depicted in Isaiah 28:11–13, which would lead to the foreign speech of foreign conquerors who would take control of the land as a result of the incredibly poor judgment of its leaders.

The third part of Isaiah 28:5–22 appears in 28:14–22, which presents a prophetic judgment speech against the Judean leadership of the country. Isaiah critiqued the Judean leadership as well as the Israelite/Ephraimite leadership of the northern kingdom of Israel. The reason for the critique of Judean leadership would have been King Ahaz's turn to the Assyrian Empire for support during the Syro-Ephraimitic War of 735–732 BCE and, later, Hezekiah's alliance with Merodach-Baladan of Babylonia as his partner in revolt against the Assyrian Empire. Isaiah was fundamentally opposed to alliance with foreign nations and their gods, and counseled reliance on YHWH alone to protect the nation in keeping with his understanding of the Davidic covenant, which called for YHWH's protection of the House of David as well as the city of Jerusalem (see Isa 7; Isa 39). He portrays the covenants with foreign powers as covenants with death, insofar as death will be the result of such relationships, and he portrays the metaphorical flood waters that will inundate Judah much like the imagery of the flood emanating from the Assyrian monarch when he metaphorically rapes Judah in Isaiah 8:5–16 by spreading his wings over the land and filling it with his own flood waters.

The second major component of Isaiah 28:5–29 is 28:23–29, which presents the allegory of the farmer to serve as prophetic instruction concerning how a farmer knows how to rely on YHWH to achieve his harvest of cumin and other agricultural products. Using the allegory of the farmer, the prophet counsels patience on the part of Judah (and Israel) and heeding the instruction of YHWH rather than an alliance to overcome the challenges posed by foreign oppressors, such as the Syro-Ephraimitic alliance or the Assyrian Empire.

III. Isaiah 29:1–24

Isaiah 29:1–24 is a prophetic instruction concerning YHWH's purpose in bringing about an assault against Ariel/Zion. Ariel (Hebrew, *ărîēl*) is oftentimes rendered as "lion of G-d,"[8] which would indicate a reference to the lion as the tribal symbol of Judah as a poetic name for Jerusalem, which was located in the tribal territory of Judah once David made the city the capital of the united kingdom of Judah and Israel. But the term also has another dimension in that it appears to be derived from the Hebrew term *har'ēl* or *ha'ărēl* in Ezekiel 43:15, which refers to the "altar hearth" of the Jerusalem Temple (often understood to be "the bosom of the earth"), insofar as a "trench" (Hebrew, *ḥêq*) is dug around the altar to collect blood, water, and any other liquids that may drain from the altar while it is in use.[9] In this manner, the Temple and its altar serve as the holy center of creation in Judean thought.

Isaiah 29:1–24 includes two major components. The first is 29:1–14, which constitutes prophetic instruction concerning YHWH as the cause of the Assyrian assault against Ariel/Zion. This section begins with a brief "woe" formula directed at Ariel/Zion in Isaiah 29:1a to indicate a warning of YHWH's intentions to bring punishment against Jerusalem. Such a contention is controversial for ancient (and modern) readers because Jerusalem is the place that David chose for his political capital and for the religious capital of the kingdom, where the Temple would be located. Jerusalem is the site for the celebration of national festivals, and YHWH's assault against such a holy place must be understood as means to purge the holy Temple and its altar from the impurity of wrongdoing on the part of the monarchy and the people in entering into foreign alliances aimed at protecting the nation from other foreign oppressors. The passage makes it clear that YHWH is the sole protector of Zion, and the leadership of the nation has erred in not recognizing this fundamental principle of Davidic ideology. The oracle employs the metaphors of one awakening from sleep, one who is blind (cf. Isa 6), and one who needs to open the sealed book, perhaps Isaiah itself, to understand the true nature of YHWH's role in relation to Jerusalem.

A second woe oracle then follows in Isaiah 29:15–24, which is formulated as prophetic instruction concerning the future realization that YHWH has delivered Jacob (Israel). This passage again begins with a brief

---

8. *HALOT* 87; see also Isa 33:7.
9. Levenson, *Sinai and Zion*, 139.

woe oracle in 28:15–16, which accuses the leadership of the nation of having been rebellious sons who deserve punishment (cf. Deut 21:18–23) for making plans to go to Egypt to seek assistance in a revolt against Assyria. During the late eighth century BCE, Egypt was ruled by the 25th Ethiopian Dynasty, which was independent of Assyria. Given Israel's past relationship with Egypt—Solomon had married the daughter of Pharaoh as his chief wife (1 Kgs 3:1)—both the northern kingdom of Israel and King Hezekiah of Judah sent envoys to Egypt in a bid to secure the Egyptians as allies in their revolts against the Assyrian Empire. But Egypt was always an unreliable ally of Judah and Israel because its distance from them—separated as it was by the Sinai Wilderness—made it difficult for Egypt to mount an assault in their support due to the length of its supply lines. Isaiah 29:17–21 makes it clear that in just a little while even the blind will see and the deaf will understand that *YHWH* is the one who will defend Jacob (Judah and Israel; cf. Isa 6). Isaiah 29:22–24 says that YHWH had redeemed Abraham in the past. When YHWH's children recognize what YHWH has done for them in days gone by, they will recognize that YHWH is acting to redeem Israel and Judah once again.

The appeal to Egypt as ally indicates that these oracles were written during the late eighth century BCE as both Israel under Hoshea and Judah under Hezekiah made appeals to Egypt for support. During the late seventh century under Josiah, Egypt was under the rule of the 26th Egyptian Saite dynasty, which was an ally of Assyria, and therefore would never have supported Judean independence from Assyria.

IV. Isaiah 30:1–33

Isaiah 30:1–33 presents a prophetic instruction speech concerning YHWH's delay in delivering the people from Assyria.[10] The passage is demarcated at the outset by the introductory "woe" (Hebrew, *hôy*) formula, which conveys a warning to the so-called "rebellious sons," i.e., Israel and Judah (cf. Isa 1:2–3). Although there is a prophetic pronouncement (Hebrew, *maśśā'*) directed to "the animals of the Negeb" in 30:6–7, this particular oracular sub-unit is apparently intended to portray the delegation traveling by caravan from Judah to Egypt to request Egypt's assistance against the Assyrian Empire. The embassy was apparently sent by King Hezekiah of Judah in preparation for his planned revolt against the Assyrian Empire in 705 BCE.

10. Sweeney, *Isaiah 1–39*, 386–401.

Such a portrayal is in keeping with the general concerns of Isaiah 30, which criticizes Judean efforts to ally with Egypt against Assyria instead of relying on YHWH, as Isaiah counsels elsewhere (see, e.g., Isa 7). The next major oracular unit in Isaiah is 31:1–9, which like most of the other sub-units in Isaiah 28–33 is introduced by the "woe" formula.

Isaiah 30:1–33 comprises two major components. The first appears in 30:1–26, which is the prophetic instruction speech proper, communicating the instruction concerning YHWH's delay in brining deliverance from the Assyrian Empire. Isaiah 30:1–26 is in turn composed of two sub-units, 30:1–11, which presents an oracular report concerning YHWH's dissatisfaction with Judah's sending an embassy to Egypt, and 30:12–26, which presents an announcement of the consequences for Judah's actions, i.e., YHWH will delay deliverance from the Assyrian Empire.

Isaiah 30:1–11 begins with a statement of the reasons for YHWH's dissatisfaction in verses 1–5, i.e., such plans run contrary to YHWH's will, insofar as YHWH expects Judah to rely exclusively on YHWH for defense. Although the embassy will travel as far as Zoan, the site of YHWH's deliverance of Israel from Egypt in the exodus (Ps 78:12), and Hanes (On), the site of the Egyptian temple dedicated to the god Re (Atum), Egypt's second largest shrine, Judah's actions constitute lack of gratitude for YHWH's actions and reliance instead on Egyptian gods in complete contradiction to the exodus tradition. As noted above, the pronouncement in 30:6–7 depicts the Judean embassy traveling through the Negev wilderness on its way to Egypt. Isaiah 30:8–11 then presents YHWH's instructions to write a document that gives witness to Judah's rebellious actions in refusing to listen to YHWH and calling for the prophets not to see the truth and to speak to them only lies. These last statements present a play on YHWH's instructions to Isaiah in Isaiah 6 to render the people blind, deaf, and dumb, because that is what they seem to want.

Isaiah 30:12–26 begins in verses 12–14, which employ the form of a prophetic judgment speech to accuse Judah of rejecting YHWH's word for something fraudulent, i.e., reliance on Egypt and its gods for assistance. Punishment will come quickly like the collapse of a broken wall that falls and is shattered into pieces like a ceramic jug. Such an image depicts a defensive wall collapsing, perhaps due to battering rams, in a siege. Isaiah 30:15–17 develops the prophetic judgment speech by claiming that Judah should have remained quiet to wait for YHWH to act, but instead fled on steeds to seek help from Egypt. Consequently the people will flee on mounts as the enemy attacks until the people are trapped on a hill top. Isaiah 30:18–26 then presents the basic announcement of salvation or restoration to indicate that YHWH will delay deliverance from Assyria. Ultimately, YHWH will provide teachers to instruct the people of Zion in YHWH's will, rain to ensure that the people are fed, and light as the people's wounds are treated and healed.

The second major sub-unit of Isaiah 30:1–33 appears in 30:27–33, which constitutes a theophanic announcement that YHWH will strike down Assyria. A theophany is a text that portrays an appearance of YHWH, generally to fight against the enemies of Israel and thereby rescue the people from danger.[11] Isaiah 30:27–28 portrays YHWH's approach from afar in raging anger to defeat those who would oppress the people, in this case, Assyria. Isaiah 30:29–33 then portrays YHWH's victory over Assyria, which has beaten Israel and Judah with the rod, much like Egypt had done in the past (see Isa 10:5–34), and celebration on Mt. Zion, the presumed site of YHWH's Temple in Jerusalem, which will follow.

Although Isaiah 30:1–33 appears to have been written in relation to Hezekiah's revolt against Assyria and his attempt to enlist Egyptian support in the late eighth century BCE, the chapter lends itself easily to Josiah's attempts to free Judah and Israel from Assyrian control a century after the time of Hezekiah. Josiah did not seek the support of Egypt, insofar as Egypt was an ally of Assyria during Josiah's reign, but his program of religious reform and national restoration was motivated in part by a reading of Isaiah and other works that now appear in the Hebrew Bible, e.g., early forms of Joshua; Judges; Samuel; Kings; Jeremiah; Hosea; Amos; Micah; and Zephaniah, among others.[12]

V. Isaiah 31:1–9

Isaiah 31:1–9 presents parenesis concerning reliance on Egyptian aid against the Assyrian Empire. Parenesis is a form of discourse, often employed in preaching, that is designed to persuade an audience with reference to a goal.[13] It combines admonition (i.e., warning, against an undesirable or faulty course of action or set of beliefs) and exhortation (a call to follow a course of action or to adopt a set of beliefs).

---

11. Sweeney, *Isaiah 1–39*, 541.
12. Sweeney, *King Josiah of Judah*.
13. Sweeney, *Isaiah 1–39*, 527.

Isaiah 28–33

Like most of the other major components of Isaiah 28–33, Isaiah 31:1–9 begins with an introductory "woe" (Hebrew, *hôy*) formula to introduce the admonition or warning against alliance with Egypt (Isa 31:1–5). The admonition warns against reliance on Egypt's military power, particularly its use of horses for its chariot corps and cavalry, neither of which is particularly useful in the hill country of Judah. The warning against military alliances with foreign nations is typical of Isaiah (Isa 2:6–21), and the prophet calls upon Jerusalem and Judah to rely on YHWH instead. Although some might see such reliance as futile, Isaiah tends to call for avoidance of confrontation and reliance on the fact that the hill country of Judah will deter potential invaders, particularly those who cannot afford to sit for months in a protracted siege of the heavily fortified Jerusalem (see Isa 7). The prophet metaphorically compares YHWH to a lion that guards its prey from shepherds or a flock of birds of prey that likewise guard their own prey from those who might try to steal it.

Isaiah 31:6–9 then presents the exhortation to return to YHWH. Isaiah 31:6 is the exhortation proper which calls upon the people to return to the one (YHWH) against whom they have rebelled. Isaiah 31:7–9 then explains the basis for the exhortation as the people recognize that idols are useless and that YHWH will ultimately defeat the Assyrian Empire, apparently invoking the imagery of YHWH's defeat of Egypt in the ancient exodus tradition (cf. Isa 30:31–33).

Isaiah 31:1–9 once again appears to be the product of Isaiah ben Amoz, who critiqued Hezekiah for his reliance on foreign powers, such as Egypt, when he was preparing for his revolt against the Assyrian Empire. And once again, an oracle calling for the downfall of Egypt would have been important in the view of King Josiah of Judah during the late seventh century BCE when he prepared to stop the Egyptians, who were attempting to send their army through the Jezreel Valley in northern Israel to support their Assyrian allies against the Babylonians at Haran (2 Kgs 22–23; 2 Chr 34–35). Unfortunately, the Egyptians killed Josiah at Megiddo, but he delayed the Egyptians long enough to prevent them from supporting the Assyrians against Babylonia at Haran. The Assyrians were defeated at Haran in 609 BCE, and the Assyrian Empire came to an end at that time. Josiah gave his life to ensure such an outcome.

VI. Isaiah 32:1—33:24

Isaiah 32:1—33:24 offers prophetic instruction concerning the announcement of a royal savior or deliverer.[14] It is demarcated at the outset by the particle *hēn* ("behold"), which marks this passage as the climactic text of Isaiah 28–33. It includes two major sub-units, both of which are concerned with a royal savior or deliverer: (1) a prophetic instruction speech about the announcement of a royal savior or deliverer in 32:1–20 and (2) a prophetic announcement of a royal savior or deliverer proper in 33:1–24. Isaiah 33:1–24 is demarcated at the outset by the "woe" (Hebrew, *hôy*) formula. Isaiah 34:1, with its summons to hear directed to the nations, begins an entirely new unit, which forms part of the introduction to the second half of the synchronic form of the book of Isaiah as a whole.

Isaiah 32:1–20 presents a prophetic instruction speech concerning the announcement of a royal savior or deliverer as the first half of Isaiah 32:1—33:24.[15] It comprises three major sub-units. The first is a disputational announcement of a royal savior or deliverer (Isa 32:1–8).[16] The second is a prophetic announcement concerning the character of the royal savior's reign, which emphasizes the emergence of salvation after disaster (Isa 32:9–19). And the third is a beatitude concerning the righteous (Isa 32:20).[17]

The disputational announcement of a royal savior or deliverer in Isaiah 32:1–8 is designed to convince its audience to abandon their view that they face only hardship and disaster in the future and to adopt a new view that the future will be far better than what they experience at present. This announcement has two basic parts. The first, Isaiah 32:1–2, is a basic announcement of a royal savior that includes an announcement of a new, righteous king and officers who will govern in righteousness (verse 1) and a metaphorical statement of their qualities (verse 2) that depicts them as a refuge from storms, etc., that will provide the people with water and shade in the wilderness. Such a statement alludes to the wilderness tradition of water provided by YHWH to Israel on the journey from Egypt to the promised land of Israel (Exod 17:1–7; Num 20:2–13). It also alludes to the portrayal of shade over Jerusalem in Isaiah 4:2–6. The second part

---

14. Sweeney, *Isaiah 1–39*, 353–58.
15. Sweeney, *Isaiah 1–39*, 409–20.
16. Sweeney, *Isaiah 1–39*, 519; Graffy, *Prophet Confronts His People*.
17. Sweeney, *Isaiah 1–39*, 515; Gerstenberger, *Psalms, Part 1*, 244–45; Gerstenberger, *Psalms, Part 2*, 511.

appears in Isaiah 32:3–8, which presents the primary point of disputation against authorities who claim that the future will entail suffering and judgment rather than blessing and hope. This text draws upon Isaiah's commission in Isaiah 6 in which YHWH instructed Isaiah ben Amoz to render the people blind, deaf, and dumb so that they would not understand, and thereby allow YHWH to accomplish the divine purposes at a time in the distant future. Isaiah 32:3–8 effectively argues that the distant future *is now* in that the blind will see, the deaf will hear, and the dumb will understand. It portrays the authorities who look toward suffering and punishment as articulate liars, who counsel the people to abandon YHWH's will, leaving the people hungry and thirsty. But those who are the benefactors of the people (Hebrew, *nādîb*) are precisely that, i.e., leaders whose goal it is to benefit the people. Such a view builds upon the portrayals of a righteous and just Davidic monarch in Isaiah 9:1–6 and 11:1–16, although no Davidic monarch is mentioned here.

The second major part of Isaiah 32:1–20 appears in verses 9–19, which is a prophetic announcement of the royal savior's reign, i.e., a reign characterized by the emergence of salvation following the past disaster.[18] This portion includes two major components. The first is a call to lament and mourn (Isa 32:9–14). It calls upon the women to mourn, which appears to reflect older Canaanite practices of mourning at the time of the fruit harvest at Sukkot, "Booths or Tabernacles," in the fall when rain is expected. In Canaanite or Ugaritic mythology, the storm god, Baal, is dead in the underworld during the dry summer season, and he is brought back to life when his consort, the goddess Anat, travels down to the underworld to rescue him and bring him back to life so that he will bring rain and fertility to the land.[19] The Mesopotamian myths of the descent of the goddesses Ishtar (Babylonian) or Inanna (Sumerian) to the netherworld to rescue the male fertility gods Tammuz (Babylonian) and Dumuzi (Sumerian) function in a similar manner.[20] Even in Israelite and Judean times in which Canaanite gods such as Anat and Baal were no longer revered, women would still conduct mourning rituals in the late summer to bring on the onset of the fall rains. During this period of mourning, cities are abandoned and the land is desolate. But the second part of this text in Isaiah 32:15–19 looks forward

18. Westermann, *Prophetic Oracles of Salvation*.

19. Wyatt, *Religious Texts from Ugarit*, 115–46; see also the Aqhat myth, Wyatt, *Religious Texts from Ugarit*, 246–312; Wright, *Ritual in Narrative*.

20. Knott, "Ishtar's (Inanna's) Descent to the Netherworld."

to the onset of joy and fertility when "a wind from on high" is poured out on the land. Such a wind appears to be the seasonal sirocco, which blows into the land of Israel and the rest of the ancient and modern Near East at times of seasonal change in the spring and the fall. Such a wind is known in Hebrew as the *Sharav* and in Arabic as the *Ḥamsin*, and it is known in the American Southwest as the Santa Ana winds.[21] These winds appear when a high pressure system settles upon the eastern deserts, thereby forcing dry, hot air to flow in reverse, east to west, blowing dust and dirt into the coastal areas and frequently doing great damage. At such times, the sun is blocked from view and the moon appears to be blood red (see Joel 3:1–5). The wind that parted the Reed Sea in the exodus narrative was such a wind, and it is viewed as an act of YHWH to deliver the people in the exodus tradition. The result will be peace, prosperity, and justice for the people as depicted in Isaiah 32:15–19.

The final portion of Isaiah 32:1–20 is the beatitude that appears in verse 20. A beatitude is a short, formulaic statement that extols the fortunate or blessed state of an individual or a people. It typically begins with statements such as "blessed are those who . . ." or "happy is he who . . . ." In the present case, Isaiah 32:20 reads, "happy are you (Hebrew, *'ašrêkem*) who sow by all the waters, who send out the feet of cattle and donkeys [to graze]." Such a beatitude emphasizes the bounty that the people will enjoy as their crops and their animals will grow.

Overall, Isaiah 32:1–20 appears to represent the words of Isaiah ben Amoz in the late eighth century BCE when Isaiah would have looked forward with hope for the installation of a new, righteous and just Davidic king (Isa 9:1–6). It also appears to presuppose the depiction of the just and righteous king who will reunite Israel and Judah in Isaiah 11:1–16, which presupposes the late seventh-century edition of the book. When read in relation to the later editions of Isaiah, the emergence of a royal savior would be understood to refer to King Cyrus of Persia in the late sixth-century edition of Isaiah and later Persian monarchs, such as Artaxerxes II, in the late fifth-/early fourth-century editions of the book.

The second part of Isaiah 32:1—33:24 appears in 33:1–24, which constitutes the prophetic announcement of a royal savior proper.[22] As noted above, this text begins with an example of the "woe" formula, and it continues through the end of Isaiah 33 until 34:1, which marks the beginning of a

---

21. See Fitzgerald, *L-rd of the East Wind*.
22. Sweeney, *Isaiah 1–39*, 420–33.

new unit that is designed to address the nations as part of the introduction to the second half of the synchronic form of the book of Isaiah.

Isaiah 33:1–24 comprises six major components. As noted in prior discussion, Isaiah 33 is a "mirror text" (German, *Spiegeltext*), which makes intertextual contexts with both the first (Isaiah 1–33) and second parts (Isaiah 34–66) of the book of Isaiah and aids in tying the book together.[23]

The first component appears in Isaiah 33:1, which presents a "woe" speech addressed to the oppressors who have betrayed and ravaged Israel and Judah to warn them that they, too, will be betrayed and ravaged. This brief statement sets the tone for what is to follow when the new royal savior or deliverer emerges. It draws on Isaiah 21:2, which portrays the impending downfall of Babylon as a betrayer is now betrayed, and Isaiah 24:16, which likewise portrays the enemies of Israel and Judah as betrayers that are now betrayed.

The second component appears in Isaiah 33:2–4, which constitutes an address to YHWH that petitions YHWH for relief from oppressors. Isaiah 33:2 presents two petitions for divine favor and for strength and salvation, and 33:3–4 elaborates on these petitions by depicting the defeat of the "roaring" oppressors like the gathering of locusts and the scattering of grasshoppers. The first image of "roaring" oppressors draws on Isaiah 17:12–14, and the metaphorical portrayal of the defeat of enemies as locusts and grasshoppers draws on Joel 1–2.

The third component appears in Isaiah 33:5–6, which addresses the audience of this text with a call to recognize that YHWH is exalted as a result of the deliverance depicted here. The language concerning YHWH's exaltation draws especially on the "Day of YHWH" language in Isaiah 2:6–21 (cf. also Isa 13). The language of justice and righteousness appears to presuppose the Davidic royal oracle of Isaiah 9:1–6 and 11:1–16.

The fourth component appears in Isaiah 33:7–13, which is the prophet's summation of the circumstances leading to the emergence of the royal savior or deliverer, formulated as a prophetic announcement of punishment.[24] The initial statement, introduced by the particle *hēn* ("behold"), points to the Arielites, i.e., the people of Ariel or Jerusalem as portrayed in Isaiah 29 who cry out loud at the devastation suffered by their land. The passage pictures the land desolate and lacking in fertility, much along the lines of Isaiah 24, and the reference to "a covenant that has been violated"

---

23. Beuken, "Jesaja 33"; Beuken, *Isaiah 28–39*, 239–77.
24. Sweeney, *Isaiah 1–39*, 530–31.

in verse 8 appears to draw on the language of Isaiah 24:5. The various parts of the land of Israel are named: viz., the Lebanon,[25] which refers to the snow-capped heights of Mount Hermon in the north; Shalom, apparently a reference to Shalem, Jerusalem;[26] Bashan, the northern Trans-Jordan;[27] and Carmel, the coastal hill country, south of Akko (Acre; see also modern-day Haifa).[28] But beginning in verse 10, YHWH states the intention to rise and be lifted up, drawing on language depicting YHWH's enthronement in the Jerusalem Temple in Isaiah 6:1 (see also Isa 2:6–21) to take action against the oppressors of Israel and Judah as one burns lime or thorns, drawing on imagery in Isaiah 1:21–26 and 5:1–7.

The fifth component (Isa 33:14–16) portrays the approach of the royal savior or deliverer as a royal entrance liturgy. The language concerning the royal savior's justice and righteousness draws once again on the royal oracles in Isaiah 9:1–6 and 11:1–16, but the entrance liturgy is based on psalmic genres that name the qualities to be possessed by one who would enter the Temple to appear before YHWH (see Pss 15; 24).[29] Here, the rhetorical questions that are typical of the entrance liturgy genre (e.g., "who may enter the house of YHWH?") are asked by the oppressors of Israel and Judah, who in asking the questions recognize that they will never gain entry.[30] Again, the language of blindness and deafness from Isaiah 6 appears, but here it characterizes the righteous savior who will be introduced by YHWH to deliver the people from oppression. The portrayal of YHWH dwelling on high again draws on the imagery of Isaiah 2:6–21.

The sixth and final component of Isaiah 33:1–24 is verses 17–24, which constitute a prophetic announcement of the vision of a royal savior or deliverer. The passage employs the visionary language that appears in the superscriptions for the book in Isaiah 1:1 and 2:1.[31] It also develops the theme of blindness from Isaiah 6, a blindness that has now come to an end. Isaiah 33:17 employs the language of vision, "your eyes will envision (Hebrew, *tehĕzeynāh*, based on the root *ḥzh*) a king in his beauty," as does 33:20, "envision (Hebrew, *ḥăzēh*) Zion, the city of our appointed times of

25. McKinny et al., "Lebanon."
26. Handy, "Shalem."
27. Blischke, "Bashan."
28. Nocquet and Dar, "Carmel."
29. Sweeney, *1–39*, 520.
30. Sweeney, *Isaiah 1–39*, 537.
31. Jepsen, "*Ḥāzâ.*"

worship." This serves to portray people who will now see YHWH's work much like the prophet himself. The rhetorical questions in verse 18 are designed to highlight the wonder and splendor of the vision to be beheld by the people. With the entrance of the royal savior, verse 19 makes it clear that no more foreign language of the oppressors will be heard (cf. 28:9-10, 11-13). Jerusalem is portrayed in verses 20-21 as a tent that will not be uprooted, much as David first established the city as the site of YHWH's holy Temple, initially portrayed as a tent in 2 Samuel 6 and Psalm 132. The imagery shifts in verse 22 to that of a mast on a sailing ship that is secured and enables the ship to travel where it is guided. And finally, in verses 23-24, YHWH emerges as the king and prince who will deliver the people, much as portrayed in Isaiah 66, so that even the lame will enjoy booty, taking up a motif that is known from 2 Samuel 5:8. But this time, the lame will be secure, which appears to presuppose the portrayal of the foreigners and the eunuchs in Isaiah 56:1-8.

Altogether, Isaiah 33:1-24 appears to be the product of the late fifth- or early fourth-century BCE edition of the book of Isaiah, insofar as it cites material from throughout Isaiah 1-32 and in some cases from Isaiah 34-66 to sum up the message of the first part of the book (Isa 1-33) and prepare the reader for the second part of the book (Isa 34-66).

5

Isaiah 34–39

I. Isaiah 34–35: Overview

ISAIAH 34–35 OFFERS A prophetic instruction concerning YHWH's power in 34:1 with the following basis for the call in 34:2–4, to return the redeemed exiles to Zion.[1] It is demarcated at the beginning by the call to attention, directed to the nations, that invites the nations of the earth to approach and listen to YHWH's instruction concerning YHWH's anger at them and intention to punish them, apparently for their role in oppressing Israel, Judah, and Jerusalem.

The textual block includes two major units. The first appears in Isaiah 34:1–17, which presents prophetic instruction concerning YHWH's power over the nations, using Edom as an example of YHWH's capacity to bring judgment against the nations. The second appears in 35:1–10, which is a prophetic oracle of salvation or restoration concerning the return of the redeemed to Zion.

The royal narratives in Isaiah 36–39 concerning YHWH's deliverance of Jerusalem and Hezekiah constitute a discrete narrative unit separate from Isaiah 34–35 which signals the conclusion of Isaiah 34–35 as a subunit within the larger, synchronic literary form of the text of Isaiah 34–54.

---

1. Sweeney, *Isaiah 1–39*, 434–37.

Isaiah 36–39 then functions as a second sub-unit within Isaiah 34–54, and Isaiah 40–54 functions as the third sub-unit within Isaiah 34–54.

Interpreters have long suspected that Isaiah 34 and 35 were written by hands later than those of Isaiah ben Amoz, even though they are included as part of Duhm's understanding of Proto-Isaiah in Isaiah 1–39. Indeed, the portrayal of Edom's demise in Isaiah 34:1–17 appears to presuppose the downfall of Edom in the fifth-fourth centuries BCE as the Nabateans began to encroach upon Edomite territory and ultimately displace the former Edomite kingdom. Isaiah 35:1–10, which portrays the return of exiled Judeans from Babylonia to Zion or Jerusalem by means of a highway through the wilderness, constitutes a portrayal of a second exodus in which Jews return to Jerusalem and the land of Israel after enduring exile in the Babylonian Empire. Although some have argued that Isaiah 35 was written by Deutero-Isaiah, most interpreters recognize the difficulty of such a claim and settle for recognizing Isaiah 35 as a text written in relation to the prophecies of Deutero-Isaiah as part of a late sixth-century edition of the book of Isaiah.

When read together as a single, two-part unit, concerned with the punishment of the nations and the restoration of the Judean exiles to Jerusalem, Isaiah 34–35 functions as an introduction to the second part of the book of Isaiah in Isaiah 34–66, which constitutes a prophetic announcement of the realization of YHWH's plans for exercising worldwide sovereignty from Zion.[2] The reasons for such a conclusion include the parallel calls for attention, respectively to Israel and to the nations in Isaiah 1 and Isaiah 34; the concern with the redemption of Zion in Isaiah 2–4; 28–33 and Isaiah 35; 40; and 49–54; the contrasting portrayals of King Ahaz ben Jotham and King Hezekiah ben Ahaz respectively in Isaiah 6:1—9:6 and Isaiah 36–39 when each is confronted with threats from invading enemies with a focus on the site of the upper pool of the Fuller's Field below the eastern walls of the city of Jerusalem; the concern with the punishment of foreign nations, especially Babylon in Isaiah 2:6–21; 13:1—23:18 and the punishment of the nations, especially Edom and Babylon in Isaiah 34; 47; and 63:1–6; the concern with the blind, deaf, dumb, and lame in Isaiah 6:1–13 and Isaiah 35:1–10; and the return of the redeemed of Israel and Judah to Jerusalem and the land of Israel by means of a highway through the wilderness in Isaiah 11:11–16; 27:12–13; 35:8–10 and Isaiah 40–48; 56:8; 62:10–12; and 66:20.

---

2. In addition to Sweeney, *Isaiah 1–39*, 435, see Evans, "Unity."

A. Isaiah 34

Isaiah 34:1–17 constitutes prophetic instruction concerning YHWH's power over the nations by employing the example of Edom.[3] The basic formal structure of this passage includes two major segments. The first is the first address to the nations concerning the destruction of Edom (Isa 34:1–15). This segment includes five major sub-units. The first is the call to attention in 34:1, directed to the nations and the world at large, in which the prophet—apparently intended to represent Isaiah ben Amoz—calls upon the nations of the world to approach and to hear YHWH's intentions to bring punishment against Edom as an example of divine power to punish nations for their roles in the oppression of Israel, Judah, and Jerusalem.

Four further sub-units, each of which is introduced by the explanatory particle *kî* ("for, because"), then follow in 34:2–15 to explain YHWH's actions. The first focuses on YHWH's intention to punish the nations, leaving their dead bodies lying about as the heavens are rolled up like a scroll and the bodies of the dead are compared to withered leaves and fruit in the aftermath of a great harvest (Isa 34:2–4). The second portrays YHWH's sword drenched in blood as the slaughter of the dead is compared to sacrificial animals that are slaughtered at the temple to be offered to YHWH for the sacred meal (Isa 34:5–6a). The third portrays the slaughter at Bozrah, the capital of Edom, metaphorically as a sacrifice for YHWH (Isa 34:6b–7). The fourth functions as a climactic announcement of punishment against Edom (Isa 34:8–15).

The second major sub-unit of the passage then appears in Isaiah 34:16–17, which presents a second address to the nations that confirms YHWH's power to punish them by stating that is YHWH's decree that brought about the punishment of Edom. This passage asks the reader of the book of Isaiah to consult the scroll of YHWH, apparently a term to refer to the book of Isaiah, in order to confirm that all the elements mentioned in this passage will be found there as statements made by YHWH through the agency of Isaiah.

As noted above, Isaiah 34 appears to have been composed in the fifth-fourth century BCE to explain the displacement of the Edomites by the Nabateans as an act of YHWH to punish Edom for its role in oppressing Israel, Judah, and Jerusalem (cf. Obadiah).[4]

---

3. Sweeney, *Isaiah 1–39*, 437–47.
4. Dicou, *Edom, Israel's Brother and Antagonist*, 105–9; Dicou, "Isaiah 34."

B. Isaiah 35

Isaiah 35:1-10 constitutes a prophetic oracle of salvation or restoration concerning the return of the redeemed Jews to Zion from Babylonian exile.[5] The formal structure of the passage includes two major components. The first is Isaiah 35:1-2, which announces rejoicing in the world by using the metaphor of the blossoming of creation. Such a correlation between the human world and the natural world of creation is inherent in YHWH's roles as master of creation, master of human events, redeemer of Israel, the one who would use Cyrus for divine purpose, and the one who would restore Zion as argued in 40:12—54:17 in the second part of the book of Isaiah. The second component appears in Isaiah 35:3-10, which is a prophetic instruction to the weak concerning the coming of YHWH and its results. Following a more detailed instruction concerning YHWH's coming in 35:3-4, Isaiah 35:5-10 presents a detailed announcement of the results. Isaiah 35:5-6a recounts the restoration of the blind and the deaf and the lame and the mute as an expression of the exiles who will now be restored to Jerusalem. Isaiah 35:6b-10 recounts the basis for the restoration as the transformation of the cosmos at large, including water that will restore the dry desert wilderness known as the Arabah in verses 6b and 7 and the corresponding restoration of the redeemed to Zion by means of a holy highway from Babylon to Zion in verses 8-10. It is clear that the exodus and wilderness traditions of the Pentateuch, particularly the motifs of the wilderness journey per se, the highway through the wilderness, the water provided to Israel in the wilderness, and the role played by creation itself in the journey, played key roles in the composition of Isaiah 35 to express the return of the Judean exiles to Jerusalem as a second exodus, this time from Babylon rather than from Egypt.[6]

Steck maintains that Isaiah 35 is an expression of a ready or prepared homecoming on the part of the exiled Jews.[7] He views Isaiah 35 as a redactional "bridge" (German, *Brücke*) between first and second Isaiah due to its role in linking the two parts of the book together. He argues that Isaiah 35 was composed during the Hellenistic period, when he maintains that the composition of the book of Isaiah was completed, primarily on the basis of

---

5. Sweeney, *Isaiah 1-39*, 447-54.

6. In addition to Sweeney, *Isaiah 1-39*, 447-54, see esp. Kiesow, *Exodustexte im Jesajabuch*; Steck, *Bereitete Heimkehr*.

7. Steck, *Bereitete Heimkehr*, 39-44.

the Qumran Isaiah scrolls, especially 1QIsa^a, which represent the earliest Hebrew scrolls of the book of Isaiah now extant.[8] Both 1QIsa^a and 1QIsa^b date to the Hellenistic period, respectively in the early and late first century BCE.[9] But Steck errs in that neither scroll is an autograph of the final edition of Isaiah in that each represents a reworking of the proto-Masoretic text of the book based on the attempts of the Qumran scribes to interpret the book of Isaiah by working their own readings into the underlying proto-Masoretic text. Insofar as the final form of the book of Isaiah presupposes the restoration of Jerusalem under the leadership of Nehemiah and Ezra in the late fifth and early fourth centuries BCE during the period in which the Achaemenid Persian Empire ruled Judah, the final composition of the book must be dated to this period.

II. Isaiah 36–39: Overview

Isaiah 36:1—39:8 presents a royal narrative concerning Hezekiah.[10] This narrative is remarkable because it is the last textual block in the book of Isaiah in which the prophet Isaiah ben Amoz explicitly appears and because different forms of the same narrative appear in 2 Kings 18:1—20:21 and 2 Chronicles 29:1—32:33. The narrative in 2 Kings 18–20 is very similar to Isaiah 36–39, although it includes many differences that suggest a different characterization and understanding of King Hezekiah. The narrative in 2 Chronicles 29–32 presents a shortened form of the narrative in Isaiah 36–39 and 2 Kings 18–20 as a framework for the introduction of narrative accounts of Hezekiah's celebration of Passover in Jerusalem and details of his reforms.[11]

In its present form, Isaiah 36–39 offers an account of Hezekiah's reign that focuses on his efforts at religious and national reform and his attempt to revolt against the Assyrian Empire, a revolt that brought about the invasion of Judah by King Sennacherib of Assyria in 701 BCE. Isaiah 36–39 comprises three distinct textual components, which are presented in reverse historical order, apparently in an effort to portray background events relevant to Hezekiah's revolt against Assyria. The first component

8. Steck, *Erste Jesajarolle*.
9. Ulrich and Flint, *Isaiah Scrolls*, 61–62, 199–200.
10. Sweeney, *Isaiah 1–39*, 454–60.
11. For a comparative study of the narratives in Isaiah 36–39, 2 Kings 18–20, and 2 Chronicles 29–32, see Ackroyd, "Biblical Interpretation."

appears in Isaiah 36:1—37:38, dated to the fourteenth year of Hezekiah's reign (701 BCE), which is a confrontation narrative about the defeat of Sennacherib's threat against Jerusalem and King Hezekiah.[12] The second appears in Isaiah 38:1–22, introduced by the temporal formula *bayyāmîm hāhēm* ("in those days"), which constitutes a royal novella concerning Hezekiah's recovery from illness.[13] The third component appears in Isaiah 39:1–8, introduced by the temporal formula *bā"ēt hahî'* ("at that time"), which constitutes a prophetic story, formulated as a dialog report, concerning Isaiah's announcement of punishment against Hezekiah on the occasion of Merodach-Baladan's embassy to Hezekiah in Jerusalem.[14]

This narrative is especially important for a number of reasons. In the first instance, it is important because Sennacherib's invasion of Judah is a known event in the ancient world, which is announced in the inscription of Sennacherib.[15] The narrative is controversial, however, because the account in the Isaian narrative (see also the Kings and Chronicles narratives) claims that Sennacherib was defeated by divine intervention and that he was forced to withdraw from Judah to return to Nineveh, his capital city, where he was assassinated in the temple of his god, Nisroch, by his own sons. Sennacherib's own account of invasion of Judah, by contrast, claims great success, as he boasts about conquering forty-six Judean cities, taking captive some 200,150 Judeans to be located elsewhere in the Assyrian Empire, seizing great quantities of booty, both in silver and gold and in goods, and bottling up King Hezekiah "like a bird in a cage" in his capital city of Jerusalem. It is striking, however, that Sennacherib does not claim to have captured, entered, and destroyed the city of Jerusalem nor does he claim to have deposed Hezekiah, which would be expected in the case of such a revolt. The fact of the matter is that Sennacherib did not take Jerusalem nor did he depose Hezekiah. The reason for his failure to accomplish these two goals lies in the fact that Hezekiah was allied with Merodach-Baladan, prince of Babylon, and the two leaders had coordinated their revolt to force Sennacherib to deal with two revolts at once. Sennacherib would have negotiated a deal to spare Jerusalem and to allow Hezekiah to remain on the throne because he had to rush to put down the Babylonian revolt. He had already devastated Judah, so Hezekiah posed little further threat against

---

12. Sweeney, *Isaiah 1–39*, 460–88.
13. Sweeney, *Isaiah 1–39*, 488–505.
14. Sweeney, *Isaiah 1–39*, 505–11.
15. Pritchard, *ANET*, 287–88.

him, but Merodach-Baladan posed a considerable threat if he succeeded in breaking away from Assyrian hegemony. In the end, both Hezekiah and Sennacherib claimed victory, and Sennacherib never did capture Merodach-Baladan.[16] Sennacherib was indeed assassinated by some of his own sons, but his assassination took place in 681 BCE.

Secondly, this narrative is important for issues of chronology in the ancient world because Sennacherib's invasion of Judah is confirmed in relation to other known events in the ancient world, and it therefore stands as the basis for reconstructing the chronology of Israelite/Judean and ancient Near Eastern chronology.

A third dimension of the narrative's importance lies in the contrast it presents between King Ahaz ben Jotham of Judah, who is portrayed in Isaiah 7 as a recalcitrant Davidic king who refuses to accept Isaiah's assurances of YHWH's ability to defend Jerusalem as promised in the Davidic covenant tradition. The result of this lack of faith is disaster for Jerusalem and Judah, which will suffer invasion by the Syro-Ephraimitic coalition and later by the Assyrian Empire. King Hezekiah ben Ahaz, by contrast, displays his faith in YHWH, at least in Isaiah 36–37 and Isaiah 38, and he is consequently delivered by YHWH from the Assyrian threat and from his own illness, as YHWH heals him through the agency of Isaiah ben Amoz. The two narratives concerning Ahaz in Isaiah 7 and Hezekiah in Isaiah 36–37 place the primary action of the narrative at the same place, by the Upper Pool of the Fuller's Field, i.e., the place where the Gihon Stream follows into the city under the base of Jerusalem's lower walls on the east by the Wadi Kidron, the major water supply of Jerusalem that would enable it to withstand siege. Whereas Ahaz refused to trust in YHWH's assurances through Isaiah, Hezekiah did trust in YHWH, and YHWH subsequently delivered Jerusalem from the Assyrian invasion and healed Hezekiah of his illness. Hezekiah then emerges as a model of faith in YHWH, in contrast to his father, Ahaz. Such an emphasis on faith in YHWH plays a key role in the late seventh century BCE when King Josiah ben Amon of Judah attempted to reform Judean religious practice and reunite the Kingdom of Judah with the territory and people of the former Kingdom of Israel. Consequently, some scholars see this interest as indicative that Isaiah 7 and Isaiah 36–37 were written as part of the late seventh-century edition of the book of Isaiah.

---

16. For discussion of historical issues, see Brinkman, "Merodach-Baladan II"; Grayson, "Assyria: Sennacherib and Esarhaddon."

Isaiah 34–39

A fourth aspect of the importance of the narrative pertains to the accounts of Hezekiah's illness in Isaiah 38.[17] The portrayal of Hezekiah's illness and cure points to the deliverance of Hezekiah and the House of David, a concern that played roles in the seventh- and sixth-century editions of the developing book of Isaiah. Insofar as concern for the deliverance of the House of David plays a role here, it would appear that a form of Isaiah 36–38 would have functioned in supporting the efforts of King Josiah of Judah to restore Davidic rule over the former northern kingdom of Israel in the late seventh century BCE and later efforts to restore the rule of the Davidic House over Judah by supporting efforts to revolt against the Persian Empire and to install Zerubbabel ben Shealtiel, the grandson of King Jehoiachin ben Jehoiakim of Judah, as the next Davidic monarch in the late sixth century BCE when the Second Temple was rebuilt (see Hag 2:20–23; Zech 6:1–15).[18]

A fifth dimension of importance pertains to Isaiah 39, which recounts Isaiah's condemnation of Hezekiah for inviting a Babylonian embassy to Jerusalem in order to plan for revolt against the Assyrian empire. This brief narrative ends with Isaiah's forecast that Hezekiah's sons would be exiled to Babylon, which actually happened when King Jehoiachin ben Jehoiakim, Hezekiah's descendant, was exiled to Babylon following the failure of King Jehoiakim's revolt against Babylon in 597 BCE (see 2 Kgs 24).[19] The presence of this threat in Isaiah 39 has prompted interpreters to conclude that Isaiah 39 was composed during the Babylonian exile and that it would therefore have been part of the late sixth-century edition of the book of Isaiah. The presence of this threat also plays a key role in explaining how the work of Deutero-Isaiah, a prophet and disciple of Isaiah ben Amoz who would have written near the end of the Babylonian exile, would have been joined to the developing book of Isaiah ben Amoz at this time. Isaiah 36–39 therefore joins Isaiah 34–35 as a second textual block that introduces readers to the second half of the book in Isaiah 34–55 (sixth-century edition) and later, Isaiah 34–66 (fifth-/fourth-century BCE edition). In this case, the portrayal of Hezekiah's faithfulness to YHWH provides a model for the late- and post-exilic Jewish community of the Babylonian exile and beyond to show faith in YHWH's efforts to restore the people of Israel and Judah to Jerusalem and to the land of Israel at large.

---

17. Ackroyd, "Interpretation"; Sweeney, *Isaiah 1–39*, 488–505.
18. Sweeney, *King Josiah of Judah*, 234–55.
19. Ackroyd, "Interpretation"; Sweeney, *Isaiah 1–39*, 505–11.

A. Isaiah 36–37

Isaiah 36:1—37:38 presents a confrontation narrative concerning the defeat of Sennacherib's threat against Jerusalem and King Hezekiah.[20] It is demarcated at the outset by the temporal formula in Isaiah 36:1 for the fourteenth year of the reign of King Hezekiah ben Ahaz of Judah, which marks the date of the invasion of Judah by the Assyrian King Sennacherib. The narrative continues through Isaiah 37:38. The temporal formula *bayyāmîm hāhēm* ("in those days") marks the beginning of the next sub-unit concerning the recovery of Hezekiah from illness in Isaiah 38:1–22.

Isaiah 36–37 has a well-defined narrative structure which recounts the negotiation between the Rab Shakeh (Hebrew, *rab-šāqēh*, lit., "chief drinker," i.e., the chief cup-bearer of King Sennacherib of Assyria) and the officials representing King Hezekiah in Jerusalem. The Assyrian Rab Shakeh's title does not indicate that he is a drunk; rather, it designates his role as the last official to serve wine and other drinks to the Assyrian king. Part of his role is to taste the drink to ensure that it is not poisoned; he risks his life on a daily basis to serve the king. Because of his proximity to the Assyrian king and the risks he takes in the king's service, the office of Rab Shakeh enables him to function as one of the chief officers and advisors of the Assyrian king. In the present instance, the Rab Shakeh has been sent by King Sennacherib of Assyria to negotiate the terms of the surrender of Jerusalem and King Hezekiah of Judah.

Isaiah 36–37 comprises seven major narrative sub-units. The first (Isa 36:1) recounts Sennacherib's invasion of Judah in 701 BCE as an introduction to the narrative.

The second (Isa 36:2–22) concerns the delivery of Sennacherib's first official message to Hezekiah by the Rab Shakeh to Hezekiah's officers standing on the walls of the city. The Rab Shakeh's position is by the Upper Pool by the road to the Fuller's Field, i.e., where the Gihon Spring flows below the eastern walls of Jerusalem facing the Wadi Kidron. The Gihon Spring is the main water source for Jerusalem, and it therefore constitutes a weak spot in the city's defenses because attacking soldiers can enter the city by means of the concealed water tunnel through which the Gihon flows into the southern part of the city of Jerusalem. Second Samuel 5:6-8 reports that David and his men conquered Jebusite Jerusalem by sending men up

---

20. Sweeney, *Isaiah 1–39*, 460–88; see also the studies of Ackroyd, noted above; Clements, *Isaiah and the Deliverance of Jerusalem*; Clements, *Isaiah 1–39*; Gonçalves, *Expédition de Sennachérib*; Seitz, *Zion's Final Destiny*; Birdsong, "Narratives About Isaiah."

the water shaft of the city, now known as "Warren's Shaft." Hezekiah's representatives include three officials: Eliakim, who was in charge of the royal palace; Shebna, the scribe; and Joah ben Asaph, the secretary or recorder.[21] The Rab Shakeh demands the unconditional surrender of Jerusalem, notes the weakness of the city which could not even find two thousand soldiers to mount horses even if he gave them the animals, mocks Judah's reliance on Egypt, and refuses to speak Aramaic instead of Hebrew so that the men defending the walls will not understand what he says. After he refuses the request by Hezekiah's officials to speak in Aramaic, the Rab Shakeh promises to give each of the men defending the city his own vine and fig tree in a new home in exile away from the land of Israel. He concludes his speech by mocking the gods of other cities conquered by Assyria who were unable to defend their people.[22]

The third sub-unit of the narrative (Isa 37:1–7) tells of Hezekiah's reaction to the Rab Shakeh's message. Upon hearing the Rab Shakeh's demands, Hezekiah dons mourning garments because he knows very well that he is unable to defend Jerusalem and that he must accept his fate. But Isaiah reassures him, and counsels him to trust in YHWH, who will defend the city and force the Assyrians to return to their own country where Sennacherib will be assassinated in his own land.

The fourth sub-unit (Isa 37:8–13) recounts how the Rab Shakeh returned to Sennacherib, who was busy besieging the city of Lachish, Judah's secondary capital in the Shephelah southwest of Jerusalem near the border with Philistia. Sennacherib sends the Rab Shakeh back to Jerusalem to reiterate his message that Jerusalem must surrender because Judah's G-d will be unable to defend the city.[23]

The fifth sub-unit (Isa 37:14–20) narrates how Hezekiah went to the Temple of YHWH in Jerusalem and laid out before YHWH the document that presents the Assyrian demands concerning the unconditional surrender of Jerusalem. He prays to YHWH for help, demonstrating his piety and

---

21. For discussion of each of these royal offices, see Fox, *In the Service of the King*, 81–96, 96–110, and 110–21 respectively. Note that Shebna is identified as the official in charge of the royal palace in Isaiah 22:15–25, but Isaiah's oracle announces that Eliakim ben Hilkiah will replace Shebna in this role.

22. For discussion of Assyrian propaganda as illustrated by Isaiah and Assyrian texts, see Machinist, "Assyria and Its Image."

23. For discussion of Lachish and its destruction during Sennacherib's 701 BCE campaign, see Ussishkin, "Lachish."

his continued faith in YHWH despite the desperate circumstances faced by the city and by himself.

The sixth sub-unit of the narrative (Isa 37:21–35) recounts Isaiah's response on YHWH's behalf. Isaiah is here portrayed as an oracular prophet, much like Moses, who serves before YHWH and receives YHWH's message directly. Isaiah is never portrayed as a priest, and it remains uncertain whether or not Isaiah serves in the Temple itself or in some other location. Isaiah communicates YHWH's word to Hezekiah in the form of two prophetic messenger speeches. The first, in Isaiah 37:21b–29, is in the form of a modified prophetic judgment speech in which YHWH promises to defeat Sennacherib, put a hook in his nose, and lead him back to his own land by the road on which he came.[24] The second, in Isaiah 37:30–35, begins with the announcement of a prophetic sign in verses 30–32 that YHWH will defend Jerusalem and defeat Sennacherib by indicating that the people of Jerusalem will survive by eating what grows in their untended fields for three years.[25] The following prophetic judgment speech in verses 33–35 reiterates YHWH's message that YHWH will defend Jerusalem and defeat Sennacherib.

The seventh and final sub-unit of the narrative (Isa 37:36–38) tells of how YHWH sent the angel of death, much as YHWH did in the plague narratives of Exodus 7–13, to strike down 185,000 Assyrian troops, how Sennacherib was forced to return to Nineveh, and how Sennacherib was assassinated by two of his own sons, Adrammelech and Sarezer, in the temple of his god, Nisroch, in Nineveh, and how Sennacherib's son Esarhaddon succeeded him on the throne of Assyria. This narrative very clearly draws on motifs from the exodus narratives in Exodus 7–13. Sennacherib was indeed assassinated by some of his sons due to their dissatisfaction with their father's decision 684 BCE to replace his son Arda-Mulissu with his youngest son, Esarhaddon, as the crown prince and successor to the throne.[26] The reasons for Sennacherib's decision are unclear. As a result of his anger and dissatisfaction with his father, Arda-Mulissu and another older brother, Nabu-shar-usar, assassinated Sennacherib in 681 BCE, apparently in a temple located in Nineveh and dedicated to an Assyrian god, perhaps Sin, the moon god.

---

24. Sweeney, *Isaiah 1–39*, 533–34.
25. Sweeney, *Isaiah 1–39*, 532.
26. Pritchard, *ANET*, 289–90; Grayson, "Assyria: Sennacherib and Esarhaddon."

There is no evidence for the slaughter of 185,000 Assyrian troops in Judah in 701 BCE by the angel of death or anyone else. The motif as portrayed here is clearly drawn from the exodus narratives, as stated above. The assassination of Sennacherib, largely as described in the narrative, did take place, although the year of the assassination was some twenty years after Sennacherib's siege of Jerusalem. Furthermore, Sennacherib himself claims victory in his own account of the siege. The most cogent explanation for these circumstances is to recognize the political realities of the situation. Sennacherib had taken the throne in the aftermath of the death of his father, Sargon II, in 705 BCE in battle in Anatolia, a disastrous defeat for the Assyrian army. It took Sennacherib some four years to rebuild and reorganize the army, which played a role in the decision by King Hezekiah of Judah and his ally, Prince Merodach-Baladan of Babylon, to revolt. The plan of the revolt was to hit Sennacherib from two sides with the presumption that Sennacherib would have to divide his army and face defeat on both sides, or put down one of the revolts to deal the other, which would enable the kingdom not attacked to take action in support of the other. Sennacherib proved to be a very able and brutal army commander, as indicated by his siege of the Judean city of Lachish and his slaughter of its inhabitants. When he conquered Lachish and most of Judah, there was little left other than Jerusalem. Although Sennacherib demanded Jerusalem's surrender, the revolt in Babylonia by Merodach-Baladan proved to be the more immediate threat in the aftermath of the campaign against Judah. Sennacherib therefore negotiated terms to allow Hezekiah to retain his throne, albeit with his sons taken as hostages to Babylonia and his tribute to Assyria increased—a great deal of booty was paid to Assyria, and Assyria was free to develop the olive oil industry in the Shephelah to support the needs of the empire. Sennacherib's victory and Hezekiah's survival enabled both monarchs to claim victory in the aftermath of the campaign, although Judah was left devastated for the next eighty or more years. Sennacherib marched the army to Babylonia to put down Merodach-Baladan's revolt. Although he succeeded in regaining control of Babylonia, at least for the remainder of his life, he never captured Merodach-Baladan, even as late as 689 BCE. Merodach-Baladan fled into the swamps of southeastern Babylonia and was never heard from again. Years later, in 652–648 BCE, a second revolt broke out, which was put down by the Assyrian army. Then in 628–627 BCE, a third revolt led by Nebopolassar, the father of Nebuchadnezzar, eventually resulted in the defeat and destruction of the Assyrian Empire in 609 BCE.

B. Isaiah 38

Isaiah 38:1–22 presents the royal novella concerning Hezekiah's recovery from illness.[27] The narrative is demarcated at the outset by the temporal formula *bayyāmîm hāhēm* ("in those days"), which places the narrative historically in relation to the account of Sennacherib's invasion of Judah in Isaiah 36–37. The temporal formula *bāʿēt hahî'* ("in that time") marks the beginning of a new sub-unit in Isaiah 39:1–8.

Isaiah 38:1–22 comprises two major literary components, each of which has its own internal structure. The first component, in Isaiah 38:1–8, presents the narrative introduction concerning the circumstances of Hezekiah's illness and recovery. This component includes three major elements, first, an account of Hezekiah's sickness (Isa 38:1); second, an account of Hezekiah's reaction to his illness in the form of a petition to YHWH for a cure (Isa 38:2–3); and third, an account of YHWH's response to Hezekiah through the prophet Isaiah ben Amoz in the form of a prophetic oracle of salvation or healing for Hezekiah (Isa 38:4–8).[28] The second component of the passage appears in Isaiah 38:9–22, which presents a narrative account of Hezekiah's letter to YHWH and its aftermath, which recounts Hezekiah's healing. Isaiah 38:9–22 comprises two major elements. The first is an account of Hezekiah's letter to YHWH, which is formulated as a report of Hezekiah's psalm of thanksgiving to YHWH (Isa 38:9–20).[29] The second is the account of Hezekiah's healing as a result of Isaiah's application of a compress, which served as a remedy for Hezekiah's affliction (Isa 38:21–22).

Isaiah 38:1–22 functions within Isaiah 36–39 as an episode that further demonstrates Hezekiah's faith in YHWH and in Isaiah ben Amoz. It therefore functions in relation to the late sixth-century edition of the book of Isaiah, which anticipates the Babylonian exile and calls upon the exiled Judeans to show faith in YHWH's capacity to redeem them from Babylonian exile and return them to Jerusalem and the land of Israel.[30] The narrative could easily function in relation to the late seventh-century edition of the book of Isaiah in the time of the program of religious reform and national restoration of King Josiah ben Amon of Judah. It is noteworthy

---

27. Sweeney, *Isaiah 1–39*, 488–505. A royal novella presents a literary account concerned with a royal figure, in this case, King Hezekiah ben Ahaz of Judah. Sweeney, *Isaiah 1–39*, 525.

28. Sweeney, *Isaiah 1–39*, 531.

29. Sweeney, *Isaiah 1–39*, 538; Gerstenberger, *Psalms, Part 1*, 14–16.

30. In addition to Sweeney, see esp. Ackroyd, "Interpretation of the Babylonian Exile."

that the Kings version of this narrative in 2 Kings 20:1–11 does not include the account of Hezekiah's letter to YHWH with its song of thanksgiving. The absence of the song in the Kings version of the narrative suggests that the Kings narrative was expanded in Isaiah by the addition of Hezekiah's song to accentuate further the depiction of Hezekiah's piety.

C. Isaiah 39

Isaiah 39:1–8 presents the prophetic story concerning Isaiah's announcement of punishment against Hezekiah on the occasion of Merodach-Baladan's embassy to Jerusalem.[31] The story appears in the form of a dialog report,[32] which recounts the dialog between Hezekiah and Isaiah over Hezekiah's actions. Isaiah condemns Hezekiah in keeping with his well-known stance against reliance on foreign powers for assistance in a time of crisis; the prophet instead calls for reliance on YHWH alone in keeping with his understanding of the Davidic covenant, which presumes YHWH's protection of the Davidic king, Jerusalem, Judah, and Israel at large (see Isa 2:6–21; 7; 36–38; 2 Sam 7).

Isaiah 39:1–8 is demarcated at the outset by the temporal formula *bā'ēt hahî'* ("in that time"), which correlates the narrative with the events recounted in Isaiah 36–37 and Isaiah 38. The narrative includes two major components. The first appears in Isaiah 39:1–2 as an account of Merodach-Baladan's embassy to Hezekiah as the setting and cause of the confrontation between Isaiah and Hezekiah. The second, Isaiah 39:3–8, recounts the three exchanges in the dialog between Isaiah and Hezekiah (Isa 39:3, 4, 5–7), which culminates in Isaiah's announcement of punishment against Hezekiah. The prophet's announcement of punishment declares that all the stores that Hezekiah has shown to the Babylonian embassy will be taken away to Babylon at some time in the future, together with Hezekiah's sons, who will serve as eunuchs in the palace of the Babylonian king. Hezekiah accepts this announcement by stating that "there will be peace and truth in my days." The narrative then functions together with the rest of Isaiah 36–39 as part of the introduction to Isaiah 40–66, which presents the prophecy of Second Isaiah and Third Isaiah at the close of the Babylonian exile in Isaiah 40–55 and in the midst of the Persian period.

---

31. Sweeney, *Isaiah 1–39*, 505–11.
32. Sweeney, *Isaiah 1–39*, 518.

Isaiah 39:1–8 thereby constitutes a composition set in the late sixth-century edition of the book of Isaiah (i.e., Isa 2–55) and it also functions in relation to the late fifth- or early fourth-century edition of Isaiah (i.e., Isa 1–66). The Kings version of the narrative in 2 Kings 20:12–19 differs only slightly from Isaiah 39:1–8. One telling difference appears in Hezekiah's response to Isaiah's prophetic announcement of punishment. Hezekiah states in 2 Kings 20:19, "shall there not be peace and truth in my days?" The use of the Hebrew phrase *hălô' im-šālôm* ("shall there not be peace?") suggests some doubt on Hezekiah's part, whereas the phrase in Isaiah 39:8, *kî yihyeh šālôm* ("for there will be peace"), is far more assertive and indicates Hezekiah's faith in YHWH and Isaiah beyond that depicted in 2 Kings 20:19. Such a difference indicates that Isaiah 39:1–8 is a modified version of 2 Kings 20:12–19 designed to accentuate Hezekiah's faith, even in the face of judgment, in the late sixth- and late fifth-/early fourth-centuries editions of the book of Isaiah.[33]

D. Compositional History

During this period, King Josiah of Judah (r. 640–609 BCE) pursued a policy of religious reform and national restoration, beginning in the twelfth year of his reign (628 BCE), which correlated with the revolt of Nebopolassar.[34] When the Babylonian army faced the Assyrians in a final battle at Haran in 609 BCE, King Josiah and the Judean army attempted to block Pharaoh Necho II at Megiddo from crossing through the Jezreel Valley in northern Israel to support his Assyrian allies. King Josiah was killed in battle for his efforts, although he succeeded in delaying the Egyptians long enough so that they did not arrive in Haran until after the battle was over. Insofar as Josiah's reforms were influenced by the exodus traditions of devotion to YHWH and YHWH's defense of the people of Israel, Isaiah 36–37, which is also heavily influenced by the exodus narrative, appears to be the product of the seventh-century BCE edition of Isaiah, designed to support King Josiah's agenda.

Much of twentieth-century scholarship on these narratives has focused on attempts to define the earlier narrative sources allegedly combined to produce the current text. Gesenius laid the foundations for such a hypothesis in his 1820–21 commentary on Isaiah with his views that Isaiah

---

33. Cf. Ackroyd, "Interpretation of the Babylonian Exile."
34. Sweeney, *King Josiah of Judah*.

36–39 were a later version of 2 Kings 18–20 and his views concerning the source division of 2 Kings 18–20.³⁵ The issue was later taken up by Stade, and Childs has been a leading proponent of this approach in more recent times.³⁶ Both of these scholars focused on the parallel account of the matter in 2 Kings 18–20, insofar as they considered it to be the more historically based account. Childs argues that there were two accounts of the Assyrian embassy to Judah. The first appears as source A in 2 Kings 18:13–16, source B1 in 2 Kings 18:17—19:9a, 36–37, and source B2 includes 2 Kings 19:9b–35. The division into sources presumes that a first Assyrian invasion resulted in Hezekiah's submission, as recounted in 2 Kings 18:13–16, and a second Assyrian invasion—as recounted in two distinct sources in B1 and B2 that have been combined—resulted in the devastation of the land. Although many scholars have accepted this analysis, there is no evidence in Assyrian records that Sennacherib invaded twice. Furthermore, if Sennacherib had been forced to invade twice, it is unlikely that he would have allowed Hezekiah to remain on the throne in the aftermath of the second invasion. Indeed, literary analysis of the final form of this text indicates that the first confrontation between Sennacherib's representatives and those of Hezekiah highlights the underlying confrontation between Sennacherib and YHWH. The second confrontation highlights Sennacherib's hubris and blasphemy insofar as Sennacherib portrays himself as the absolute power in the universe over and against YHWH. But such a sequence merely heightens the dramatic tension of the narrative and provides the basis for YHWH's response: to defeat Sennacherib's army and send him back to his own land where he will be murdered by his own sons in the temple of his own god. Overall, this model offers little by which to understand the historical realities of the Judean/Babylonian revolt of King Hezekiah of Judah and Prince Merodach-Baladan of Babylon. Instead, it contributes to understanding the literary dimensions of the text.

An especially fruitful literary analysis of this narrative emerges when one compares the two very similar accounts in Isaiah 36–37 and 2 Kings 18–20. Although these two accounts are nearly identical, Wildberger's highlighting of the differences between them proves to be particularly useful in

---

35. Gesenius, *Jesaia*, 932–1008; see esp. the discussion by Seitz, *Zion's Final Destiny*, 48–118.

36. Stade, "Anmerkungen zu 2 Kö. 15–21"; Childs, *Isaiah and the Assyrian Crisis*, 69–103; Childs, *Isaiah*, 259–87, esp. 260–64.

identifying the different emphases in each.[37] Following his detailed commentary on Isaiah 36–39, Wildberger presents a synoptic comparison of the two narratives in which he shades the different readings between the two texts to emphasize their distinctive readings. His chart notes that 2 Kings 18–20 includes 2 Kings 18:14–16 at the beginning of the narrative but that it is absent in Isaiah 36–37. This brief passage recounts Hezekiah's initial surrender and payment of tribute to Sennacherib—indeed, some of its figures match those mentioned in Sennacherib's account of his campaign. The major insight provided by this reading, however, is to indicate that Hezekiah initially succumbed to the Assyrian attack, but Sennacherib continued the campaign anyway, thereby portraying Sennacherib as an evil and dishonest conqueror and Hezekiah as faithless king who did not rely on YHWH at the outset. A second major difference is the presentation of Hezekiah's prayer of thanksgiving to YHWH after he had been healed of his wound in Isaiah 38:9–22, which demonstrates his faithfulness to YHWH, whereas 2 Kings 20:6–11 presents only brief narrative comments concerning the healing, which does not display Hezekiah's piety in the manner that the Isaiah narrative does. Otherwise, the differences between the two narratives are minor, but those of the Isaiah narrative function as a means to emphasize Hezekiah's piety whereas those of the Kings narrative raise questions about Hezekiah's faithfulness to YHWH and his decisions during the Assyrian siege of Judah.[38] The account of Hezekiah's reign in 2 Chronicles 29–32 is a heavily modified version of the narrative presented in 2 Kings 18–20.

It is also noteworthy that both versions of the narrative, Isaiah 36–39 and 2 Kings 18–20, conclude with Isaiah's reprimand of Hezekiah for showing the Babylonian ambassadors of Merodach-Baladan the equipment and provisions that were stored in the Jerusalem Temple in preparation for the revolt against Assyria. Isaiah's reprimand includes a statement that Hezekiah's sons would be taken into exile to Babylon, a judgment to which Hezekiah accedes. This narrative conflicts with the message of comfort apparent in the account of YHWH's deliverance of Jerusalem and Hezekiah and YHWH's healing of Hezekiah, but it makes eminent sense in both Isaiah and Kings in that it points forward to the Babylonian exile. The exile is apparent in Isaiah immediately following Isaiah 36–39 in Isaiah 40–66,[39]

---

37. Wildberger, *Isaiah 28–39*, 359–479, esp. 481–93.

38. In addition to the analysis in my *Isaiah 1–39*, 460–88, see also Sweeney, *1–2 Kings*, 397–424.

39. See now Poulsen, *Black Hole in Isaiah*.

and in Kings, the Babylonian exile is apparent in the regnal account of King Manasseh ben Hezekiah in 2 Kings 21:1–18, which holds Manasseh responsible for the destruction of Jerusalem and the Babylonian exile due to his many sins, and 2 Kings 24–25, which recounts the events leading up to the Babylonian exile and the exile itself. The two forms of the narrative play key roles in anticipating the Babylonian exile in both Isaiah and Kings.

The compositional history of Isaiah 36–39 is therefore complicated, but the following observations aid in reconstructing the process. The account of YHWH's defeat of Sennacherib in Isaiah 36–37 appears to have been written as part of the late seventh-century Josianic edition of the book of Isaiah, insofar as it emphasizes the exodus tradition of YHWH's deliverance of Israel, a motif that appears throughout Isaiah 1–35 to point to YHWH's deliverance of Israel from Assyria and Egypt, a close ally of Assyria during the seventh century BCE. The narrative was included in the seventh-century BCE Josianic edition of the book of Kings, where it was embellished with the shorter account of YHWH's healing of Hezekiah to demonstrate YHWH's power to deliver the faithful Hezekiah from his wound. The account of Isaiah's encounter with King Ahaz in Isaiah 7 was composed as part of the seventh-century edition of the book to provide contrast with Hezekiah and therefore to hold out Hezekiah as a model of piety in Josiah's time. But in the aftermath of the death of Josiah at the hands of Pharaoh Necho at Megiddo in 609 BCE and the subsequent destruction of Jerusalem and the Temple of Solomon, and the Babylonian exile in 598–597, 588–586, and 582 BCE, the Kings narrative was expanded with the account of Hezekiah's reception of the embassy of Merodach-Baladan, the Babylonian prince, to anticipate the Babylonian exile and to hold Hezekiah responsible in part, although primary responsibility remains with his son, Manasseh. With the appearance of the late sixth-century edition of the book of Isaiah, the narrative was employed in the book to anticipate the Babylonian exile, as in the earlier edition, but the portrayal of Hezekiah was idealized by the deletion of the account of his initial surrender to Sennacherib, the addition of the full account of his prayer of thanksgiving to YHWH, and the other modifications made to the narrative to portray him as a model of piety for the Jewish people in the time of the exile so that they might be returned to Jerusalem in a second exodus, this time from Babylon rather than from Egypt. Isaiah 36–39 remained in the late fifth-/early fourth-century edition of the book of Isaiah so that Hezekiah could serve as a model of piety during the reforms of Nehemiah and Ezra.

6

Isaiah 1–39
Concluding Remarks

ISAIAH 1–39 NEVER STOOD as an independent prophetic book, at least not in its present canonical form. As the preceding discussion of the synchronic final form of the book and the diachronic process of its formation demonstrates, the book of Isaiah is the product of at least some four hundred years of literary development from the time of the late eighth-century prophet Isaiah ben Amoz through the late fifth-/early fourth-century work of writers collectively known as Trito-Isaiah, some of whom worked during the time of the restoration of Jewish life in Jerusalem and Judah during the middle of the Persian period. Some would even take the process further than that into the Greco-Roman period when the earliest Hebrew manuscripts of the book of Isaiah were written as part of the Judean wilderness library at Qumran.

Ironically, many commentaries are written on Isaiah 1–39 as if it was an independent prophetic book. When considered separately from the rest of the book, Isaiah 1–39 focuses especially on the future of Davidic kingship among its many concerns. But analysis of the final form of the entire book of Isaiah demonstrates that the book reconsidered the Davidic covenant to apply to the entire people of Israel in Isaiah 55, and Isaiah 44:28 and 45:1 name King Cyrus of Persia, not a Davidic monarch, as YHWH's messiah and Temple-builder. By the end of the book in Isaiah 66, YHWH emerges as the true king.[1]

Although the present form of Isaiah 1–39 never stood as an independent, self-standing book, the process of the book of Isaiah's formation begins with oracles and perhaps narratives that can be traced back to the time of the prophet himself. All of these oracles and narratives likely appear in the present form of Isaiah 1–39, but they do not constitute the entirety of the present form of these chapters. As the preceding discussion has shown, Isaiah 1–39 includes many texts, both oracular and narrative, that date to editions of the book of Isaiah that appeared long after the lifetime of the late eighth-century prophet, such as the posited late seventh-century edition of the book that was produced during the reign of King Josiah ben Amon of Judah to support his ultimately failed program of religious reform and national restoration; the late sixth-century edition of the book that was produced by anonymous writers, such as the so-called Deutero- or Second Isaiah, at the time of the conclusion of the Babylonian exile when King Cyrus the Great of Persia conquered Babylon and was named by the priests of Marduk to be Babylon's divinely chosen ruler; and the final edition of the book written during the late fifth or early fourth century BCE by writers collectively known as Trito-Isaiah to support the reforms of Nehemiah and Ezra during the rule of the Achaemenid Persian Empire.

In addition to the reconstruction of the diachronic formation of the book of Isaiah offered here, studies have shown that other books of the Hebrew Bible were informed by texts from the developing book of Isaiah, particularly the other prophetic books of the Hebrew Bible, beginning with the developing book of Kings that appeared in successive editions during the reign of King Hezekiah ben Ahaz of Judah in the later eighth century and the reign of King Josiah ben Amon of Judah during the late seventh century BCE, and during the sixth-century BCE Babylonian exile;[2] the books of Jeremiah that appeared in both the shorter form of the book that became the basis for the Greek Septuagint version of Jeremiah in the late sixth century BCE and the longer, proto-Masoretic Hebrew form of the book that appeared in relation to the reforms of Nehemiah and Ezra;[3]

---

1. In addition to the above discussion and the relevant commentary in Sweeney, *Isaiah 1–39* and *Isaiah 40–66*, see Sweeney, "Reconceptualization of the Davidic Covenant in Isaiah."

2. Sweeney, *King Josiah of Judah*, 33–177; Sweeney, *1–2 Kings*.

3. Sweeney, "Reconceptualization of the Davidic Covenant in the Books of Jeremiah"; Sweeney, "Jeremiah Among the Prophets"; Sweeney, "Hope and Resilience."

the developing book of Ezekiel, that appeared as early as the end of the Babylonian exile and the beginning of the Persian period in the late sixth or early fifth century BCE;[4] the developing book of the Twelve Prophets that follow a similar course of development in the late sixth and the later fifth or early fourth centuries BCE;[5] the books of Chronicles and Ezra-Nehemiah that appeared successively during the middle Persian period;[6] and the book of Daniel, that emerged during the second-century BCE Hasmonean revolt against the Syrian-Seleucid Empire. In all cases, texts from Isaiah were quoted or referenced frequently as these books interacted intertextually with the writings now found in the book of Isaiah.[7]

There are also the many textual versions of Isaiah that first appear as proto-Masoretic Hebrew texts among the Dead Sea Scrolls of Qumran, beginning in the second century BCE;[8] the Septuagint Greek version of the book of Isaiah that was allegedly written in the first century BCE and appears in many Christian Greek manuscripts beginning with the fourth-century CE Codex Vaticanus and the fourth-century CE Codex Sinaiticus;[9] the Syriac Peshitta manuscripts that appear as early as the fifth century CE;[10] the Latin Vulgate manuscripts that represent the fourth-century CE translation by Jerome, recognized as a saint in Christianity;[11] the Aramaic Targum Jonathan, that allegedly first appeared in the Talmudic period in the fifth or sixth century CE;[12] and later editions, such as the Judeo-Arabic translation of Isaiah by R. Saadia Gaon (892–942 CE),[13] among many others.

It is clear that the book of Isaiah is the most frequently cited prophetic book in the Jewish Haftarot tradition of prophetic texts that are read to accompany the weekly reading of the Torah in the Jewish worship service.[14]

---

4. Sweeney, "Ezekiel's Debate with Isaiah"; Sweeney, *Reading Ezekiel*.

5. Sweeney, *Twelve Prophets*; Sweeney, "Swords into Plowshares"; Sweeney, "Book of the Twelve and Kingship."

6. See 2 Chr 29–32; Ackroyd, "Interpretation"; Sweeney, "Distinctive Roles of the Prophets."

7. Sweeney, "End of Eschatology in Daniel?"

8. Brooke, "Isaiah in the Qumran Scrolls."

9. Ngunga, "Isaiah in Greek."

10. Kooij, *Alten Textzeugen des Jesajabuches*, 258–98.

11. Anni Laato, "Isaiah in Latin."

12. Tooman, "Isaiah in Aramaic."

13. Derenbourg and Derenbourg, *Version Arabe d'Isaïe*.

14. Fishbane, *Haftarot*.

Indeed, Isaiah is well-known in the Talmud as a book of comfort that is placed first among the latter prophets due to its historical setting in the time of Isaiah ben Amoz or alternatively following Jeremiah and Ezekiel because of its focus on comfort or restoration.[15] In Christianity, it is the most frequently quoted biblical book after the book of Psalms that plays a key role in depicting the life and teachings of Jesus, recognized as the messiah in Christianity.[16] In both Judaism and Christianity, the refrain sung by the Seraphim in Isaiah 6:3, "Holy, holy, holy is the L-rd of Hosts! The whole earth is full of his glory," appears prominently in the liturgy of both traditions. Isaiah even finds a place in modern institutions, such as the United Nations, where Isaiah 2:2–4, with its message of peace among the nations of the world, with swords turned into plowshares and spears turned into pruning hooks, is carved onto the so-called Isaiah Stone, set in Ralph J. Bunche Park, just across the street from the United Nations Headquarters Building in New York.[17] And the questions raised by the book of Isaiah continue to dominate theological thinking, such as the post-Shoah theological discussion taking place in Judaism and Christianity in the aftermath of the Holocaust, the messianic tradition of Christianity, and the emergence of modern Zionism in Judaism, which, like the book of Isaiah, calls for the restoration of the Jewish homeland in the land of Israel.[18]

The book of Isaiah is one of the most influential books of the Bible in both Judaism and Christianity, and Isaiah 1–39 plays a very large role in that influence in both traditions.[19]

---

15. See b. Baba Batra 14b–15a. For discussion of the reception of the book of Isaiah in Judaism, albeit heavily influenced by Christian theological concerns, see Antti Laato, "Isaiah in Ancient, Medieval, and Modern Jewish Traditions"; Antti Laato, *Message and Composition of the Book of Isaiah.*

16. Moyise, "Isaiah in the New Testament."

17. Sweeney, "Isaiah 1–39," 678.

18. Sweeney, "Post-Shoah Readings of Isaiah."

19. For a full and detailed discussion of the reception history of the book of Isaiah, see Sawyer, *Isaiah Through the Centuries.*

Appendix

Form Criticism and the Structure of Isaiah

The Vision of Isaiah Ben Amoz
Prophetic Exhortation to Jerusalem and Judah to Adhere to YHWH (1-66)

I. **CONCERNING YHWH's plans for worldwide sovereignty at Zion (1-33)**
   A. PROLOGUE TO THE BOOK OF ISAIAH: Introductory parenesis concerning YHWH's intention to purify (1)
   B. PROPHETIC INSTRUCTION: Concerning YHWH's projected plans to establish worldwide sovereignty at Zion: announcement of the Day of YHWH (2-33)
      1. Prophetic announcement concerning the preparation of Zion for its role as the center for YHWH's world rule (2-4)
      2. Prophetic instruction concerning the significance of Assyrian judgment against Israel: Restoration of Davidic rule (5-12)
      3. Prophetic announcement concerning the preparation of the nations for YHWH's world rule (13-27)
         a. Pronouncements concerning the nations (13-23)
            i. Pronouncement concerning Babylon et al. (13-14)
            ii. Pronouncement concerning Moab (15-16)
            iii. Pronouncement concerning Damascus (17-18)

iv. Pronouncement concerning Egypt (19–20)
v. Pronouncement concerning the Wilderness of the Sea (21:1–10)
vi. Pronouncement concerning Dumah (21:11–12)
vii. Pronouncement concerning Arabia (21:13–17)
viii. Pronouncement concerning Valley of Vision (22)
ix. Pronouncement concerning Tyre (23)

b. Prophetic announcement of YHWH's new world order: Prophecy of salvation for Zion/Israel (24–27)
   i. Prophetic announcement concerning YHWH's punishment of earth (24)
   ii. Prophetic announcement of YHWH's blessing of the earth and its results for Zion (25–27)

4. Prophetic instruction concerning YHWH's plans for Jerusalem: Announcement of a royal savior (28–33)
   a. Prophetic instruction concerning YHWH's purpose in bringing Assyrian hegemony (28)
   b. Prophetic instruction concerning YHWH's purpose in bringing assault against Ariel/Zion (29)
   c. Prophetic instruction concerning YHWH's delay in delivering people from Assyria (30)
   d. Parenesis concerning reliance on Egyptian aid against Assyria (31)
   e. Prophetic instruction concerning announcement of a royal savior (32–33)
      i. Prophetic instruction speech concerning announcement of royal savior (32)
      ii. Prophetic announcement of royal savior proper (33)

II. **CONCERNING the realization of YHWH's plans for worldwide sovereignty at Zion (34–66)**
   A. PROPHETIC INSTRUCTION: Concerning the realization of YHWH's worldwide sovereignty at Zion (**34–54**)
      1. Prophetic instruction concerning YHWH's power to return the redeemed exiles to Zion (34–35)
         a. Prophetic instruction concerning YHWH's power over the nations: example of Edom (34)
         b. Prophetic oracle of salvation/restoration concerning the return of the redeemed to Zion (35)

2. Royal narratives concerning YHWH's deliverance of Jerusalem and Hezekiah (36–39)
   a. Confrontation story concerning defeat of Sennacherib's threat against Jerusalem (36–37)
   b. Royal novella concerning Hezekiah's recovery from illness (38)
   c. Prophetic story concerning Isaiah's announcement of punishment against Hezekiah on occasion of Merodach-Baladan's embassy: dialogue report (39)
3. Prophetic instruction that YHWH is maintaining covenant and restoring Zion (40–54)
   a. Renewed prophetic commission to announce YHWH's restoration of Zion (40:1–11)
   b. Instruction proper: YHWH is maintaining covenant and restoring Zion (40:12—54:17)
      i. Contention: YHWH is master of creation (40:12–31)
      ii. Contention: YHWH is master of human events (41:1—42:13)
      iii. Contention: YHWH is redeemer of Israel (42:14—44:23)
      iv. Contention: YHWH will use Cyrus for the restoration of Zion (44:24—48:22)
      v. Contention: YHWH is restoring Zion (49:1—54:17)
B. PROPHETIC EXHORTATION: To adhere to YHWH's covenant (55–66)
   1. Exhortation proper (55)
   2. Substantiation: prophetic instruction concerning the reconstituted nation in Zion (56–66)
      a. Prophetic instruction concerning proper observance of covenant (56–59)
      b. Prophetic announcement of salvation for the reconstituted nation (60–62)
      c. Prophetic instruction concerning the reconstituted nation (63–66)

The structure diagram above presents the formal structure and generic character of the book of Isaiah as established in Marvin A. Sweeney, *Isaiah 1-39, with an Introduction to Prophetic Literature*, FOTL 16 (Grand Rapids: Eerdmans, 1996) and Marvin A. Sweeney, *Isaiah 40-66*, FOTL (Grand

Rapids: Eerdmans, 2016). Form represents the formal presentation of a text, and genre represents the typical elements of language that inform the formal character of the text.

Form criticism may be defined as follows:

> Form criticism is a foundational, dynamic, and continually evolving exegetical method employed in modern critical interpretation of biblical texts. It analyzes the formal features of a text, including its unique syntactical and semantic form or literary structure and its typical linguistic genres that give shape to the text and function within it to facilitate its expression. Form criticism functions both synchronically to analyze the present literary form of the text and diachronically to ascertain and examine its compositional history in relation to its postulated written and oral stages. It works in tandem with other critical methodologies, such as rhetorical criticism, redaction criticism, tradition-historical criticism, textual criticism, canonical criticism, newer literary criticisms, social-scientific analysis, and linguistics in the interpretation of biblical texts. Form criticism is intimately concerned with the societal, historical, literary, and conceptual settings in which the biblical texts function, in which they were produced, and in which they are read.[1]

Brief examples of genres employed in this structure diagram are as follows:

CONFRONTATION STORY: A sub-genre of the prophetic story that focuses on a confrontation between the prophet and his or her opponents.

ORACLE: A broad generic category that designates communication from a deity, often through an intermediary such as a priest, seer, or prophet.

PARENESIS: An address to an individual or group that seeks to persuade with reference to a god.

PRONOUNCEMENT (Hebrew, *maśśā'*): A prophetic discourse in which the prophet attempts to explain how YHWH's actions are manifested in the realm of human affairs.

PROPHETIC ANNOUNCEMENT: A broad collecting generic term for an unsolicited (in contrast to a solicited prophetic oracle) announcement of a prophet concerning future events or future actions of YHWH.

---

1. Sweeney, "Form Criticism: The Question," 251–72, 251–52 (page numbers from the reprint in *Vision of the Holy*).

PROPHETIC COMMISSION: An authoritative charge to a prophet given by a superior to a subordinate.

PROPHETIC EXHORTATION: An address form employed by a prophet to persuade an audience to adopt a particular course of action.

PROPHETIC INSTRUCTION: A writing or discourse by a prophet, chiefly in imperative mode, that offers guidance to an individual or group by setting forth particular values or prescribing rules of conduct.

PROPHETIC ORACLE OF SALVATION/RESTORATION: A sub-genre of the Prophetic Announcement of Salvation or Blessing to individuals, groups, or the nation.

PROPHETIC STORY: A type of historical story in which a prophetic figure plays a central role and carries the interpretative motifs that express the narrator's interests.

ROYAL NARRATIVE: A genre of ancient Egypt literature that presents the king as an ideal figure of strength, piety, and success.

ROYAL NOVELLA: A long, prose narrative about a royal figure produced by a literary artisan for a particular purpose or purposes.

VISION REPORT: The description by a prophet of what he or she sees (vision) or hears (audition) in an inner prophetic perception.

Please note that while this outline of Isaiah is terminologically precise in its use of form-critical categories, the main body of the book will sometimes speak of units of biblical text using a variety of other descriptors. This is simply to allow for stylistic variation. For form-critical precision, please use this outline.

Bibliography

Ackroyd, Peter R. "The Biblical Interpretation of the Reigns of Ahaz and Hezekiah." In *Studies in the Religious Tradition of the Old Testament*, 181–92. London: SCM, 1987.
———. "The Book of Isaiah." In *The Interpreter's One-Volume Commentary on the Bible*, edited by C. M. Laymon, 79–104. Nashville: Abingdon, 1971.
———. "The Death of Hezekiah: A Pointer to the Future?" In *Studies in the Religious Tradition of the Old Testament*, 172–80. Nashville: Abingdon, 1971.
———. "Historians and Prophets." In *Studies in the Religious Tradition of the Old Testament*, 121–51. Nashville: Abingdon, 1971.
———. "An Interpretation of the Babylonian Exile: A Study of II Kings 20 and Isaiah 38–39." In *Studies in the Religious Tradition of the Old Testament*, 152–71. Nashville: Abingdon, 1971.
———. "Isaiah 1–12: Presentation of a Prophet." In *Studies in the Religious Tradition of the Old Testament*, 79–104. Nashville: Abingdon, 1971.
———. "Isaiah 36–39: Structure and Function." In *Studies in the Religious Tradition of the Old Testament*, 105–20. Nashville: Abingdon, 1971.
———. *Studies in the Religious Tradition of the Old Testament*. London: SCM, 1987.
Anderson, Bernhard W. "Exodus and Covenant in Second Isaiah and Prophetic Tradition." In *The Mighty Acts of G-d: In Memoriam G. Ernest Wright*, edited by F. M. Cross et al., 339–60. Garden City, NY: Doubleday, 1976.
———. "Exodus Typology in Second Isaiah." In *Israel's Prophetic Heritage*, edited by B. W. Anderson and W. Harrelson, 177–95. London: SCM, 1962.
Baumann, Gerlinde. *Love and Violence: Marriage as Metaphor for the Relationship Between YHWH and Israel in the Prophetic Books*. Translated by L. M. Maloney. Collegeville, MN: Liturgical, 2003.
Berges, Ulrich. *Das Buch Jesaja: Komposition und Endgestalt*. HBS 16. Freiburg: Herder, 1998.
———. *Jesaja 55–66*. HThKAT. Stuttgart: Herder, 2022.
Beuken, Willem A. M. *Isaiah II. Volume 2: Isaiah 28–39*. Historical Commentary on the Old Testament. Leuven: Peeters, 2000.
———. *Jesaja 28–39*. HThKAT. Freiburg: Herder, 2010.
———. "Jesaja 33 als Spiegeltext im Jesajabuch." *ETL* 67 (1991) 5–35.

Bibliography

Birdsong, Shelley L. "The Narratives About Isaiah and Their Relationship with 2 Kings and 2 Chronicles." In *The Oxford Handbook of Isaiah*, edited by L.-S. Tiemeyer, 95–110. Oxford: Oxford University Press, 2020.

Blenkinsopp, Joseph. *Isaiah 1–39*. AB 19. New York: Doubleday, 2000.

———. *Isaiah 40–55*. AB 19A. New York: Doubleday, 2002.

———. *Isaiah 56–66*. AB 19B. New York: Doubleday, 2003.

Blischke, Mariecke V. "Bashan." In *EBR* 3:581.

Brinkman, J. A. "Merodach Baladan II." In *Studies Presented to A. Leo Oppenheim*, 6–53. Chicago: The Oriental Institute at the University of Chicago, 1964.

Brooke, George, J. "Isaiah in the Qumran Scrolls." In *The Oxford Handbook of Isaiah*, edited by L.-S. Tiemeyer, 429–50. Oxford: Oxford University Press, 2020.

Budde, Karl. *Jesajas Erleben: Eine gemeinverständliche Auslegung der Denkschrift des Propheten (Kap. 6,1—9,6)*. Gotha: Leopold Klotz, 1928.

Carr, David M. "Reaching for Unity in Isaiah." *JSOT* 57 (1993) 61–80.

———. "Reading Isaiah from Beginning (Isaiah 1) to End (Isaiah 65–66): Multiple Modern Possibilities." In *New Visions of Isaiah*, edited by. R. F. Melugin and M. A. Sweeney, 188–218. JSOTSup 214. Sheffield, UK: Sheffield Academic Press, 1996.

Childs, Brevard S. *Isaiah: A Commentary*. OTL. Louisville, KY: Westminster John Knox, 2001.

———. *Isaiah and the Assyrian Crisis*. Studies in Biblical Theology II/3. London: SCM, 1967.

Clements, Ronald E. "Beyond Tradition History: Deutero-Isaianic Development of First Isaiah's Themes." In *Old Testament Prophecy*, 78–92. Louisville, KY: Westminster John Knox, 1996.

———. "The Immanuel Prophecy of Isaiah 7:10–17 and Its Messianic Interpretation." In *Old Testament Prophecy*, 65–77. Louisville, KY: Westminster John Knox, 1996.

———. *Isaiah 1–39*. NCeB. London: Marshall, Morgan, and Scott, 1980.

———. *Isaiah and the Deliverance of Jerusalem: A Study of the Interpretation of Prophecy in the Old Testament*. JSOTSup 13. Sheffield, UK: JSOT, 1980.

———. *Old Testament Prophecy: From Oracles to Canon*. Louisville, KY: Westminster John Knox, 1996.

———. "The Prophecies of Isaiah and the Fall of Jerusalem in 587 B.C." *VT* 30 (1980) 421–36.

———. "The Prophecies of Isaiah to Hezekiah Concerning Sennacherib." In *Old Testament Prophecy*, 35–48. Louisville, KY: Westminster John Knox, 1996.

———. "The Unity of the Book of Isaiah." In *Old Testament Prophecy*, 93–104. Louisville, KY: Westminster John Knox, 1996.

Cogan, Mordecai, and Haim Tadmor. *2 Kings*. AB 11. Garden City, NY: Doubleday, 1988.

Collins, John J. "Introduction: The Genre Apocalypse Reconsidered." In *Apocalypse, Prophecy, and Pseudepigraphy: On Jewish Apocalyptic Literature*. Grand Rapids: Eerdmans, 2016.

Conrad, Edgar W. *Reading Isaiah*. OBT. Minneapolis: Fortress, 1991.

Cook, L. Stephen. *On the Question of the "Cessation of Prophecy" in Ancient Judaism*. TSAJ 145. Tübingen: Mohr Siebeck, 2011.

Cooper, Jerrold S. "Assyrian Prophecies, the Assyrian Tree, and the Mesopotamian Origins of Jewish Monotheism, Greek Philosophy, Christian Theology, Gnosticism, and Much More." *JAOS* 120 (2000) 430–44.

Cross, Frank M. "The Council of YHWH in Second Isaiah." *JNES* 12 (1953) 274–77.

Bibliography

Day, John. *G-d's Conflict with the Dragon and the Sea*. Cambridge: Cambridge University Press, 1985.
Dearman, Andrew, ed. *Studies in the Mesha Inscription and Moab*. Atlanta: Scholars, 1989.
Derenbourg, Joseph, and Hartwig Derenbourg. *Version Arabe d'Isaïe de R. Saadia ben Josef al-Fayyoûmî*. Paris: Ernest Leroux, 1896.
De Vries, Simon J. *From Old Revelation to New: A Tradition-Historical and Redaction-Critical Study of Temporal Transitions in Prophetic Prediction*. Grand Rapids: Eerdmans, 1995.
Dicou, Burt. *Edom, Israel's Brother and Antagonist: The Role of Edom in Biblical Prophecy and Story*. JSOTSup 169. Sheffield, UK: Sheffield Academic Press, 1994.
———. "Literary Function and Literary History of Isaiah 34." *BN* 58 (1991) 30–45.
Dillmann, August. *Der Prophet Jesaia*. 5th ed. KHAT 5. Leipzig: Hirzel, 1890.
Dothan, Trude, and Seymour Gitin. "Tel Miqne (Ekron)." In *NEAEHL* 5:1952–58.
Duhm, Bernhard. *Das Buch Jesaia*. 5th ed. 1892. HKAT III/1. Göttingen: Vandenhoeck & Ruprecht, 1968.
Eichhorn, Johann Gottfried. *Einleitung in das Alte Testament*. 5 vols. Göttingen: Rosenbusch, 1820–24.
Ephal, Israel. *The Ancient Arabs: Nomads on the Borders of the Fertile Crescent, 9th–5th Centuries B.C.* Jerusalem: Magnes Press, Hebrew University, 1984.
Erlandsson, Seth. *The Burden of Babylon: A Study of Isaiah 13:2—14:23*. ConBibOT 4. Lund: Gleerup, 1970.
Evans, Craig A. "The Unity and Parallel Structure of Isaiah." *VT* 38 (1988) 129–47.
Ewald, Heinrich Georg August. *Die Propheten des Alten Bundes*. 2nd ed. 2 vols. Göttingen: Vandenhoeck & Ruprecht, 1867–68.
Finkelstein, Israel. "The Archaeology of the Days of Manasseh." In *Scripture and Other Artifacts: Essays on the Bible and Archaeology in Honor of Philip J. King*, edited by M. D. Coogan et al., 169–87. Louisville, KY: Westminster John Knox, 1994.
Fishbane, Michael. *Haftarot*. JPS Commentary on the Bible. Philadelphia: Jewish Publication Society, 2002/5762.
Fitzgerald, Aloysius, F. S. C. *The L-rd of the East Wind*. CBQMS 34. Washington, DC: The Catholic Biblical Association of America, 2002.
Flannery Dailey, Frances. *Dreamers, Scribes, and Priests: Jewish Dreams in the Hellenistic and Roman Eras*. SJSJ 90. Leiden: Brill, 2004.
Fohrer, Georg. "Jesaja 1 als Zusammenfassung der Verkündigung Jesajas." In *Studien zur Alttestamentlichen Prophetie (1949–1965)*, 148–66. BZAW 99. Berlin: Töpelmann, 1967.
Fox, Nili Sacher. *In the Service of the King: Officialdom in Ancient Israel and Judah*. Cincinnati: Hebrew Union College Press, 2000.
Friedländer, M. *The Commentary of Ibn Ezra on Isaiah*. 1873. Repr., New York: Feldheim, n.d.
Gerstenberger, Erhard. *Psalms, Part 1, with an Introduction to Cultic Poetry*. FOTL 14. Grand Rapids: Eerdmans, 1988.
———. *Psalms, Part 2, and Lamentations*. FOTL 15. Grand Rapids: Eerdmans, 2001.
Gesenius, Wilhelm. *Philologisch-kritischer und historischer Commentar über den Jesaia*. 2 parts. Leipzig: Vogel, 1820–21.
Giovino, Mariana. *The Assyrian Sacred Tree: A History of Interpretation*. OBO 230. Göttingen: Vandenhoeck & Ruprecht, 2007.

BIBLIOGRAPHY

Gitay, Yehoshua. *Isaiah and His Audience: The Structure and Meaning of Isaiah 1–12*. SSN. Assen, The Netherlands: Van Gorcum, 1991.

———. "Reflections on the Study of Prophetic Discourse: The Question of Isaiah I 2–20." *VT* 33 (1983) 207–21.

Gitin, Seymour. "Seventh Century B.C.E. Cultic Elements in Ekron." In *Proceedings of the Second International Congress on Biblical Archaeology, June 1990*, 248–58. Jerusalem: Israel Exploration Society, 1993.

———. "Tel Miqne-Ekron: A Type Site for the Inner Coastal Plain in the Iron Age II Period." In *Recent Excavations in Israel: Studies in Iron Age Archaeology*, edited by S. Gitin and W. G. Dever, 23–58. AASOR 49. Winona Lake, IN: Eisenbrauns, 1989.

Goedicke, H. "The End of 'So, King of Egypt.'" *BASOR* 171 (1963) 64–66.

Goelt, Ogden. "Hathor." In *EBR* 11:408–10.

Gonçalves, Francolino J. *L'expédition de Sennachérib en Palestine dans la littérature hébraïque ancienne*. Louvaine-La-Neuve: Institut Orientaliste, 1986.

Gosse, Bernard. *Isaïe 13,1—14,23 dans la tradition des oracles contre les nations*. OBO 78. Göttingen: Vandenhoeck & Ruprecht, 1988.

Graffy, Adrian. *A Prophet Confronts His People: The Disputation Speech in the Prophets*. AnBib 104. Rome: Biblical Institute Press, 1984.

Grayson, A. K. "Assyria: Sennacherib and Esarhaddon (704–669 B.C.)." In *The Cambridge Ancient History, III, Part 2, The Assyrian and Babylonian Empires and Other States of the Near East, from the Eighth to the Sixth Centuries B.C.*, edited by J. Boardman et al., 103–41. Cambridge: Cambridge University Press, 1991.

———. "Assyrian Civilization: The Monarchy." In *The Cambridge Ancient History, III, Part 2, The Assyrian and Babylonian Empires and Other States of the Near East, from the Eighth to the Sixth Centuries B.C.*, edited by J. Boardman et al., 194–228. Cambridge: Cambridge University Press, 1991.

Halpern, Baruch. *The First Historians: The Hebrew Bible and History*. San Francisco: Harper and Row, 1988.

Handy, Lowell K. "Shalem." In *ABD* 5:1152–53.

Hasel, Gerhard F. *The Remnant: The History and Theology of the Remnant Idea from Genesis to Isaiah*. Berrien Springs, MI: Andrews University Press, 1974.

Hays, Christopher B. *The Origins of Isaiah 24–27: Josiah's Festival Scroll for the Fall of Assyria*. Cambridge: Cambridge University Press, 2019.

Hibbard, J. Todd. *Intertextuality in Isaiah 24–27*. FAT 2:16. Tübingen: Mohr Siebeck, 2006.

Hitzig, Ferdinand. *Der Prophet Jesaja*. Heidelberg: Winter, 1833.

Holt, Else K., et al, eds. *Concerning the Nations: Essays on the Oracles Against the Nations in Isaiah, Jeremiah, and Ezekiel*. LHBOTS 612. London: Bloomsbury, 2015.

Hurowitz, Victor (Avigdor). "Isaiah's Impure Lips and Their Purification in Light of Akkadian Sources." *HUCA* 60 (1989) 39–89.

Jacobsen, Thorkild. *The Sumerian King List*. Chicago: The University of Chicago Press, 1939.

———. *The Treasures of Darkness: A History of Mesopotamian Religion*. New Haven, CT: Yale University Press, 1976.

Jepsen, A. "Ḥāzâ." In *TDOT* 4:280–90.

Jones, Brian C. *Howling Over Moab: Irony and Rhetoric in Isaiah 15–16*. SBLDS 157. Atlanta: Scholars, 1996.

Kaiser, Otto. *Isaiah 1—12: A Commentary*. OTL. Translated by J. Bowden. Philadelphia: Westminster, 1983.

Bibliography

———. *Isaiah 13–39: A Commentary*. OTL. Translated by R. A. Wilson. Philadelphia: Westminster, 1974.

Katzenstein, H. Jacob. *The History of Tyre: From the Beginning of the Second Millennium B.C.E. Until the Fall of the Neo-Babylonian Empire in 538 B.C.E.* Jerusalem: Schocken Institute, Jewish Theological Seminary, 1973.

Kiesow, Klaus. *Exodustexte im Jesajabuch: Literarkritische und Motivgeschichtliche Analysen*. OBO 24. Göttingen: Vandenhoeck & Ruprecht, 1979.

Kim, Hyun Chul Paul. "Day of the L-rd." In *EBR* 6:299–301.

———. *Reading Isaiah: A Literary and Theological Commentary*. Reading The Old Testament. Macon, GA: Smyth and Helwys, 2016.

Klein, Ralph W. *2 Chronicles*. Hermeneia. Minneapolis: Fortress, 2012.

Knott, Elizabeth Ann. "Ishtar's (Inanna's) Descent to the Netherworld." In *EBR* 13:387–90.

Korpel, Marjo. "Leviathan." In *EBR* 16:292–96.

Knierim, Rolf P. "Criticism of Literary Features: Form, Tradition, and Redaction." In *The Hebrew Bible and Its Modern Interpreters*, edited by D. A. Knight and G. M. Tucker, 123–65. Chico, CA: Scholars, 1985.

———. "Form Criticism Reconsidered." *Interpretation* 27 (1973) 435–48; reprinted in *Reading the Hebrew Bible for a New Millennium: Form, Concept, and Theological Perspective, Volume 2: Exegetical and Theological Studies*, edited by W. Kim et al., 42–71. Harristown, PA: Trinity, 2000.

Kooij, Arie van der. *Die alten Textzeugen des Jesajabuches: Ein Beitrag zur Textgeschichte des alten Testaments*. OBO 35. Göttingen: Vandenhoeck & Ruprecht, 1981.

———. *The Oracle of Tyre: The Septuagint of Isaiah 23 as Version and Vision*. VTSup 71. Leiden: Brill, 1998.

Kratz, Reinhard Gregor. *Kyros im Deuterojesaja Buch*. FAT 1. Tübingen: Mohr Siebeck, 1991.

Laato, Anni Maria. "Isaiah in Latin." In *The Oxford Handbook of Isaiah*, edited by L.-S. Tiemeyer, 489–503. Oxford: Oxford University Press, 2020.

Laato, Antti. "Isaiah in Ancient, Medieval, and Modern Jewish Traditions." In *The Oxford Handbook of Isaiah*, edited by L.-S. Tiemeyer, 507–30. Oxford: Oxford University Press, 2020.

———. *Message and Composition of the Book of Isaiah: An Interpretation in the Light of Jewish Reception History*. DCLS 46. Berlin: de Gruyter, 2022.

Lack, Rémi. *La Symbolique du Livre d'Isaïe*. AnBib 59. Rome: Biblical Institute Press, 1973.

Lenowitz, Harris. *The Jewish Messiahs: From the Galilee to Crown Heights*. Oxford: Oxford University Press, 1998.

Levenson, Jon D. *Creation and the Persistence of Evil: The Jewish Drama of Divine Omnipotence*. San Francisco: Harper and Row, 1988.

———. *Sinai and Zion: An Entry into the Jewish Bible*. Minneapolis: Winston, 1985.

———. "The Temple and the World." *JR* 64 (1984) 275–98.

Luckenbill, Daniel David. *Ancient Records of Assyria and Babylonia, Part Two*. London: History and Mysteries of Man, 1989.

Machinist, Peter. "Assyria and Its Image in First Isaiah." *JAOS* 103 (1983) 719–37.

Macintosh, A. A. *Isaiah XXI: A Palimpsest*. Cambridge: Cambridge University Press, 1980.

Mazar, Amihai. *Archaeology of the Land of the Bible, 10,000–586 B.C.E.* New York: Doubleday 1990.

Bibliography

Mazar, B., and Y. Shiloh. "Jerusalem: The Early Periods and the First Temple Period." In *NEAEHL* 2:698–712.

Mazar, E., et al. "Jerusalem." In *NEAEHL* 5:1801–17.

McKinny, Chris, et al. "Lebanon." In *EBR* 15:1191–203.

Merlo, Paolo. "Asherah." In *EBR* 2:975–80.

Meyers, Carol L. *The Tabernacle Menorah: A Synthetic Study of a Symbol from the Temple Cult.* ASORDS 2. Missoula, MT: Scholars, 1976.

Miller, J. M. *Archaeological Survey of the Kerak Plateau.* ASOR Archaeological Reports 1. Atlanta: Scholars, 1991.

———. "Moab and the Moabites." In *Studies in the Mesha Inscription and Moab*, edited by A. Dearman, 1–40. Atlanta: Scholars, 1988.

Mowinckel, Sigmund. *Jesaja-Disiplene: Profetien fra Jesaja til Jeremia.* Oslo: Achehoug (Nygaard), 1926.

———. *The Spirit and the Word: Prophecy and Tradition in Ancient Israel.* Edited by K. C. Hanson. Minneapolis: Fortress, 2002; a republication of Mowinckel, *Prophecy and Tradition: The Prophetic Books in the Light of the Study of the Growth and History of the Tradition.* ANAO. Oslo: Dybwad, 1946.

Moyise, Steve. "Isaiah in the New Testament." In *The Oxford Handbook of Isaiah*, edited by L.-S. Tiemeyer, 531–41. Oxford: Oxford University Press, 2020.

Ngunga, Abi T. "Isaiah in Greek." In *The Oxford Handbook of Isaiah*, edited by L.-S. Tiemeyer, 451–68. Oxford: Oxford University Press, 2020.

Nielsen, Kirsten. *There Is Hope for a Tree: The Tree as Metaphor in Isaiah.* JSOTSup 65. Sheffield, UK: JSOT Press, 1989.

Nocquet, Danny, and Shimon Dar. "Carmel." In *EBR* 4:988–93.

Parpola, Simo. "The Assyrian Tree of Life: Tracing the Origins of Jewish Monotheism." *JNES* 52 (1993) 161–208.

Paul, Shalom. *Isaiah 40–66.* ECC. Grand Rapids: Eerdmans, 2012.

Pitard, Wayne T. *Ancient Damascus: A Historical Study of the Syrian City-State from Earliest Times Until Its Fall to the Assyrians in 732 B.C.E.* Winona Lake, IN: Eisenbrauns, 1987.

Polaski, Donald C. *Authorizing an End: The Isaiah Apocalypse and Intertextuality.* BIS 50. Leiden: Brill, 2001.

Poulsen, Frederik. *The Black Hole in Isaiah: A Study of Exile as a Literary Theme.* FAT 125. Tübingen: Mohr Siebeck, 2019.

Pritchard, James B. *The Ancient Near East in Pictures.* Princeton, NJ: Princeton University Press, 1969.

———. *Ancient Near Eastern Texts Relating to the Old Testament.* Princeton, NJ: Princeton University Press, 1969.

Rendtorff, Rolf. *Canon and Theology: Overtures to an Old Testament Theology.* Translated by M. Kohl. Minneapolis: Fortress, 1993.

———. "The Composition of the Book of Isaiah." In *Canon and Theology*, 146–69. Minneapolis: Fortress, 1993.

———. "Isaiah 6 in the Framework of the Composition of the Book." In *Canon and Theology*, 170–80. Minneapolis: Fortress, 1993.

———. "Isaiah 56:1 as a Key to the Formation of the Book of Isaiah." In *Canon and Theology*, 181–89. Minneapolis: Fortress, 1993.

Roberts, Jimmy Jack McBee. *First Isaiah.* Hermeneia. Minneapolis: Fortress, 2015.

Bibliography

Sawyer, John F. A. *Isaiah Through the Centuries*. Wiley Blackwell Bible Commentaries. Chichester, UK: Wiley Blackwell, 2018.

Schmidt, Brian B. "Marzeah." In *EBR* 17:1234-36.

Seitz, Christopher R. "The Divine Council: Temporal Transition and New Prophecy in the Book of Isaiah." *JBL* 109 (1990) 229-47.

———. "How Is the Prophet Isaiah Present in the Latter Half of the Book? The Logic of Chapters 40-66 in the Latter Half of the Book." *JBL* 115 (1996) 219-40.

———. *Zion's Final Destiny: The Development of the Book of Isaiah. A Reassessment of Isaiah 36-39*. Minneapolis: Fortress, 1991.

Stade, B. "Miscellan: Anmerkungen zu 2 Kö. 15-21." *ZAW* 6 (1886) 156-89.

Steck, Odil Hannes. *Bereitete Heimkehr: Jesaja 35 als redaktionalle Brücke zwischen dem Ersten und dem Zweiten Jesaja*. SBS 121. Stuttgart: Katholisches Bibelwerk, 1985.

———. *Die erste Jesajarolle von Qumran (1QIsa): Schreibweise als Leseanleitung für ein Prophetenbuch*. SBS 173/1-2. Stuttgart: Katholisches Bibelwerk, 1998.

Stromberg, Jacob. *Isaiah After Exile: The Author of Third Isaiah as Reader and Redactor of the Book*. Oxford: Oxford University Press, 2011.

Sweeney, Marvin A. *1-2 Kings: A Commentary*. OTL. Louisville, KY: Westminster John Knox, 2007.

———. *1-2 Samuel*. NCBC. Cambridge: Cambridge University Press, 2023.

———. "The Book of Isaiah in Recent Research." *Currents in Research: Biblical Studies* 1 (1993) 141-62; reprinted in *Recent Research on the Major Prophets*, edited by A. J. Hauser, 78-92. Sheffield: Sheffield Phoenix, 2008.

———. "The Book of the Twelve and Kingship." In *The Book of the Twelve: Composition, Reception, and Interpretation*, edited by L.-S. Tiemeyer and J. Wöhrle, 489-506. VTSup 184. Leiden: Brill, 2020.

———. "The End of Eschatology in Daniel? Theological and Socio-Political Ramifications of the Changing Contexts of Interpretation." In *Form and Intertextuality in Prophetic and Apocalyptic Literature*, 248-61. FAT 45. Tübingen: Mohr Siebeck, 2005.

———. *Exodus*. CCC. Eugene, OR: Cascade, forthcoming, 2025.

———. "The Distinctive Roles of the Prophets in the Deuteronomistic History and the Chronicler's History." In *The Oxford Handbook of the Historical Books of the Hebrew Bible*, edited by B. E. Kelle and B. A. Strawn, 201-13. Oxford: Oxford University Press, 2020.

———. "Ezekiel's Debate with Isaiah." In *Reading Prophetic Books*, 185-202. Tübingen: Mohr Siebeck, 2014.

———. "Form Criticism." In *To Each Its Own Meaning: An Introduction to Biblical Criticisms and Their Applications*, edited by S. L. McKenzie and S. R. Haynes, 58-89. Louisville, KY: Westminster John Knox, 1999; reprinted in *Visions of the Holy*, 21-53. Atlanta: SBL, 2023.

———. "Form Criticism: The Question of the Endangered Matriarchs in Genesis." In *Visions of the Holy*, 251-72. Atlanta: SBL, 2023.

———. "Hope and Resilience in the Books of Jeremiah." In *The Oxford Handbook of Jeremiah*, edited by L. Stulman and E. Silver, 420-37. Oxford: Oxford University Press, 2021.

———. "Isaiah (Book and Person): I. Hebrew Bible/Old Testament." In *EBR* 13:297-305.

———. *Isaiah 1-4 and the Post-Exilic Understanding of the Isaianic Tradition*. BZAW 171. Berlin: de Gruyter, 1988.

Bibliography

———. "Isaiah 1–39." In *The Old Testament and Apocrypha: Fortress Commentary on the Bible*, edited by Gale Yee et al., 673–97. Minneapolis: Fortress, 2014.

———. *Isaiah 1–39, with an Introduction to Prophetic Literature*. FOTL 16. Grand Rapids: Eerdmans, 1996.

———. *Isaiah 40–66*. FOTL. Grand Rapids: Eerdmans, 2016.

———. "Jeremiah Among the Prophets." In *The Book of Jeremiah: Composition, Reception, and Interpretation*, edited by J. R. Lundbom et al., 26–44. VTSup 188. Leiden: Brill, 2018.

———. *Jewish Mysticism: From Ancient Times Through Today*. Grand Rapids: Eerdmans, 2020.

———. *King Josiah of Judah: The Lost Messiah of Israel*. Oxford: Oxford University Press, 2001.

———. "New Gleanings from an Old Vineyard: Isaiah 27 Reconsidered." In *Early Jewish and Christian Exegesis: Studies in Memory of William Hugh Brownlee*, edited by C. A. Evans and W. F. Stinespring, 51–66. Atlanta: Scholars, 1987.

———. "On the Road to Duhm: Isaiah in Nineteenth-Century Critical Scholarship." In *"As Those Who Are Taught": The Interpretation of Isaiah from the LXX to the SBL*, edited by C. Mathews McGinnis and P. K. Tull, 243–61. SBLSym 27. Atlanta: SBL, 2006.

———. *The Pentateuch*. CBS. Nashville: Abingdon, 2017.

———. "Political Perspective in the Book of the Twelve: The Case of Zechariah." In untitled festschrift for James D. Nogalski. BZAW. Berlin: de Gruyter, forthcoming, 2025.

———. "Post-Shoah Readings of Isaiah." In *The Oxford Handbook of Isaiah*, edited by L. S. Tiemeyer, 542–58. Oxford: Oxford University Press, 2020.

———. *The Prophetic Literature*. IBT. Nashville: Abingdon, 2005.

———. *Reading Ezekiel: A Literary and Theological Commentary*. Reading the Old Testament. Macon, GA: Smyth and Helwys, 2013.

———. "Reading the Final Form of Isaiah as a Persian Period Text." In *The History of Isaiah: The Formation of the Book and Its Presentation of the Past*, edited by J. Stromberg and J. T. Hibbard, 527–37. FAT 150. Tübingen: Mohr Siebeck, 2021.

———. *Reading the Hebrew Bible After the Holocaust: Engaging Holocaust Theology*. Minneapolis: Fortress, 2008.

———. *Reading Prophetic Books: Form, Intertextuality, and Reception in Prophetic and Post-Biblical Literature*. FAT 89. Tübingen: Mohr Siebeck, 2014.

———. "The Reconceptualization of the Davidic Covenant in the Books of Jeremiah." In *Reading Prophetic Books*, 167–84. Tübingen: Mohr Siebeck, 2014.

———. "The Reconceptualization of the Davidic Covenant in Isaiah." In *Reading Prophetic Books*, 94–113. Tübingen: Mohr Siebeck, 2014.

———. "Swords into Plowshares or Plowshares into Swords? Isaiah and the Twelve in Intertextual Perspective on Zion." In *Visions of the Holy: Studies in Biblical Literature and Theology*, 517–32. SBLResBS 105. Atlanta: SBL, 2023.

———. "Synchronic, Diachronic, and Intertextual Dimensions of the Davidic and Exodus/Wilderness Motifs in the Book of Isaiah: Gains and Losses of a One-View Reading of the Book of Isaiah." To be published in a volume of essays edited by Ulrich Berges, based on the papers presented at the Leuven Biblical Colloquium on the Book of Isaiah, August 5–7, 2024. Leuven: Peeters, forthcoming.

Bibliography

———. *Tanak: A Theological and Critical Introduction to the Jewish Bible*. Minneapolis: Fortress, 2012.
———. "The Ten Sefirot." In *Dictionary of Deities and Demons in the Bible*, edited by K. van der Toorn et al., 837–43. 2nd ed. Leiden: Brill, 1999.
———. "Textual Citations in Isaiah 24–27: Toward an Understanding of the Redactional Function of Chapters 24–27 in the Book of Isaiah." In *Reading Prophetic Books*, 64–78. Tübingen: Mohr Siebeck, 2014.
———. *The Twelve Prophets*. 2 vols. Berit Olam. Collegeville, MN: Liturgical, 2000.
———. *Visions of the Holy: Studies in Biblical Theology and Literature*. SBLResBS 105. Atlanta: SBL, 2023.
———. "Where Were You When They Came for Me? The Role of the Reader in Relation to the Eternal Covenant in the Book of Isaiah." In *The Function of the Reader in the Formation and Reception of the Book of Isaiah*, edited by A. L. H. M. van Wieringen and S. Jang, 73–85. Leiden: Brill Schöningh, 2024.
———. *Zephaniah*. Hermeneia. Minneapolis: Fortress, 2003.
Tooman, William A. "Isaiah in Aramaic." In *The Oxford Handbook of Isaiah*, edited by L. S. Tiemeyer, 469–88. Oxford: Oxford University Press, 2020.
Tucker, Gene M. "Prophetic Superscriptions and the Growth of a Canon." In *Canon and Authority*, edited by G. W. Coats and B. O. Long, 56–70. Philadelphia: Fortress, 1977.
Tull, Patricia K. *Isaiah 1–39*. SHBC. Macon, GA: Smyth and Helwys, 2010.
Tull Willey, Patricia. *Remember the Former Things: The Recollection of Previous Texts in Second Isaiah*. SBLDS 161. Atlanta: Scholars, 1997.
Ulrich, Eugene, and Peter W. Flint, eds. *Qumran Cave 1. II: The Isaiah Scrolls*. DJD 32, Parts 1 and 2. Oxford: Clarendon, 2010.
Ussishkin, David. "Lachish." In *NEAEHL* 3:897–911.
———. *The Village of Silwan: The Necropolis from the Period of the Judean Kingdom*. Jerusalem: Israel Exploration Society and Yad Izhak Ben-Zvi, 1993.
Vainstub, Daniel. "Carthage." In *EBR* 4:1013–15.
Vermeylen, J. *Du prophète d'Isaïe à l'apocalyptique. Isaïe I–XXXV, miroir d'un Demi-millénaire d'expérience religieuse en Israël*. 2 vols. EB. Paris: Gabalda, 1977–78.
Westermann, Claus. *Prophetic Oracles of Salvation in the Old Testament*. Louisville, KY: Westminster John Knox, 1991.
Widengren, Geo. *The King and the Tree of Life in Ancient Near Eastern Religion*. Uppsala: Almqvist and Wilksell, 1951.
Wieringen, Archibald L. H. M. van. *The Implied Reader in Isaiah 6–12*. BibInt 34. Leiden: Brill, 1998.
Wieringen, Archibald L. H. M. van, and Sehoon Jang, eds. *The Function of the Reader in the Formation and the Reception of the Book of Isaiah*. Leiden: Brill, 2024.
Wiesehöfer, Josef. "Meses, Media." In *EBR* 18:286–89.
Wiklander, Bertil. *Prophecy as Literature: A Text-Linguistic and Rhetorical Approach to Isaiah 2–4*. ConBibOT 23. Stockholm: Gleerup, 1984.
Wildberger, Hans. *Jesaja 1–12*. BKAT X/1. Neukirchen-Vluyn: Neukirchener Verlag, 1972; ET, *Isaiah 1–12*, Continental Commentary, translated by T. H. Trapp. Minneapolis: Fortress, 1991.
———. *Jesaja 13–27*. BKAT X/2. Neukirchen-Vluyn: Neukirchener Verlag, 1978; ET: *Isaiah 13–27*. Continental Commentary, translated by T. H. Trapp. Minneapolis: Fortress, 1997.

Bibliography

———. *Jesaja 28–39*. BKAT X/3. Neukirchen-Vluyn: Neukirchener Verlag, 1982; ET: *Isaiah 28–39*. Continental Commentary, translated by T. H. Trapp. Minneapolis: Fortress, 2002.

Williamson, H. G. M. *The Book Called Isaiah: Deutero-Isaiah's Role in Composition and Redaction*. Oxford: Clarendon, 1994.

———. *Isaiah 1–5*. ICC. London: T&T Clark, 2006.

———. *Isaiah 6–12*. ICC. London: T&T Clark, 2018.

Wright, David P. *Ritual in Narrative: The Dynamics of Fasting, Mourning, and Retaliation Rites in the Ugaritic Tale of Aqhat*. Winona Lake, IN: Eisenbrauns, 2001.

Wyatt, N. *Religious Texts from Ugarit*. Sheffield, UK: Sheffield Academic Press, 1998.

Index

Ackroyd, Peter R., 3, 6–7, 13, 26–27, 36, 108, 111–12, 116, 118, 124
Anderson, Bernhard W., 21, 42

Baumann, Gerlinde, 21, 63
Berges, Ulrich, 3, 22
Beuken, Willem A. M., 17–18, 89, 101
Birdsong, Shelley L., 112
Blenkinsopp, Joseph, 4, 11, 13, 22, 45, 65, 69
Blischke, Mariecke V., 102
Brinkman, J. A., 70, 110
Brooke, , George J., 124
Budde, Karl, 45

Carr, David M., 12, 28
Childs, Brevard S., 4, 13, 22, 45, 68, 73, 119
Clements, Ronald E., 3, 6–8, 37, 112
Cogan, Mordecai, 66
Collins, John J., 80–81
Conrad, , Edgar W., 28
Cook, L. Stephen, 11, 78
Cooper, Jerrold S., 55
Cross, Frank M., 21

Dar, Shimon , 102
Day, John, 87
De Vries, Simon J., 38–39, 54, 64–65, 68–69, 79, 84
Dearman, Andrew, 63
Derenbourg, Joseph, 124

Derenbourg, Hartwig, 124
Dicou, Burt, 106
Dillmann, August, 4
Dothan, , Trude, 32
Duhm, Bernhard, 2, 4, 13, 36, 105

Eichhorn, Johann Gottfried, 3–4
Ephal, Israel, 71
Erlandsson, Seth, 15, 61
Evans, Craig A., 8,18,105
Ewald, Heinrich Georg August, 4

Finkelstein, Israel, 32
Fishbane, Michael, 124
Fitzgerald, Aloysius, F.S.C., 39, 60, 100
Flannery-Dailey, Frances, 11
Flint, Peter W., 2, 108
Fohrer, Georg, 8, 10, 27, 31
Fox, Nili Sacher, 75, 113
Friedländer, Michael, 3

Gerstenberger, Erhard, 62, 85, 98, 116
Gesenius, Wilhelm, 4, 118–19
Giovino, Mariana, 55
Gitay, Yehoshua, 11, 31, 46
Gitin, Seymour, 32
Goedicke, Hans, 66
Goelt, Ogden, 35
Gonçalves, Francolino J., 112
Gosse, Bernard, 61, 70
Graffy, Adrian, 73, 98
Grayson, A. K., 55, 110, 114

Index

Halpern, Baruch, 46
Handy, Lowell K., 102
Hasel, Gerhard F., 31, 42
Hays, Christopher B., 16, 59, 80, 82–83
Hibbard, J. Todd, 79
Hitzig, Ferdinand, 4
Holt, Else K., 15
Hurowitz, Victor (Avigdor), 47

Jacobsen, Thorkild, 55
Jepsen, A., 28, 102
Jones, Brian C., 62

Kaiser, Otto, 45, 69
Katzenstein, H. Jacob, 76–77
Kiesow, Klaus, 21, 43, 107
Kim, Hyun Chul Paul, 4, 74
Klein, Ralph W., 20, 29
Knierim, Rolf P., 4, 73
Knott, Elizabeth Ann, 99
Kooij, Arie van der, 78, 124
Korpel, Marjo, 87
Kratz, Reinhard Gregor, 22

Laato, Anni Maria, 124
Laato, Antti, 125
Lack, Rémi, 28
Lenowitz, Harris, 52
Levenson, Jon D., 59, 81, 93
Luckenbill, Daniel David, 77

Machinist, Peter, 113
Macintosh, A. A., 70–72
Mazar, Amihai, 32
Mazar, Benjamin, 74
Mazar, Eilat , 74
McKinny, Chris, 102
Merlo, Paolo, 35
Meyers, , Carol L., 35
Miller, J. Maxwell, 62
Mowinckel, Sigmund, 27
Moyise, Steve, 125

Ngunga, Abi T., 124
Nielsen, Kirsten, 35, 54–55
Nocquet, Danny, 102

Parpola, Simo, 55
Paul, Shalom, 2
Pitard, Wayne T., 63
Polaski, Donald C., 79
Poulsen, Frederik, 18, 35, 120
Pritchard, James B., 32, 35, 48, 63, 67–68, 73, 76, 109, 114

Rendtorff, Rolf, 3, 7
Roberts, Jimmy Jack McBee, 38

Sawyer, , John F. A., 125
Schmidt, Brian B., 91
Seitz, Christopher R., 10, 18, 21, 112, 119
Shiloh, Yigal , 74
Stade, Bernhard, 119
Steck, Odil Hannes, 18, 107–8
Stromberg, Jacob, 3, 7
Sweeney, Marvin, 3–4, 6–8, 10, 12–16, 18–24, 27–37, 40–59, 61–62, 64–67, 69, 71–74, 76, 78, 80, 82–88, 90, 94, 96, 98, 100–102, 104–9, 111–12, 114, 116–18, 120, 123–25, 129–30

Tadmor, Haim, 66
Tooman, William A., 124
Tucker, Gene M., 10, 30, 37, 59
Tull, Patricia K., 7
Tull Willey, Patricia, 7

Ulrich, Eugene, 2, 108
Ussishkin, David, 113

Vainstub, Daniel, 77
Vermeylen, Jacques, 84

Westermann, Claus, 99
Widengren, Geo, 55
Wieringen, Archibald L. H. M. van, 3, 14
Wiesehöfer, Josef, 60
Wiklander, Bertil, 8, 13, 36
Wildberger, Hans, 13, 21, 26–27, 38, 45, 64–65, 68, 119–20
Williamson, H. G. M., 3, 7, 11, 13, 28, 30, 37–38, 42–43
Wright, David P., 99
Wyatt, Nicholas, 91, 99

www.ingramcontent.com/pod-product-compliance
Lightning Source LLC
Chambersburg PA
CBHW031457160426
43195CB00010BB/1016